Melville's Mirrors

Studies in American Literature and Culture:
Literary Criticism in Perspective

Brian Yothers, Series Editor
(*El Paso, Texas*)

About *Literary Criticism in Perspective*

Books in the series *Literary Criticism in Perspective* trace literary scholarship and criticism on major and neglected writers alike, or on a single major work, a group of writers, a literary school or movement. In so doing the authors — authorities on the topic in question who are also well-versed in the principles and history of literary criticism — address a readership consisting of scholars, students of literature at the graduate and undergraduate level, and the general reader. One of the primary purposes of the series is to illuminate the nature of literary criticism itself, to gauge the influence of social and historic currents on aesthetic judgments once thought objective and normative.

Melville's Mirrors

Literary Criticism and America's Most Elusive Author

Brian Yothers

Rochester, New York

Copyright © 2011 Brian Yothers

All Rights Reserved. Except as permitted under current legislation,
no part of this work may be photocopied, stored in a retrieval system,
published, performed in public, adapted, broadcast, transmitted,
recorded, or reproduced in any form or by any means,
without the prior permission of the copyright owner.

First published 2011 by Camden House
Reprinted in paperback 2019

Camden House is an imprint of Boydell & Brewer Inc.
668 Mt. Hope Avenue, Rochester, NY 14620, USA
www.camden-house.com
and of Boydell & Brewer Limited
PO Box 9, Woodbridge, Suffolk IP12 3DF, UK
www.boydellandbrewer.com

Paperback ISBN-13: 978-1-64014-053-0
Paperback ISBN-10: 1-64014-053-0
Hardcover ISBN-13: 978-1-57113-509-4
Hardcover ISBN-10: 1-57113-509-X

Library of Congress Cataloging-in-Publication Data

Yothers, Brian, 1975–
  Melville's mirrors: literary criticism and America's most elusive author / Brian Yothers.
    p. cm.
  Includes bibliographical references and index.
  ISBN-13: 978-1-57113-509-4 (acid-free paper)
  ISBN-10: 1-57113-509-X (acid-free paper)
  1. Melville, Herman, 1819–1891—Criticism and interpretation—History. I. Title.
  PS2387.Y68 2011
  813'.3—dc23

2011023807

This publication is printed on acid-free paper.
Printed in the United States of America.

*In memory of Esther Yothers (1942–1988)
and Leslie Jayasuriya (1927–2010)*

Contents

Preface to the Paperback Edition: Melville's Critical Reception at His Bicentennial — ix

Acknowledgments — xvii

References to Herman Melville's Works — xix

Introduction: Seeking Melville — 1

1: Defining Melville: The Melville Revival and Biographical and Textual Criticism — 7

2: Literary Aesthetics and the Visual Arts — 29

3: Melville's Beard I: Religion, Ethics, and Epistemology — 59

4: Melville's Beard II: Gender, Sexuality, and the Body — 96

5: Aspects of America: Democracy, Nationalism, and War — 119

6: "An Anacharsis Clootz Deputation": Race, Ethnicity, Empire, and Cosmopolitanism — 150

Epilogue: Encountering Melville — 174

Works Cited — 181

Index — 207

Preface to the Paperback Edition: Melville's Critical Reception at His Bicentennial

AUGUST 1, 2019, WILL MARK the two-hundredth anniversary of Herman Melville's birth, and it marks roughly a century of sustained scholarly attention to his work that followed the work of recovery that began at (and in some cases even before) his death on September 28, 1891. It seems appropriate, then, to bring *Melville's Mirrors* up to date for Melville's bicentennial year, given that 2019 is a year of considerable celebration of Melville's life, work, and legacy.

Two hundred years after his birth, Herman Melville continues to tantalize. In the seven years since the first publication of *Melville's Mirrors*, the range of engagement with Melville's work has continued to expand, both through extensions of well-established avenues of inquiry and through newer approaches that have reflected the urgent issues of the second decade of the twenty-first century. The volume of scholarship devoted to Melville has continued to increase dramatically; as of December 2018, the MLA International Bibliography lists 6,638 hits for "Melville, Herman" in the category "Primary Subject Author." This puts him well ahead of any of his mid-nineteenth-century contemporaries—Hawthorne, Poe, Emerson, Dickinson, Stowe, Thoreau, Douglass, or Mark Twain—and suggests that he continues to be the dominant figure in nineteenth-century American literary studies, with only William Faulkner (twentieth century) and Henry James (nineteenth and twentieth centuries) challenging him in scholarly attention in the broader canon of literature from the United States. In practical terms, this continued attention means that there are 648 new MLA listings for Melville since 2012, a far greater volume of work than any preface could address, but a body of work for which I will nonetheless sketch the outlines.

One question that I posed to myself as I began this preface was whether there was a chapter that I would have written had I been composing the volume in 2018 that I did not include in 2011. I am inclined to think that the most likely chapter I would have added would have been one dealing with the scientific, technological, and climatic implications of Melville's work. As literary criticism has responded to the climate crisis that is the defining threat of our time, Melville's work has come to seem all the more resonant, and such work as Michael Jonik's *Herman Melville and the Politics of the Inhuman* (2018), Wyn Kelley's brief but provocative "Lauding the Inhuman Sea" (2015), Jennifer Schell's essay "'We Account the Whale Immortal': Fantasies of Ecological Abundance and Discourses of Extinction in Herman Melville's *Moby-Dick*" (2014), Timothy Sweet's "'Will He Perish?': *Moby-Dick* and Nineteenth-Century Extinction Discourse" (2018), and the joint Melville Society/ Emily Dickinson Society panel on "Dickinson, Melville, and Posthuman Poetics" have all addressed the ways in which Melville studies has looked beyond the human, both in broadly philosophical terms and particularly in the face of ecological crisis. Schell's *"A Bold and Hardy Race of Men": The Lives and Literature of American Whalemen* (2013), and Hester Blum's ongoing work on the Arctic also set Melville's work in a broader context closely connected with ecology as well as the elements of class suggested by their focus on sailors. Philip Hoare's *Leviathan, or The Whale*, published in 2009, has continued to draw attention precisely because the depth of Hoare's engagement with natural history. Other approaches to Melville and science have emerged in Meredith Farmer's essay "Herman Melville and Joseph Henry at the Albany Academy; or, Melville's Education in Mathematics and Science" (2016) and Eileen McGinnis's "'Change Irreverent': Evolution and Faith in 'The Encantadas' and *Clarel*" (2017), focusing respectively on Melville's own education in the sciences and his engagement with the work of Charles Darwin. Mary K. Bercaw Edwards edited a special issue of *Extracts* in *Leviathan* (2015) that explored the thirty-eighth voyage of the *Charles W. Morgan* (the participation of literary scholars in the voyage was organized by Bercaw Edwards with support from the National Endowment for the Humanities)[1] and the reactions by twenty-first century scholars to the experience of being aboard a nineteenth-century whaling vessel, shedding further light on Melville and his lived environment, and supplementing Bercaw Edwards's *Cannibal Old Me: Spoken Sources in Melville's Early Works* (2009), which served to illuminate the lives and language of sailors as they shaped Melville's literary imagination.

Melville biography and textual scholarship might seem to be the least likely field discussed in the 2011 chapters to make substantial progress in the 2010s, given its venerable role in Melville studies. And yet the field continues to be productive of major statements on the theory of biography and discoveries in the practice of biography. In biographical studies, Hershel Parker's *Melville Biography: An Inside Narrative* (2013) constituted both an acerbic critique of rivals in the field of whom Parker disapproved, and, more appealingly, a reflective guide to the process of writing

---

[1] From 1969 to 2005, the *Melville Society Extracts* were the society's house organ; since then they have been published as a department within *Leviathan: A Journal of Melville Studies*.

literary biography. It also provided insights that extended Parker's earlier work. John Bryant, meanwhile, presented work from his biography-in-progress of Melville at several Melville Society conferences, whetting the appetite of participants in those conferences for his contribution to the field, which promised a wider-ranging engagement with questions of race, gender, and the historical crises that had shaped the United States than had yet been encountered in Melville studies. In textual studies, the majestic Northwestern-Newberry edition of Melville's work was finally brought to completion with the 2017 publication of *Billy Budd, Sailor and Other Uncompleted Writings*. Two important new Norton Critical editions emerged in this period: Hershel Parker's third Norton Critical Edition of *Moby-Dick*, and Robert S. Levine's and Cindy Weinstein's new Norton Critical Edition of *Pierre; or, The Ambiguities*. Katie McGettigan's *Herman Melville, Modernity, and the Material Text* (2017) showed how textual scholarship could inform critical readings of Melville's work more deeply, illustrating that criticism, theory, and scholarship need not be divorced from each other.

Meanwhile, digital projects that engage with Melville have only expanded since 2011. Two major projects that were already in full swing by 2011 were the *Melville Electronic Library*, for which John Bryant is general editor and Wyn Kelley associate editor, and *Melville's Marginalia Online*, with Steven Olsen-Smith as general editor and Peter Norberg as associate general editor and Dennis Marnon as bibliographical editor. The *Melville Electronic Library* continued to expand its range of projects, including substantial exhibits on Melville's collection of prints, Melville's poetry and the Civil War, and the dimensions of travel in Melville's work alongside scholarly editions of *Billy Budd* and *Moby-Dick* that illustrated Bryant's "fluid text" theory of textual editing. *Melville's Marginalia Online* began to make its editions of books that Melville owned and/or annotated searchable and produced substantial new editions of his marginalia to Milton, Homer, and Emerson, among others. Of particular note was the fact that Dawn Coleman worked with Melville's volumes of the works of William Ellery Channing, pointing out that his engagement with the famous Unitarian minister's thought had been much more substantial than had previously acknowledged, and documenting her insights in both the 2015 Critical Introduction to the edition published on *Melville's Marginalia Online* and two substantial essays: "Melville and the Unitarian Conscience" (2017) and "Mahomet's Gospel and Other Revelations: Discovering Melville's Hand in *The Works of William E. Channing*" (2015). Wyn Kelley published several important pieces on the value of digital approaches to Melville in print: a book, co-edited with Henry Jenkins, *Reading in a Participatory Culture: Remixing "Moby-Dick" in the English Classroom*, was published in 2013, and two important book chapters, "'This Matter of Writing': Melville and the Manuscript Page"

(2017) and "Melville by Design" (2018) extended Kelley's earlier work on Melville and the Digital Humanities.

The question of form continues to exert fascination for Melville scholars. Notably, Samuel Otter and Elisa Tamarkin published substantial book chapters on Melville's aesthetics and the visual arts, "Melville, Poetry, Prints" (Otter, 2018) and "A Final Appearance with Elihu Vedder" (Tamarkin, 2018; an earlier version was published in *Leviathan* in 2016). Geoffrey Sanborn's brief book-length study *The Value of Herman Melville* (2018) shows the continuity of concerns with form, notably in Sanborn's dialogue with Warner Berthoff's *The Example of Herman Melville* (1962).

One of the most substantial treatments of Melville's influence on the visual arts was Elizabeth Schultz's 1995 study *Unpainted to the Last: "Moby-Dick" and Twentieth-Century American Art*. In 2019, to celebrate Melville's bicentennial year, Schultz published a substantial sequel to this magisterial work in *Leviathan*. Several briefer pieces have also been highly illuminating with regard to Melville's influence on the visual arts: Dawn Coleman's 2016 review essay "Whales in Cincinnati" and a cluster of pieces in a special 2013 issue of *Leviathan* devoted to "Artists and Adaptation." Matt Kish's *Moby-Dick in Pictures* (2011) generated considerable excitement among Melville scholars with its ambitious provision of an illustration for every page in Melville's most memorable book. These works continued the tradition of artistic responses to Melville that appeared in the late-twentieth-century work of Frank Stella and in Robert del Tredici's *Floodgates of the Wonder-World: A Moby-Dick Pictorial* (2001), along with the work of many other artists. Robert K. Wallace continued to be a leading figure in the study of Melville's relation to both the visual arts and music, publishing *Heggie and Scheer's Moby-Dick: A Grand Opera for the Twenty-First Century* (2013) and continuing his research into Melville's own collection of prints. Melville's poetry commanded increasing attention as well, notably in an important volume edited by Sanford E. Marovitz, *Melville as Poet: The Art of "Pulsed Life"* (2013) and in two substantial pieces dealing with Melville's late works of poetry: Gillian Osborne's "Herman Melville: Queen of the Flowers" (2016) and Martin Kevorkian's "Faith Among the Weeds: Melville's Religious Wildings Beyond These Deserts" (2017). Kevorkian also was the author of a substantial consideration of Melville's late work alongside that of Emerson and Hawthorne: *Writing Beyond Prophecy: Emerson, Hawthorne, and Melville after the American Renaissance* (2013).

Religious and philosophical questions have loomed large in Melville scholarship throughout its history, and the last seven years have seen resurgence in scholarship on these matters. Daniel Herman's *Zen and the White Whale* (2014) delved into connections between *Moby-Dick* and Buddhism, while Dawn Coleman's *Preaching and the Rise of the American Novel*

(2013) showed that the nineteenth-century Protestant sermonic tradition was crucial to understanding Melville's work. Brian Yothers's *Sacred Uncertainty: Religious Difference and the Shape of Melville's Career* (2015) examined Melville's engagement with varieties of religious pluralism and controversy, both within and beyond the boundaries of Western monotheistic thought, while Jonathan A. Cook's *Inscrutable Malice: Theodicy, Eschatology, and the Biblical Sources of "Moby-Dick"* (2012) provided the most thorough and perceptive accounting for Melville's engagement with his biblical sources to date. In *Visionary of the Word: Melville and Religion* (2017), a group of scholars assembled by Cook and Yothers considered the range of ways in which Melville's skeptical engagement with religious faith helped to define his work, including a massive essay by Cook on "*Clarel* and the Victorian Crisis of Faith" and an exploration of "Melville's Asia, Melville's Missionaries" by Yothers. Laura Lopez Pena's *Beyond the Walls: Being with Each Other in Herman Melville's "Clarel"* (2015) offered a powerful and ambitious reading of Melville's long poem *Clarel*, a work profoundly connected to religious and philosophical questions alike.

In a more secular, philosophical vein, Branka Arsić and K. L. Evans edited a substantial volume, *Melville's Philosophies* (2018) and Corey McCall and Tom Nurmi produced a parallel volume, *Melville among the Philosophers* (2017), with an afterword by Cornel West, bringing Melville's engagement with philosophy back to the center of Melville studies. K. L. Evans's own *One Foot in the Finite: Melville's Realism Reclaimed* (2017) offered the bold contention that Melville was distinctive among nineteenth-century American writers in his embrace of specifically philosophical Realism. David Faflik's *Melville and the Question of Meaning* (2018) offered a consideration of the interplay between democracy and form and combined close attention to the artistic, philosophical, and political dimensions of Melville's work.

Studies of gender and sexuality in Melville likewise continue to flourish. David Greven's *Gender Protest and Same-Sex Desire in Antebellum American Literature: Margaret Fuller, Edgar Allan Poe, Nathaniel Hawthorne, and Herman Melville* (2014) and his 2017 essay "In the Name of the Father: *Billy Budd* and the Critics from the Melville Revival to Cold War America" served to expand on his already impressive contributions to the study of sexuality in nineteenth-century American literature. Meanwhile, Rasmus Simonsen's "Melville's Chimney: Queer Syntax and the Rhetoric of Architecture" (2015), Christian Reed's "The Bachelor and the Orphan" (2015), and Matthew Knip's "Homosocial Desire and Erotic Communitas in Melville's Imaginary: The Evidence of Van Buskirk" (2016) offered new directions from emerging scholars for the study of Melville and sexuality.

Jason Franks's edited volume *A Political Companion to Herman Melville* (2013) provided a substantial addition to the flourishing body of scholarship on Melville and American democracy and nationalism, and Jennifer Greiman's single-author volume *Democracy's Spectacle: Sovereignty and Public Life in Antebellum American Writing* (2011) situated Melville within broader forms of nineteenth-century American democratic thought. Colin Dayan's "Bartleby's Screen" (2015) and John Cyril Barton's *Literary Executions: Capital Punishment and American Culture, 1820–1925* (2014) provided important and original contributions to law-and-literature scholarship on Melville.

Christopher Freeburg's *Melville and the Idea of Blackness* (2012) was the most substantial contribution on the subject of Melville and race to emerge in the last seven years given its substantial treatment of both Melville's novels, centrally *Moby-Dick*, and his short fiction, most crucially "Benito Cereno." Greg Grandin's *The Empire of Necessity: Slavery, Freedom, and Deception in the New World* (2015) vastly enlarged the contexts for considering "Benito Cereno" in light of New World Slavery and transatlantic cultural and religious encounters. John Bryant's ambitious and compelling essay "How Billy Grew Black and Beautiful: Versions of Melville in the Digital Age" (2014) had the effect of bringing together digital and archival scholarship on Melville with scholarship on race in Melville's works. Brian Pellar's *"Moby-Dick" and Melville's Anti-Slavery Allegory* (2017) made the stimulating if counterintuitive claim that nearly everything in *Moby-Dick* could be explained as part of an elaborate anti-slavery allegory. The cosmopolitan side of Melville studies was reinforced in such publications as Jeffrey Einboden's studies of Arabic, Persian, and Hebrew translations of Melville's work in *Nineteenth-Century US Literature in Middle Eastern Languages* (2013) and "'Billy's Rendering of the Matter': Global Translations of *Billy Budd, Sailor*" (2017), Leyli Jamali's "Herman Melville in Iran" (2018), and Karen Tei Yamashita's "Call Me Ishimaru" (2016).

In addition to the digital resources described above, *Leviathan: A Journal of Melville Studies* continues to be the major venue for scholarship on Melville, and in its present incarnation is edited by Samuel Otter, with Brian Yothers as associate editor, Dawn Coleman as book review editor, and Mary K. Bercaw Edwards as *Extracts* editor. The Melville Society Cultural Project, led by Mary K. Bercaw Edwards, Wyn Kelley, Timothy Marr, Christopher Sten, and Robert K. Wallace, continues to play a substantial role in reaching out to the wider community through, among other endeavors, the annual *Moby-Dick* Marathon reading at the start of each New Year in New Bedford, an event that, thanks to the efforts of Colin Dewey, now has a counterpart in California near the anniversary of the first British publication of *The Whale*, as *Moby-Dick* was known before its subsequent American publication gave it the name by which we know it. The Melville Society continues to underwrite these endeavors and to be a powerful source for the preservation of Melville's work and legacy.

As the third century since Herman Melville's birth looms, his influence in both literature and the arts and in literary studies continues to expand, and this new edition of *Melville's Mirrors* marks the continuing development of a field of critical response that in its range of concern and aspiration parallels that of the author to which it is devoted.

El Paso, Texas
December 31, 2018

Acknowledgments

THE PROCESS OF WRITING THIS BOOK reminded me constantly of the debt that we all owe to the thousands of men and women who have contributed to the vitality of Melville studies over the past century, and in a sense this entire project is an acknowledgment of indebtedness to these scholars and critics. Some scholars deserve special mention here because of their personal kindness to me: John Bryant, Wyn Kelley, Scott Norsworthy, Peter Norberg, Jonathan Cook, Dawn Coleman, Mary K. Bercaw Edwards, Cody Marrs, Jennifer Greiman, Zachary Hutchins, Meredith Farmer, Timothy Marr, Dennis Berthold, Douglas Robillard, Robert K. Wallace, Mark McCullough, Liam Corley, and William Potter. Andrew Delbanco's seminar on Melville's short fiction at the National Humanities Center helped to start me thinking more comprehensively about the development of Melville criticism, and my association with Steven Olsen-Smith's *Melville's Marginalia Online* coupled with Olsen-Smith's extraordinary scholarly generosity has left an indelible mark on my own development as a Melvillean. Samuel Otter has been unfailingly encouraging and was the source of many helpful suggestions for the revision of this manuscript, and it has been a great privilege to work with Sam on *Leviathan* over the last six years. He is a model of scholarship, tact, and commitment to Melville studies.

Several of my mentors from Purdue University have continued to be sources of wisdom and encouragement long after I matriculated: G. R. Thompson, Kristina Bross, Robert Paul Lamb, Wendy Flory, Ann Astell, Muriel Harris, and John Duvall. Kathleen Maloney, Celeste Heinze, Ryan Johnson, Holly McBee, Alison Baker, James Palmer, Malini Johar Schueller, Rob Davidson, Henry Hughes, Steven Frye, Eric Carl Link, and Derek Parker Royal have demonstrated that Purdue alumni form a particularly supportive network.

At the University of Texas at El Paso, Maggy Smith, David Ruiter, and Evelyn Posey as English department chairs and Patricia Witherspoon, Steve Crites, and Denis O'Hearn as deans of the College of Liberal Arts have been consistently supportive of my research. UTEP's Interlibrary Loan has supplied me with numerous books and articles. I owe especial thanks to the members of the literature faculty: Meredith Abarca, Shelley Armitage, Ezra Cappell, John A. R. Dick, Ruben Espinosa, Mimi Gladstein, Robert Gunn, Lawrence Johnson, Deane Mansfield-Kelley, Lois Marchino, Marion Rohrleitner, Thomas Schmid, Barbara Zimbalist,

Andrew Fleck, Joseph Ortiz, and Tony Stafford, for the supportive environment to which each has contributed. Charles Ambler, Adam Arenson, Beth Brunk-Chavez, Sandra McGee Deutsch, Kate Mangelsdorf, Roy Mathew, Doug Meyers, Jonna Perrillo, Brenda Risch, Brad Cartwright, and Sue Stanfield have all been helpful interlocutors beyond the boundaries of my program.

At Camden House, Jim Walker has been the source of endless encouragement, support, and thoughtful editorial suggestions. Scott Peeples has provided helpful editorial advice and insightful responses to my work. Many thanks also to Ryan Peterson and John Blanpied for their careful work in the copyediting process and to Jane M. Best for her expert guidance through the production process. Working with such a superb editorial team has been a true pleasure.

In my family, Willard Yothers, Yvonne Jayasuriya, Carmeline Jayasuriya, Rosanne Weerackoon, and Heather Maraldo have all shown their belief in me and my scholarly efforts. The Weaver family of Goshen, Indiana, particularly my grandparents Harold and the late Magdalena Weaver, my aunts Lucy and Elsie Weaver, and my uncles Glenn and the late John Weaver, have been a source of much strength and support. The two people to whom this book is dedicated, Esther Yothers and Leslie Jayasuriya, are not here to see this book's publication, but each has shaped me in ways I can only begin to hint at here. Finally, to express adequately the gratitude that I owe to Maryse Jayasuriya will require a lifetime.

References to Herman Melville's Works

THE STANDARD EDITION of Herman Melville's works, and the one cited throughout this volume, is the Northwestern-Newberry edition of *The Writings of Herman Melville* (1968–), published by Northwestern University Press and the Newberry Library and edited by Harrison Hayford, Hershel Parker, and G. Thomas Tanselle. The specific volumes are listed below, with variations among the editors noted when relevant. They are cited in the text in parentheses by short title and page number.

Typee, A Peep at Polynesian Life (Vol. 1). 1968.
Omoo, A Narrative of Adventures in the South Seas (Vol. 2). 1968.
Mardi and the Voyage Thither (Vol. 3). 1970.
Redburn, His First Voyage (Vol. 4). 1969.
White-Jacket, or The World in a Man of War (Vol. 5). 1970.
Moby-Dick, or The Whale (Vol. 6). 1988.
Pierre, or the Ambiguities. (Vol. 7). 1971.
Israel Potter, His Fifty Years of Exile (Vol. 8). 1982.
Piazza Tales and Other Prose Pieces, 1839–1860 (Vol. 9). Edited by Harrison Hayford, Alma MacDougall, and G. Thomas Tanselle. 1987. This volume includes, along with the other Piazza Tales, "Bartleby, the Scrivener," *Benito Cereno*, and *The Encantadas*, as well as uncollected prose pieces from the 1840s and 1850s, most notably Melville's most famous review, "Hawthorne and His Mosses."
The Confidence-Man, His Masquerade (Vol. 10). 1984.
Published Poems (Vol. 11). Edited by Robert C. Ryan, Alma MacDougall Reising, Harrison Hayford, G. Thomas Tanselle. 2009. This volume includes *Battle-Pieces*, *John Marr and Other Sailors*, and *Timoleon*.
Clarel, A Poem and Pilgrimage in the Holy Land (Vol. 12). 1993.
Billy Budd, Sailor, and Other Uncompleted Writings (vol. 13). Edited by Hershel Parker, Harrison Hayford, Alma A. MacDougall, Robert A. Sandberg, and G. Thomas Tanselle. 2017. Includes *Weeds and Wildings, Parthenope*, and other uncompleted fiction and poetry.
Correspondence (Vol. 14). Edited by Lynn Horth. 1993.
Journals (Vol. 15). Edited by Howard Horsford and Lynn Horth. 1989.

Introduction: Seeking Melville

THE SUMMER AND FALL OF 2010 and the early months of 2011 saw unlikely portents of the persistent allure of America's most thoroughly canonized novel and the elusive author behind it. Television viewers and web surfers contemplating the purchase of a smartphone were assured that a major cell-phone provider's latest offering could take the place of Captain Ahab's charts in tracking Moby Dick around the world. Readers of *Nature* learned that a particularly fearsome fossil whale, similar to a sperm whale but with teeth on its upper jaw, had been discovered in Peru, and given a name that reflected the author of *Moby-Dick*'s ongoing fascination for cetologists: *Leviathan melvillei*. America's forty-fourth president confessed via his Facebook page that *Moby-Dick* ranked with Toni Morrison and the Bible among his favorite literary works. Indeed, even as I was putting the finishing touches on this introduction in February 2011, the *New York Times* reported that a sunken ship named *Two Brothers* commanded by George Pollard, whose whale ship *Essex* served as one of Melville's models for the story of the *Pequod*, the doomed vessel on which Ishmael sailed in *Moby-Dick*, had been discovered six hundred miles off the coast of Honolulu. It seemed that "the invisible police officer of the fates" was not done with Herman Melville yet (*Moby-Dick* 7).[1]

And yet, the author who was responsible for Moby Dick, Captain Ahab, Bartleby, and Billy Budd seemed oddly obscure. Unlike the white-haired, white-suited Mark Twain or the broad-browed, melancholy Edgar Allan Poe, Melville's image was not immediately recognizable, nor did the mention of his name conjure a specific list of character traits that students and the general public could use to orient themselves to the man. The images of Melville resided rather behind his books, and in the portions of libraries and bookstores frequented mainly by scholars. The names of Moby Dick, Captain Ahab, Bartleby, Billy Budd, and even Starbuck, are widely known among the reading public, but the neither the name nor the image of Melville himself seems to come to mind as quickly as do his titles or characters. Moreover, the idea that Melville had a great deal to say about matters as diverse as art, religion, philosophy, politics, travel, and poetry can come as a surprise to those who either were assigned *Moby-Dick* in high school (or feel they should have been) and associated Melville largely with either cetology or the quirkiness of Bartleby. Even among scholars of American literature, Melville can seem a cipher: the abundantly canonized author whose work seems to stand more as a trope for the aesthetic or nationalist preoccupations of an earlier generation of scholars than as a figure worthy of being read afresh. Thus, curiously, Melville circa 2011 can seem both startlingly omnipresent and revered and curiously unrecognized and marginal.

Who was Herman Melville? What does he mean for American culture? What does he mean for the history of literary art? Why is he at once so ubiquitous and so elusive? If these questions have only been suggested, and not discussed, by public representations of Melville, they have constituted an ongoing obsession for many literary scholars. Perhaps the magnitude of literary scholars' obsession with answering these questions has something to do Melville's own habitual privacy — the way that he hid his private thoughts by limiting his correspondence and journals, and the way in which he hid in plain sight in his fiction and poetry through his use of narrative framing and the riddling, ironic personae that he created for his narrators.

Melville himself serves as an early and illustrious commentator on the subject of the difficulty associated with constructing a meaningful picture of an author, particularly one so multifaceted as himself. A recurring motif in Melville's work is that of the mirror, and it is from that motif that this study derives its title. In *Mardi*, for example, Melville's narrator discusses the metaphor of the mirror explicitly, using it to explain the literary possibilities of the sea:

> Now as the face of a mirror is blank, only borrowing character from what it reflects, so in a calm in the Tropics, a colorless sky overhead, the ocean, upon its surface, hardly presents a sign of existence. The deep blue is gone; and the glassy element lies tranced, almost as viewless as the air. (48)

Melville thus identified clearly what would become one of the great challenges for his critics, the capacity of art, here discussed through the metaphor of the sea, to take on the characteristics of its surrounding context. Melville extended the metaphor of the sea as mirror to powerful effect in the opening chapter of *Moby-Dick*, where Ishmael relates his version of the story of Narcissus, in which the image in the water before Narcissus — his own — becomes "the ungraspable phantom of life" (5). In *Pierre*, Melville developed this concept still more explicitly in relation to the writing of books, arguing that "all the great books in the world are but the mutilated shadowings-forth of invisible and eternally unbodied images in the soul; so that they are but the mirrors, eternally reflecting to us our own things" (284). Small wonder that one of Melville's most acute readers, Milton Stern, noted in his essay "Towards 'Bartleby the Scrivener'" that "Melville made mirrors" when constructing his texts, meaning that Melville's work tends to admit of various and contradictory readings, depending on his readers' predilections (14). I would add that this very quality means that Melville continues to make mirrors, as literary scholars and critics produce understandings of his work that are both their own and ineluctably shaped by Melville's artistic and philosophical vision.

In addition to his Protean capacity to be more or less what his readers wish him to be, Melville also was characterized by another trait that contributed substantially to his personal elusiveness and to the elusive quality of his work. This trait might best be seen by considering the visual images of Melville that have come down to us from the nineteenth century. In only one of them do we see any approximation of Melville's unadorned face — the earliest of his portraits painted in 1847 by Asa S. Twitchell, in which he is still a young man and a blossoming literary celebrity with a modest beard and no mustache, but not yet the author of *Moby-Dick*. After this early portrait, the Melvilles that we see are all hidden behind beards: in 1861, 1870, and 1885, Melville is increasingly hirsute in his portraits and photographs.

The beard which conceals Melville's face is also explicitly, if humorously, addressed in his work, once again in *Pierre*, which is perhaps the most revelatory and most potentially misleading of all of Melville's works as a picture of Melville himself as a writer. In *Pierre* Melville writes:

> It had always been one of the lesser ambitions of Pierre, to sport a flowing beard, which he deemed the most noble corporeal badge of the man, not to speak of the illustrious author. But as yet he was beardless; and no cunning compound of Rowland and Son could force a beard which would arrive at maturity in any reasonable time for the frontispiece. (253)

Pierre was published in 1852, just as Melville was making the transition from the young man with the goatee in his first portrait to the thoroughly bewhiskered elder of later representations. In this passage, he explicitly, if ironically, connects the beard to ideas of wisdom and literary profundity and genius. Melville's beard, then, was not simply a decision in terms of fashion, but rather a self-conscious effort to create an authorial persona that ultimately became accepted among many of his critics — and an effort that Melville was himself prepared to satirize. Melville's beard can stand as a potent symbol for his capacity to evade, tantalize, and frustrate his readers, increasing rather than diminishing uncertainty.

My intention in this study is both to create a meaningful taxonomy of the various critical mirrors used to understand Melville's work, and to evaluate the degree to which these critical perspectives are successful in getting behind Melville's beard, and revealing knowledge that would not otherwise be accessible to us as readers of Melville's work. The arrangement of the chapters is intended to revise conventional critical taxonomies based on "schools" of criticism and to point out family resemblances among studies of Melville that otherwise might seem distant from each other in intent and critical methodology and ideology.

This study tracks the development of Melville criticism and scholarship from the explosion of Melville scholarship in the Melville Revival of the 1920s to the present time. The study is organized around a few central strands that have recurred over the decades in Melville scholarship. Chapter 1 deals with both the Melville Revival and the ongoing efforts in textual and bibliographical scholarship to create a historically accurate picture of Melville that transcends both the narcissistic tendency to find ourselves in Melville and Melville's own authorial hiddenness. Of particular interest are the efforts of Melville scholars to discover the sources of Melville's art in his engagement with his own reading, thus indicating Melville's creative use of the literary mirrors available to him.

Chapter 2 examines Melville's position as a literary artist and as a figure who was shaped as a writer by his own encounter with the visual arts and whose work helped to inspire a great deal of visual art. The theme of this chapter is less the quest for an authentic Melville than the aesthetic qualities of Melville's work, and the potential of Melville's aesthetics to shape and be shaped by others. I have deliberately combined critical work that could be variously described as belonging to the fields of the New Criticism, Post-Structuralism, and Cultural Studies. Both Melville and his critics have been characterized by an inspired eclecticism in relation to the arts, and my goal has been to honor this eclecticism rather than to reduce it to a single narrative.

Chapter 3 takes Charles R. Anderson's complaints about the obscuring effects of Melville's beard — both literally and figuratively in the sense of Melville's status as a nineteenth-century sage — and considers the religious and philosophical significances of Melville's body of work and the efforts of literary critics and scholars in delineating these significances. Throughout his career, Melville was obsessed with questions of faith, doubt, and religious difference. This chapter explores critical representations of Melville as a believer, a skeptic, and an inhabitant of a variety of gradations in between these two polar tendencies in relation to religion. It also considers Melville's positions as a thinker, a novelist admired as much for the depth of his ideas and the complexity of his philosophical entanglements as for the plots of his novels. As the progression of the chapter shows, Melville's work continues to be tremendously productive of religiously and philosophically oriented readings, and in recent years the question of ethics has come particularly to the fore in readings of Melville.

A side of Melville's personal life that has contributed to recent scholarly inquiry has been his relationship to his family (including allegations of misogyny, alcoholism, and abuse) and the possibility that his often emotionally charged relationships with other men constitute evidence of homoerotic desire or homosexual identity. Chapter 4 addresses these other sides of the trope of Melville's beard that have been explored by scholars more recently: whether Melville's beard concealed not just a novelist and sage, but also a man of powerful and conflicting emotional and sexual impulses. The chapter explores in turn Melville's representations of and relationships with women, Melville's erotically charged representations of and relationships to other men, and Melville's treatment of the body and disability. The disabled body has only recently become a major subject for discussion among Melville critics, but once critics began to look for disability in Melville's works, it quickly became evident that this was a truly pervasive theme, and it seems appropriate that a chapter devoted to Melville's treatment of the body should close with a consideration of his representation of traits that are shared by characters from Ahab to Bartleby to Billy Budd.

From the earliest days of Melville's scholarship, there has been a tension between Melville's status as a significant author in the context of world literature and Melville's status as a characteristically American author. Chapter 5 explores the American face of Herman Melville, noting in particular the ways in which critical accounts of Melville's Americanness have tended to mirror the changing understandings of America that have developed in response to the major historical events and crises of the twentieth and twenty-first centuries. Melville has been examined with particular urgency by scholars seeking to understand such issues as American nationalism and exceptionalism, American law and democracy, and war and violence in American culture, and this chapter is organized around these three interrelated strands in Melville scholarship.

Melville is perhaps America's transnational novelist par excellence, and chapter 6 takes up such matters as race, slavery, imperialism, and transnationalism in his work. Melville was from the beginning of his career a writer of global scope: his first two novels, *Typee* (1846) and *Omoo* (1847), are both fictionalized versions of the young Melville's own travels from New England to the South Pacific; his third, *Mardi* (1849), takes as its occasion a literal voyage through the South Pacific that becomes increasingly allegorical; his fourth novel, *Redburn* (1849), offers an account of a transatlantic voyage; his fifth novel, *White-Jacket* (1850), is a narrative of life aboard a United States naval vessel. *Moby-Dick* (1851) represented a culmination of this tendency, with its "Anacharsis Clootz deputation drawn from all the isles of the earth" (121), from which this chapter's title is taken. The critics discussed in this chapter both analyze the development of the transnational in Melville's early career and illustrate its persistence in his later years through *Clarel* (1876) and the posthumously published *Billy Budd*. The interrelated topics of race, slavery, and imperialism have also proved to be areas of substantial interest for critics of *Moby-Dick*, *Benito Cereno* (1856), *Battle-Pieces* (1867), and *Clarel*, with significant overlap between scholars of transnationalism and imperialism and scholars of race and slavery. This chapter therefore discusses the development of readings of Melville's treatment of antebellum slavery and the civil war alongside the transnational component of his work.

Throughout this study, my overriding concern is with delineating both the evolution of representations of Melville in critical texts and the ways in which these representations become more than mere representations: a central thesis here is that we do know Melville better as a result of the scholarly efforts of the last century. In a review of an earlier volume in the Camden House Literary Criticism in Perspective series (Scott Peeples's *The Afterlife of Edgar Allan Poe* [2004]), the distinguished American literary scholar Nina Baym (who also figures in these pages), suggested that the volume demonstrated a will to believe in the critic's mission. It is my hope that this volume affirms a similar will to believe in the vocation of literary criticism and scholarship. Our understanding of Melville himself, and of his world and ours, is richer because of the critical mirrors held up to the author of *Moby-Dick* by the scholars whose work is considered in the following pages. To them, both those I know personally and have thanked in the acknowledgments to this volume and those I know only through their words, I, and indeed all lovers of Melville's work, owe a profound debt of gratitude.

Notes

[1] See the AT&T Blackberry Torch commercial "Searching for Moby Dick" (available on YouTube); "Call me Leviathan melvillei," *Nature News*, June 30, 2010; Barack Obama's Official Facebook Page, Info: Favorite Books; McKinley, Jesse. "No Moby-Dick: A Real Captain, Twice Doomed," *New York Times* Feb. 2011, A1.

1: Defining Melville: The Melville Revival and Biographical and Textual Criticism

Herman Melvill was born on August 1, 1819. Herman Melville, having acquired a first bright and then gradually tarnished literary reputation, a final "e" at the end of his surname, and varied life experiences as a son, brother, schoolmaster, sailor, deserter, novelist, husband, father, lecturer, poet, grandfather, and customs official, died in semi-obscurity on September 28, 1891. It seems fair to assert that Herman Melville, the towering and alternately worshipped and reviled figure at the center of the American literary canon, was born (or re-born, as the case may be) sometime in the second half of the second decade of the twentieth century. In those years of war, revolution, disease, and chaos, writers on both sides of the Atlantic began projects that would create the "Melville Revival" of the 1920s and would push Melville from the status of a semi-obscure cult figure in the history of maritime writing to that of America's most taught, most debated, and most tantalizingly elusive writer.

It is certainly possible to overstate the degree to which Melville had vanished from public consciousness prior to the Melville Revival. He was never completely forgotten, and he had passionate advocates from the point at which he lost the bulk of his audience in the early 1850s through the end of his life and on until the cusp of the centennial of his birth in 1919. Moreover, as Brian Higgins and Hershel Parker demonstrated in their 1995 collection *Herman Melville: The Contemporary Reviews*, Melville's works were never without perceptive and appreciative reviewers, however much the consensus of early reviewers turned against Melville after the publication of *Moby-Dick* (1851) and *Pierre* (1852).[1]

The earliest retrospective indications that Melville's fame as an author might outlive him appeared before his death, and, curiously, came not from Americans seeking the Great American Novel, but rather from English writers interested in sea fiction. As early as 1884, English sea writer W. Clark Russell was arguing that *Moby-Dick* was not only Melville's "finest work," but was in fact comparable to Blake's artwork and the poetry of Coleridge and Milton (in Higgins, 117–18). A year later, Robert Buchanan published a poem praising Melville with a footnote that described him as the "one great imaginative writer fit to stand shoulder to shoulder with Whitman" in North America (119). Another English sea writer, the aptly named H. S. Salt, lauded Melville in 1889 for his sense of humor and his powers of observation. Melville was also the subject of several early biographies in the 1890s. Melville's longtime friend Arthur Stedman sought to stir up interest in Melville's work immediately following his death in 1891 in a series of brief biographical sketches. Another friend, Joseph Edward Adams Smith, wrote the earliest effort at an extended biography in a nine-installment series published in the Pittsfield, Massachusetts, *Evening Journal* in 1892. Both of these biographies indicate the loyalty that Melville inspired in his friends, but neither abounds in insights regarding the quality of much of Melville's work — this is indicated in no small degree by the fact that Melville's short story from the 1850s, "Cock-a-Doodle-Doo," gets roughly equal billing with *Moby-Dick* from both Smith and Stedman. Titus Munson Coan, meanwhile, held out the lasting merit of *Typee* in an essay in the Boston *Literary World* (116–19).

Finally, the most prolonged tribute to Melville from the years before the Melville Revival came from a Canadian scholar, Archibald MacMechan, who argued forcefully for the idea that *Moby-Dick* in particular among Melville's works gave voice to specifically American literary themes and styles. Meanwhile, as Frank Jewett Mather, Jr., was to note in his centenary essay on Melville in 1919, literary luminaries such as Robert Louis Stevenson, Charles Warren Stoddard, and John La Farge had all expressed admiration for Melville's body of work. Melville's chief reviver, Raymond Weaver, was himself able to cite triumphantly the praise of Melville expressed by John Masefield, England's great poet of the sea, who referred to *Moby-Dick* as a "wild, beautiful romance," in which Melville "seem[ed] to have spoken the very secret of the sea" (in Weaver, 25).

Nonetheless, there is no evading the fact that something special happened in the development of Melville's literary reputation in the years surrounding the end of the First World War, and the most spectacular transformation in his reputation came as the result of a conversation between a young Columbia University instructor, Raymond Weaver, and the revered Columbia literary scholar Carl Van Doren. Weaver's account of the conversation was first published in Hershel Parker's *The Recognition of Herman Melville* (1967). Van Doren indicated to his junior colleague that he had been giving some thought to the upcoming centenary of Melville's birth, and that as Melville was "a wonderful old boy," Weaver might find it worth his while to write up an article on the obscure author (Parker, *Recognition*, vii). Weaver made two stunning discoveries that served to alter the course of his life. The first was the magnificent prose of Melville's early novels, culminating in *Moby-Dick*, and the second was absence of any major scholarly biography of this superb writer. In retrospect, Weaver looked back on the days during which he wrote the book that resulted from these two discoveries, *Herman Melville: Mariner and Mystic* (1921), with astonishment, relating in his account of the genesis of the project that he considered it "piracy" in those early days if he was asked to pay more than a dollar for first editions of *Moby-Dick*. These same first editions for which Weaver scorned to pay a dollar in 1920 sold for over $200 before the end of the 1920s (*Recognition*, viii). A quick Google search reveals that first editions of *Moby-Dick* are currently advertised at prices running from $28,000 to $85,000 in 2010. With the publication of Weaver's biography in 1921, the days when Melville could be regarded as an obscure writer or a curiosity in American literary history were gone forever.

In hindsight, it is easy to see the flaws in Weaver's groundbreaking biography. Weaver was introducing to the world of literary scholarship a figure who had generated little prior scholarly interest, so he had two main sources of information about Melville: documents and memories supplied by members of the Melville family, most particularly Melville's granddaughter, Elizabeth Melville Metcalf, and the accounts provided by first-person narrators in Melville's novels. Weaver, as has been frequently noted, found that the most effective method of filling in holes in Melville's biography was to assume that Melville's first-person narrators were stand-ins for Melville himself. Thus, when Weaver describes Melville's young adulthood and his first transatlantic voyage, he quotes extensively from *Redburn*. When he discusses Melville's time in the Pacific, he quotes from *Typee*, *Omoo*, and, most problematically of all, Ishmael's narration in *Moby-Dick*. The unwary reader is likely to receive the impression that these quotations are entries in a private journal instead of the musings of characters in Melville's novels. Just how much this use of the novels' narrators distorted the record of Melville's life became clear in the period from 1937–1952, when studies by William Gilman, Howard Vincent, Wilson Heflin, Merrell Davis, and Charles R. Anderson tracked the relationship between fact and fiction in Melville's novels, and revealed that even in Melville's most fact-oriented novels, there is a wide variance between the narrators' accounts and what we know about Melville's own history.

Moreover, Weaver's account of Melville's career seems strangely misshapen from the perspective of twenty-first century Melville scholarship, and Weaver's misprisions may account for some of the enduring distortions in how Melville's career is viewed. For Weaver, the last forty years of Melville's life are something between a tragedy and a farce, and Weaver's biography implies strongly that it would have been much better had Melville died after the publication of *Pierre*, rather than continuing to live and write into the early 1890s. The two chapters that deal with Melville's entire post-*Moby-Dick* career in Weaver's biography are entitled "The Great Refusal" and "The Long Quietus," and run to under fifty pages between them, much of which consists of direct quotations from Melville or his correspondents, and all of which indicates that intellectually and artistically, these years constituted a living death for Melville.

Melville himself might not have appreciated having his existence truncated in this manner, but to some degree that is the point: Weaver's biography was less an account of the mundane existence of a flesh and blood man who wrote novels than a dark hagiography for the modern era. In reflecting on the questions about Melville's sanity raised by critics and family members alike, Weaver first identified a soul-destroying "saneness" as the characteristic of nineteenth-century America, and then argued that Melville's resistance to the broader "sanity" of his culture associates him with "poets, prophets, and saints" throughout history (18). Lest Weaver's readers should fall into the error of regarding Melville as a run-of-the-mill poet, prophet, or saint, Weaver proceeded in the same paragraph to associate Melville with Socrates and Jesus Christ. Considered in this light, it is perhaps unsurprising that Weaver seemed to suggest that Melville should have died at the age of thirty-three.

The cost of this myth-making is that the arc of Melville's career became restricted for Weaver to the seven years from the writing of *Typee* to the publication of *Pierre*, which caused Weaver to ignore for the most part such major fiction and poetry as *The Piazza Tales* (1856), *The Confidence-Man* (1857), *Battle-Pieces* (1866), *Clarel* (1876), virtually all of Melville's late poetry, and, surprisingly in light of the fact that it was Weaver who eventually first published an edition of Melville's posthumous masterpiece, *Billy Budd*. In sum, Weaver's biography misrepresented Melville's early novels by overestimating their congruence with his life and dismissed all of his short fiction and poetry and his last full-length novel with hardly any analysis at all.

Despite all these flaws, *Herman Melville: Mariner and Mystic* remains an astonishing achievement. Weaver took a nearly forgotten writer, who was judged by many of his more generous contemporaries to be a minor, if nonetheless talented, writer of travel narratives and sea fiction, and transformed him into the central figure in the history of the American novel. Weaver accomplished this in part due to his profound imaginative empathy with the temper of Melville's work. If Weaver was not the first to recognize the greatness of *Moby-Dick* (as we have seen, W. Clark Russell was making the argument for the centrality of *Moby-Dick* among Melville's works in the 1880s) he certainly was the first to construct a sustained narrative out of Melville's career that made *Moby-Dick* its climax and persuaded a substantial audience that this choice was warranted. Weaver's most egregious weakness — his denigration of Melville's work and life from 1852 through 1891 — is also in some ways his greatest strength. The story that Weaver tells is, in its essentials, the story that subsequent Melville biographers have elaborated upon: a young man who has earned his fame and fortune through writing popular narratives of travel based on his own experience finds that these narratives no longer express his deepest intellectual and spiritual aspirations, and heroically rejects writing novels that sell in order to write a masterpiece that will be unrecognized in the author's time, but will ultimately come to be recognized as one of the most magnificent expressions of the human spirit. If this sounds like a common-sense summary of Melville's career through the publication of *Moby-Dick*, it is a measure of the degree to which all readers of Melville are intellectual descendents of Weaver now.

In what is perhaps the most important statement on Melville's significance in Weaver's study, Weaver lists the three great accomplishments of Melville's literary career: His "literary discover[y]" of the South Seas, his interpretation of the world of sailors, and finally, his authorship of *Moby-Dick*, which, Weaver said, with a trace of hyperbole, was "after the order of Melchizedek, without issue and without descent" (25). It is notable that Melville's later work is absent from this synopsis, and characteristic that Weaver again refers to Melville in terms generally used for a prophet or savior. These are two of the three attributes of Weaver's work that every Melville scholar since has either adopted or inveighed vigorously against. The third attribute of Weaver's work that has spawned intense argument ever since is his placement of Captain Ahab, rather than the narrator Ishmael, at the center of *Moby-Dick*. For Weaver, Ahab is the hero of the novel because of his Promethean persona and his "spiritual daring" (332). This point of view has often been disparaged, as we shall see, on the grounds that Ahab is a crazed tyrant, and the more ambivalent and humble Ishmael has come for Ahab's condemners to be the most important figure in the novel. That the debate that Weaver sparked continues can be seen in one of the most ambitious studies of the young twenty-first century, Clare Spark's *Hunting Captain Ahab: Psychological Warfare and the Melville Revival* (2001). I shall have more to say about Spark in chapter 5, but for the moment it suffices to observe that Spark sees the subsequent rejection of Weaver's admiration for Ahab as a disastrous detour away from the radical potential of Melville's great novel. Weaver may have been superseded, but the controversies that first appear in his work go on.

Weaver's other enduring contribution to Melville studies came through the field of textual criticism as the result of the assistance that he received from an important Melville scholar who was also a Melville family member: Eleanor Melville Metcalf. Weaver was given an unpublished and unedited manuscript that had been preserved in a breadbox by Metcalf that dealt with the strange story of a handsome young sailor who was impressed into the British Navy and executed for mutiny.[2] That manuscript, which we now know as *Billy Budd*, proved to be one of Melville's most enduring works, and it was Weaver who edited the first edition of the novella ever published. As with his biography, Weaver's textual work on *Billy Budd* has been revised significantly, but Weaver's editorial recovery of this magnificent late work of fiction is by itself sufficient to make him a towering figure in the history of the effort to define the contours of Melville's body of work.

The length of the shadow that Weaver casts in Melville studies, both as a figure to be resisted and as an inescapable forbear, becomes evident when one considers the direction of biographical criticism on Melville in the 1920s and beyond. John Freeman, Melville's first British biographer, drew almost exclusively on Weaver's biographical researches in his 1926 study *Herman Melville*, and like Weaver, he accepted most of Melville's early work as straight autobiography, plundering *Typee*, *Omoo*, and *Redburn* for supposedly biographical details that later researchers proved to be fictitious. The change that had been wrought in Melville's literary reputation in the 1920s becomes clear when we consider that Freeman deemed it possible to refer to Melville in passing in his opening sentence as "the most powerful of all the great American writers" (1). This would have come as news to even Melville's most ardent admirers a decade earlier, but by 1926 it could seem somewhat like common sense. Freeman extended the critical recovery of Melville in this biography with his consideration of *Billy Budd*, which Weaver's textual editing had by this point made known to the community of scholars, and he introduced a theme that would prove one of the most enduring in *Billy Budd* criticism: the idea that in this final work, Melville had finally reached a state of peace with the philosophical, religious, and artistic questions with which he had wrestled throughout his life (136), thus rejecting Weaver's portrait of a Melville who was disillusioned to the end. Freeman provided an important corrective to Weaver's biography by considering Melville's short fiction of the 1850s much more carefully. Weaver had glossed over works like "Bartleby the Scrivener" and "Benito Cereno" without recognizing their literary merit, but Freeman praised both highly as well as drawing attention to the sketch "The Chola Widow" in *The Encantadas*. Freeman unfortunately proved even less receptive to Melville's poetry than Weaver, however, most notably in his airy assertion that in a world with cinema, there was really no need for a long descriptive poem like *Clarel*, Melville's 1876 epic on the subject of faith, doubt, and cross-cultural dialogue (166).

Lewis Mumford, in his 1929 biography, charitably moved the date of Melville's "real" death back from 1852 to the time of Melville's completion of the closing scene of *Billy Budd*, when Billy cries "God bless Captain Vere!" just before his execution. That he did so was indicative of a transformation in Melville's reputation that had occurred in no small part as a result of Weaver's efforts. By the end of the 1920s, it was simply no longer possible to ignore the fact that Melville had been anything but silent from 1852 until 1891, and that his output during that period had included both superlative short fiction (most notably "Bartleby," "Benito Cereno," and *Billy Budd*) and voluminous poetry, as well as his last full-length novel, *The Confidence-Man*. Mumford, like Freeman, relied heavily on Weaver's primary research into Melville's life, but much more than Freeman, he reinterpreted the meaning of this research. The brilliance of Mumford's reinterpretation lay in his ability to take concepts directly from Melville's writing and reading — "Timonism," as a descriptor for Melville's post-*Moby-Dick* disillusionment, for example — and to use these terms to organize the course of Melville's life and career. Because of Mumford's eagerness to allow Melville to tell his own story as much as possible by means of quotation and paraphrase, Mumford evaded the error that Weaver and Freeman made of discounting Melville's later work, and he was thus able to construct a new trajectory for Melville's career. In Mumford's telling, Melville does rise to the peak of his powers in *Moby-Dick*, but rather than following this artistic triumph and commercial failure with a "long quietus" he works steadily as a chastened, disillusioned, and often misanthropic writer, finally achieving a resolution to his anguished quest for meaning when he writes the concluding scene of *Billy Budd*, at which point he is ready for death. Mumford recognized the presence of tragedy in Melville's life, but he saw Melville's personal story reaching a redemptive conclusion — a viewpoint that was enabled in part by the fact that his estimate of the artistic qualities of Melville's later work (and particularly his poetry) was higher than that of Weaver or Freeman.

What ties Weaver, Freeman, and Mumford together is the sense of imaginative identification with Melville that is at the core of their books. The triumph achieved by these studies is that they effectively resurrected Melville's literary reputation and made him a kind of literary contemporary of 1920s modernism. Moreover, once Mumford had completed his biography, the default understanding of the trajectory of Melville's career was firmly in place. It is fair to say that the Melville that most students meet in introductory college courses is still more or less the Melville who appears in Mumford's biography, for better or for worse. What is missing in their work, however, is a sense of the nineteenth-century man on whom the early twentieth-century cultural signifier was based. Who was Herman Melville? What views, if any, did he have on Nature, Art, Politics, Religion, or Philosophy apart from those placed in the mouths of his characters? What are the sources of Melville's art in his life, his reading, and his conversations with contemporaries? Did his cultural milieu mean anything to him other than as an oppressive environment against which he was determined to rebel? As it became clear that Melville's place as a major writer was secured, these questions became increasingly urgent, and from the 1930s to the 1950s, scholars drawn into Melville's orbit were increasingly intent on answering them. The Melville of the 1920s had been a Promethean artist bitterly estranged from his society; the Melville of the 1930s and 1940s would be a man of his times as well as a critic of those times.

If Melville's recuperation as a major author was the work in no small part of scholars at Columbia, his emergence as an author whose life we can discuss with some confidence was the fruit of the efforts of a remarkably tenacious group of scholars associated with Yale University. As Sanford Marovitz has noted in a recent essay on the Melville Revival, Stanley T. Williams was the dissertation director of a series of Melvilleans who helped connect the mythologized Melville of the first generation of twentieth-century biographers to the flesh and blood man who wrote fiction and poetry from his residences in New York and Massachusetts between the 1840s and 1890s. Harrison Hayford, who will figure repeatedly throughout my account of the history of Melville studies, was among these students, as were such eminent Melvilleans who appear in later chapters as James Baird, Walter Bezanson, Merrell R. Davis, Charles Feidelson, Elizabeth Foster, William H. Gilman, Tyrus Hillway, Henry F. Pommer, Merton M. Sealts, Jr., and Nathalia Wright (Marovitz, 'Revival," 523). The overwhelming effect of the efforts of Williams and his students was to redirect Melville studies from retrospective mythologizing of the great author to painstaking, often heroic, research into the details of his life.

Another critic who valued biographical fact-gathering, Willard Thorp, did not publish a full-length book on Melville, but he laid the foundation for the biographical renaissance of the 1940s. Thorp collected much of Melville's major work into a one-volume collection in 1938, and he supplied a substantial addition to our knowledge about Melville the human being in the introductory material for the volume. Thorp's interest in Melville's economic situation was extended in William Charvat's important 1943 article in *American Literature*, "Melville's Income," which tabulated the exact amounts of money that Melville had received for his writing throughout his literary career.

William H. Gilman (a member of the fact-oriented Yale group), Charles Roberts Anderson, and Wilson Heflin all contributed tremendously to excavating specific segments of Melville's early career and debunking misunderstandings of the relationship between Melville's life and work that grew out of the frenzied efforts of the early leaders of the Melville Revival. Of these three biographers, Charles Roberts Anderson was the earliest and the most wide-ranging. If Weaver found himself making the counter-intuitive case that Melville was both among America's greatest writers and a sort of literary sage when he began his biography of Melville, Anderson found himself revising the consensus that Weaver had fostered. Curiously, Anderson seems to have had a quarrel with Melville's beard — which he saw as standing in for a wider misapprehension of Melville as an author who was important because he was tortured and profound, rather than, as Anderson argued, because he was a "joyous" narrator of the experience of travel who rather liked being a popular author at first, and knew that he was good at it (7). In his introduction, Anderson noted sardonically that Melville's life had been the subject of rather more discussion than his work in much of the criticism published as of 1939, and that the discussion of Melville's life had dealt much more with portraits of his philosophy based on guesswork than on the knowable facts about Melville's experiences. Anderson sought to deal in knowable facts rather than guesswork, and he sought to establish that Melville's greatness consists not in his philosophy of life, but in his ability to narrate romances of the sea. As a result of this agenda, Anderson's work had the effect of rehabilitating the works that, before the Melville Revival, had seemed Melville's most enduring but had since lost status — *Typee* and *Omoo* — and while Anderson acknowledged *Moby-Dick*'s greatness, he saw it as consisting more in its status of a brilliantly arranged "romance of the sea" than as a piece of metaphysical wisdom literature. Anderson's work also had the effect of establishing clearly that Melville's work in *Typee* and *Omoo* was no naïve account of unadulterated personal experience. In painstaking detail, Anderson established that Melville had borrowed heavily from works by prior travelers such as David Porter, G. H. von Langsdorff, C. S. Stewart, and William Ellis in *Typee* and *Omoo*, and he also tracked the ways in which Melville had, in the early portions of *Typee*, exaggerated the evidence that the Taipii (Typee is Melville's variant on the more commonly accepted name) engaged in cannibalism in order to make his defense of the Taipii later in the novel more rhetorically impressive. Anderson also tracked down some significant source material for *Moby-Dick*, including works such as Thomas Beale's *The Natural History of the Sperm Whale*, J. Ross Browne's *Etchings of a Whaling Cruise*, and Joseph C. Hart's *Miriam Coffin*, all of which Melville referenced in *Moby-Dick*, and all of which contributed much more to the substance of the novel than Melville was willing to admit. Anderson also called attention to the function of propaganda in *White-Jacket*, emphasizing well in advance of critical movements like New Historicism the cultural work that Melville's earlier and more popular novels were doing in nineteenth-century America, particularly in relation to Melville's scathing critique of flogging in the U.S. Navy.[3]

If Anderson dealt a death-blow to the idea that *Typee*, *Omoo*, and *White-Jacket* were unadulterated autobiography, William H. Gilman did the same service in relation to Melville's fourth novel, *Redburn*. Gilman's careful research into Melville's life and his comparison of the facts he uncovered demonstrated clearly that *Redburn*, like the South Seas novels, was highly crafted and fictionalized, and not a reliable source of biographical data. Howard P. Vincent's *The Trying-Out of Moby-Dick* (1949) and Wilson Heflin's 1952 Vanderbilt dissertation "Herman Melville's Whaling Years," meanwhile, contributed to a much clearer sense of the relationship between Melville's biography and his construction of *Moby-Dick*, and established that, when it came to that construction, the writings of others mattered at least as much as Melville's personal experiences, and quite likely more. Heflin's landmark dissertation was published posthumously in 2004, and is thus now widely available to readers of Melville.

The years immediately before and after 1950, falling as they did around the centennial of *Moby-Dick*'s 1851 publication, resulted in a tremendous flurry of biographical activity about Melville among both dedicated Melvilleans and scholars of American literature more broadly construed.

The earliest of these studies, Richard Chase's *Herman Melville: A Critical Study* (1949) was notable less for its original insights into Melville's life than for its incorporation of Melville into the development of the fledgling discipline of American Studies, and indeed, Chase's appropriation of Melville at this crucial moment in the development of the field has had profound consequences for how Melville has been interpreted by scholars of American Studies ever since. For Chase, Melville offered a model for developing a new vision of liberalism, more informed by tragedy and uncertainty than earlier, more optimistic varieties of liberalism. As will be shown in chapter 4, Chase's thesis resulted in sharp attacks on both Chase's "Cold-War liberalism" and Melville's alleged role as a model for American Cold War thinking.

Newton Arvin, who published a biography with the straightforward title of *Herman Melville* in 1950, serves as a link between Weaver and Mumford's early Melville biographies and the recurrent tendency in Melville scholarship to turn back to Melville's artistic accomplishments. It is indicative of the presence of these dueling tendencies in biographical criticism on Melville that in Andrew Delbanco's recent biography of Melville, Delbanco refers back to Arvin as the predecessor whose work he finds most valuable (citing Arvin five times in his index, and Howard not at all), and Hershel Parker refers back to Leon Howard as the author of the "standard" Melville biography prior to Parker's own biography. In some ways, Arvin seemed hardly to be a biographer in the conventional sense. Through his early chapters, he dealt primarily with facts about Melville's early life that were already widely known by the late 1940s, and once he started to write in earnest about Melville's literary career, he virtually abandoned Melville's outward life altogether. The one area where Arvin extended prior biographical scholarship was in his consideration of the Melville-Hawthorne relationship, which drew upon Arvin's own prior work as a biographer of Nathaniel Hawthorne.

Where Arvin excelled was in his tracking of Melville's use of language throughout his body of work. In doing so, Arvin reversed several conventional opinions of the relative value of Melville's early work. While the scholars of the 1920s and 1930s tended to focus most on *Typee* (both because it was Melville's first novel and because of its popularity) and

Mardi (because of its strong allegorical component), Arvin argued that Melville's expanded awareness of the possibilities of language and narrative in *Omoo* and *Redburn* made them the most important milestones among Melville's pre-*Moby-Dick* work. The unquestionable center of Arvin's biography, both literally and metaphorically, was his consideration of *Moby-Dick*. He devoted a full fifty-page chapter to a careful formal consideration of the novel, and he closed it with a hypothesis that seems remarkably prescient in the context of twenty-first century debates about the environment: he suggests that "cosmic submissiveness" — a willingness to submit to Nature with the same reverence with which the Calvinist preacher in *Moby-Dick* Father Mapple submitted to his God — might be the ultimate upshot of the conclusion of *Moby-Dick* (Arvin, 192–93). Arvin gave much of the rest of Melville's career short shrift, but he saw the concept of "cosmic submissiveness" reprised in the "Nunc Dimittis" quality of *Billy Budd*, which he somewhat incautiously suggested was universally accepted to be a narrative of reconciliation (292–99).

Jay Leyda can seem in retrospect like one of Melville's own monomaniacal characters. A student of Russian cinema, Leyda believed that he could best preserve Melville's legacy by assembling primary documents associated with Melville's life and work in chronological order and allowing them to speak for themselves as much as possible. The result, *The Melville Log* (1951), is surely among the most ambitious achievements in the history of American literary scholarship. Over the course of two 900 page volumes, Leyda arranged selections from Melville's published work, journals, and letters; reviews of Melville's work; public documents associated with Melville (such as tax records); and letters, journals, and diaries written by Melville's associates and family members. In addition to being an influence on all subsequent Melville biographical scholarship, Leyda's *Log* is also an ongoing project: during his lifetime, Leyda began to collaborate with Hershel Parker on the development of and expanded *Melville Log*, and Parker has continued the project since Leyda's death in 1988.

Leon Howard's *Herman Melville* (1951) is forever linked with Leyda's *Log* by design. Howard explicitly, and by agreement with Leyda, sought to create a factual narrative of Melville's life that could be read side-by-side with *The Melville Log*. If Leyda collected the facts about Melville's life with almost unimaginable zeal, Howard provided a theoretical justification for such a fact-based approach by lambasting critics whom he believed speculated irresponsibly about Melville's life and character based on his works. Howard's biography was to remain the most authoritative study of the details of Melville's life until the publication of Hershel Parker's two-volume biography in 1996 and 2002 and Laurie Robertson-Lorant's one-volume biography in 1996. Despite its formidable successors, Howard's biography is still worthwhile reading. Howard possessed a knack for highlighting details in Melville's life that had broad cultural resonances, and that have disappeared from more recent biographies. For example, Howard noted that Isaac Montgomery, a close associate of Melville in Hawaii, was despised by Protestant missionaries in part because of his interest in promoting Roman Catholicism as a counterweight to Protestant missionary influence in the Hawaiian islands (Howard, 68–70). Given both the vitriolic attacks on Melville as a potential Catholic secret agent in the contemporary missionary press and the ambivalent sympathy for Catholicism that many have discerned in Melville's later poetry, it seems a shame that such a detail has not been discussed in Melville biographies more recent than Howard's. Howard's biography was also notable for the acerbic critique that he directed at scholars and critics, who, he believed, were more interested in finding themselves in Melville than in investigating the details of his own life. Howard rebuked what he saw as a solipsistic tendency in Melville criticism to recreate Melville's major works as material for practical criticism that would validate whatever the current critical theory might be, and he suggested that a demythologized approach to gathering up the facts of Melville's life as an antidote. Ironically, more recent scholars have found precisely the sort of solipsism in Howard's account of Melville's marriage as a scene of Melville's torment at the hands of a neurotic wife. Melville scholars acquainted with Howard personally, most notably Harrison Hayford, later suggested in *Melville's Evermoving Dawn* that this account had considerably more to do with Howard's own experiences than with anything he discovered about Melville's marriage (Garner et al., 230).

Many of Melville's biographers seem to feel and claim a kinship with the creator of Ishmael, Ahab, and the great white whale, but Eleanor Melville Metcalf was the only major biographer of Melville who could claim a blood relationship to the author himself. Metcalf was Melville's granddaughter, and she was able to recall in *Herman Melville: Cycle and Epicycle* (1953) the experience of pulling on Melville's beard while sitting on his lap as a small child and listening to him as he told stories from his travels. Metcalf's book provided a more human picture of Melville than had yet appeared, and it shed considerable light on the relationships Melville had with his family members and members of his literary milieu. Moreover, although documents associated with the Melville and Gansevoort families and Melville's literary associates made up the bulk of Metcalf's book, the commentary that she interspersed between them showed a truly Melvillean capacity to cut directly to the heart of the matter. The fact that Metcalf published her work after the flurry of Melville biographies around the centennial of *Moby-Dick* meant that these biographies were dated almost from the start in their treatment of Melville's personal life.

By the time the next major Melville biography had been published after the burst of work in the early 1950s, nearly a quarter of a century had passed.[4] Edwin Haviland Miller's biography was significantly indebted for its details to the work done by Leyda and Howard in at mid-century, but Miller sought to extend and modernize the critical conversation about Melville's life and its relation to his work by means of psychoanalytic theory. Perhaps more than any Melville biography before or since, Miller's biography was shaped by large conceptual frames that depended on neither the close attention to Melville's literary works that had characterized the Melville biographies by Weaver, Freeman, Mumford, and Arvin, nor the close attention to the details of Melville's day-to-day life that characterized the work of Anderson, Gilman, Heflin, Vincent, Leyda, Howard, Hayford, Sealts, or Metcalf. Taking Melville's identification of his narrator in *Moby-Dick* with the biblical figure Ishmael, Miller found in Melville's family structure a repetition of the biblical story of Abraham and his children. Melville's father Allan thus becomes Abraham. His mother Maria Gansevoort Melville becomes Sarah. His elder brother Gansevoort, the favored son in the family until his death in the mid-1840s, becomes Isaac. Not surprisingly, Herman himself becomes Ishmael. One might note that this requires some rearranging of the furniture of the biblical account, given that Ishmael is older than Isaac and becomes an outcast because his mother is not Sarah, but her slave Hagar. The point of all this typologizing is not, however, to make the Melville family conform to the story of the patriarchs of the Hebrew scriptures, but rather to make family relationships broadly construed central to Melville's literary production. The emphasis on family relationships would prove productive in later studies by Michael Paul Rogin, Laurie Robertson-Lorant, and Hershel Parker, but in Miller's study the usefulness of this emphasis was restricted by the fact that Miller was interested in the Melvill(e) family not as a group of historical figures, so much as psychological types who could be seen to have wounded Herman's spirit in artistically productive ways. Furthermore, they all bow gracefully out of the picture in Miller's telling once Melville's only real family emerges: Nathaniel Hawthorne, who according to Miller was both Melville's most important erotic interest and his most meaningful, and wounding, father figure.

Because Miller's biography is so thesis-driven, it is consistently hampered by an inability to take seriously any elements in Melville's body of work that does not conform to Miller's thesis. For example, "The Whiteness of the Whale," long one of the most debated and renowned chapters in *Moby-Dick*, becomes for Miller something between an extended joke and a deliberate authorial red herring, on the grounds that Ishmael's expressed horror at the color white as the "colorless all-color of Atheism" cannot be meant seriously by a writer as skeptical as Melville. Moments like this vitiate what is otherwise an admirable quality of Miller's biography: his willingness to consider Melville as a sometimes frail and conflicted man, rather than merely as a transcendent artist.

Although two decades passed after Miller's biography before another major biography of Melville was published, biographical criticism was not silenced in the interim. Miller's biography coincided with a major discovery from an unlikely source. The Unitarian minister and historian Walter D. Kring unearthed two important facts about Melville. First, Kring discovered a letter from Samuel Shaw, Elizabeth Shaw Melville's brother, to Henry Whitney Bellows, her minister at All Soul's Unitarian Church in New York City, that suggested that Shaw might stage a kidnapping in order to enable Elizabeth to leave Herman, whom Shaw believed to be in a precarious mental state. Second, Kring discovered a membership list from All Soul's Unitarian Church from the 1880s that demonstrated that Melville had chosen to become a full member of the church in the mid-1880s. Kring published both of these findings in an essay co-authored with Jonathan Carey entitled "Two Discoveries Concerning Herman Melville" in the *Proceedings of the Massachusetts Historical Society* in 1975, and he published an expanded version in 1981 in a pamphlet edited by Hershel Parker and Donald Yannella and entitled *The Endless, Winding Way in Melville*. The Shaw-Bellows letter proved quite explosive, touching off a controversy that culminated in Elizabeth Renker's article "Herman Melville, Wife-Beating, and the Written Page," which was initially published in *American Literature* in 1994 and was reprinted in Renker's 1998 book-length study *Strike through the Mask: Herman Melville and the Scene of Writing*, and Cathy Davidson and Jessamyn Hatcher's influential 2002 collection *No More Separate Spheres!* What had previously been a vague rumor of possible domestic violence on Melville's part had become a question that no biographer could completely ignore. Kring's second discovery, by contrast, proved eminently ignorable, and it remains to be seen when a full account of the significance of Melville's late adoption of Unitarianism will be written. The only study to address it in any length is Kring's own *Herman Melville's Religious Journey* (1997), which was hampered by the fact that as Kring himself confessed, Kring was neither a Melville scholar nor a literary critic in the broader sense.[5]

By the 1990s, Melville biography might have been expected to go into eclipse, given the general move toward cultural studies and away from large-scale treatments of single authors during the last decade of the twentieth century and the first decade of the twenty-first. If anything, however, the 1990s and 2000s proved to be a time period of sustained engagement with Melville's life that exceeded any previous period. Stanton Garner's *The Civil War World of Herman Melville* (1993) was the first of a cavalcade of biographically based studies of Melville during the 1990s. Garner built his study around his research into Melville's family, social, and political connections in New York in the 1860s as a deeply interested observer of the Civil War. Because Garner's focus is primarily on Melville's relationship to war and nationalism, I will reserve most of my discussion of his study for chapter 5, but clearly no account of Melville biography is complete without him.

Whether or not Melville himself had a problem with women (a matter that will be taken up in more detail in chapter 4) there is no doubt that Melville scholarship in the early years tended to portray Melville's work in aggressively, and sometimes almost exclusively, masculine terms and that this tendency has had unfortunate implications for our understanding of Melville's work in more recent years. Among other problems, the tendency of some early scholars to find misogyny (sometimes seemingly with an air of approbation) in Melville's life and work has meant that it has at times been taking for granted that Melville had little to say to women and was not significantly influenced by women. Laurie Robertson-Lorant's 1996 biography of Melville provided a useful corrective to this deforming tendency in Melville biography. Robertson-Lorant made careful use of the letters and journals written by the women in Melville's life to demonstrate both that Melville depended emotionally and intellectually on his relationships with women, and that the women in Melville's life were compelling figures in their own right. In particular, Robertson-Lorant refuted misogynistic portraits of Elizabeth Shaw Melville as a hindrance to Melville's creativity by citing witty letters that she wrote as a teenager, Melville's dependence on her for editing and copying his work, and most touchingly, the renewed affection that developed between the husband and wife late in life and was recorded in many of the poems that Melville wrote in the 1880s. Through her careful analysis of the Melvilles' marriage, Robertson-Lorant also called into question facile portraits of Melville himself as a wife-beating misogynist. Moreover, Robertson-Lorant approached the questions about Melville's sexuality, alcoholism, and mental health in a judicious spirit that truly illuminated that relationship between Melville's life and work rather than simply sensationalizing it.

A great virtue of Hershel Parker's massive two-volume biography of Melville, the first volume of which was published in 1996, and the second in 2002, is that it recovers figures from Melville's family history who have often been reduced to caricatures (perhaps most spectacularly in Miller's biography). Allan Melvill, Herman's father, ceases to be simply an improvident failure as he is in most Melville biographies and becomes a witty letter-writer and a master of the conventions of late eighteenth-century rhetoric. Previous Melville biographies revealed why Allan's failures and early death contributed to Herman's streak of melancholy; Parker's helps us to see why Allan was a not unworthy sire for one of world literature's most verbally inventive authors. Gansevoort Melville as well is considered more closely here then elsewhere, and instead of simply portraying Gansevoort as the favored older brother who serves as a necessary foil for the underrated Herman, Parker revealed through careful study of Gansevoort's *Index Rerum* (the record that Gansevoort kept of his own reading and intellectual development) that Gansevoort's reading contributed to Herman's own intellectual and artistic growth and to the fund of images and allusions available to him when he was writing works ranging from *Moby-Dick* to *Clarel* (*Herman Melville*, 1:109–35).

The most frequent criticism of Parker's biography has been that it lacks selectivity: Parker is blamed for seeming unwilling to exclude any fact about Melville, his family, his friends, or his publishers, however mundane. The heft of Parker's two volumes ensures that these complaints are not without merit, and yet it is hard for scholars who want to comprehend the history of Melville the man to wish the bulkiness of Parker's study away. What Parker provides the dedicated reader of Melville is a rich and detailed picture of a powerful and inventive mind responding to the large-scale pressures of Melville's own historical epoch (although race and class get less treatment than is merited), the smaller-scale pressures of Melville's family environment and his circle of friends, and Melville's profound engagement with the a tremendous volume of literature from around the globe.

Parker's reconstruction of Melville's life and milieu is astonishing, and yet there are puzzling moments in the biography. For example, when discussing "Bartleby the Scrivener," Parker argues that the story continues Melville's satire on Unitarianism from *Pierre*, and he adduces the narrator's non-attendance of a sermon he had planned to see at Trinity Church as evidence (2:176). Surely it is counterintuitive to find evidence for Melville's scorn for Unitarianism in a potentially derisive reference to a church that, in addition to being an Episcopal church, actually has the central element in traditional Christian doctrine that Unitarianism rejects in its very name! Indeed, Parker's treatment of Melville's personal religious history is marred by an assumption about Melville's hostility toward Unitarianism that the very biographical facts Parker discusses, and in many cases brings to light as a result of his own heroic scholarly endeavors, seem not to bear out. As imposing as Parker's monumental biography is, the process of interpreting Melville's personal choices, and particularly, those related to religion, is not yet at an end.

The potential of biographical criticism to continue to inspire and transform critical considerations of Melville's work appears particularly clearly in Parker's 2008 study *Melville: The Making of the Poet*. Readers who consult this volume expecting prolonged readings of Melville's published poetry will be disappointed to find that the poetry that Melville produced comes in for relatively little discussion. Instead, what Parker does in this volume (and what he announces in the introduction that he intends to do) is to lay the groundwork for future considerations of Melville's poetic technique by exploring at length Melville's reading of canonical European poetry and the development of his knowledge of poetic theory, metrics, and prosody.

After Parker, any new Melville biography has to justify its existence on some grounds other than comprehensiveness. Elizabeth Hardwick's slender biography of Melville, published in 2000, takes the opposite tack from Parker in that it leaves the facts about Melville's life largely as it found them, and attempts, like Arvin's biography before it, to probe the inner meaning of Melville's life, particularly as revealed through his fiction. The brevity of Hardwick's biography means that it breaks little new factual ground, but it does serve the purpose of providing a brief, lyrically written, and up-to-date account of Melville's development as a writer for readers who are unfamiliar with earlier biographies and who lack the stamina to undertake reading the lengthier and more recent ones.

Writing in Parker's wake as well, Andrew Delbanco staked his claim to greatness as a Melville biographer in 2005 on his acuity as a close reader of the language of Melville's great prose works and his capacity to weave an account of Melville's intellectual and artistic development into a history of Melville's cultural moment. Delbanco's biography is more ambitious in its scope than Hardwick's, and seeks to revive the minority tradition in Melville biography of considering Melville primarily as a developing literary artist. What distinguishes Delbanco's work most strikingly from earlier work in this vein by Weaver, Freeman, Mumford, and Arvin, however, is his mastery of the body of American Studies scholarship devoted to Melville that has developed since the 1950s. Throughout his biography, Delbanco moves seamlessly from haunting explications of Melville's supple and ingenious use of language to considerations of his often caustically critical interactions with the ideologies of race and gender that prevailed among his contemporaries in nineteenth-century America. This structure allows Delbanco to illuminate the mutual interpenetration of culture and aesthetics in Melville's work. As with his earlier work on the Puritans, moreover, Delbanco is able to write with a deep sympathy about the affective qualities of Melville's work and vision. Less fortunately, Delbanco follows Weaver and Freeman in regarding Melville's poetry as being of a considerably lower order of achievement than his best prose, a decision which is likely to strike devotees of Melville's poetry as a missed opportunity, given Delbanco's virtuosity as a close reader of Melville's prose.

The impulse to revive a blended biographical and aesthetic approach to Melville's life was expressed beautifully again in 2008 in Wyn Kelley's *Herman Melville: An Introduction*. Kelley uses Melville's correspondence with Hawthorne on the subject of a new novel built around the story of a young woman named Agatha (this is the story that Hershel Parker claimed in his biography of Melville ultimately took the form of a lost novel by Melville entitled *The Isle of the Cross*). While earlier critics of Melville's short fiction had incorporated the Agatha narrative into their arguments, Kelley's careful attention to the intersection between Melville's life and work in the Agatha letters represented a genuine advance in biographical criticism of Melville. Melville suggested first that Hawthorne write a novel based on Agatha's story, and then said that he would take the story up himself if Hawthorne was not interested. Kelley used Melville's discussion in his letters to Hawthorne as a spring board for analyzing his creative process, particularly his use of sources in building each of his major works. Kelley's study thus showed a way forward for biographical studies of Melville: by incorporating both the attention to factual biographical detail of the school of Melville biography associated with Parker and Howard and the sensitivity to form associated with Arvin and Delbanco, she demonstrated that aesthetic and biographical studies of Melville can profit by continued and intensified intermingling.

Textual Criticism

Not only was Raymond Weaver Melville's first major biographer, but he was also the scholar who inaugurated a rich tradition of Melvillean textual criticism by bringing out the first published edition of Melville's posthumous masterpiece *Billy Budd*. As with Weaver's biography, however, his textual scholarship proved both essential and flawed, and as a result, the most important development in textual scholarship following Weaver was the corrected edition of *Billy Budd*, which was completed by Harrison Hayford and Merton M. Sealts, Jr. in 1962. Hayford and Sealts were not the first to revise Weaver's original transcription; Weaver revised his 1924 version himself in 1928, and F. Barron Freeman revised Weaver's 1928 version in 1948, but the Hayford and Sealts version of *Billy Budd* has been accepted as by far the most authoritative since the early 1960s.

Two impressive monuments of textual scholarship helped both to cement Melville's standing as a major author and to shape the ways in which his fiction, poetry, and journals have been read ever since. The 1940s and 1950s saw the publication of the Hendricks House edition of Melville's works, and this edition was absorbed and superseded by a herculean labor of scholarship, the Northwestern-Newberry edition, which is at the present time and for the imaginable future the definitive edition of all Melville's work, including his journals and correspondence. The renowned textual scholars G. Thomas Tanselle, Harrison Hayford, and Hershel Parker were the general editors of the Northwestern Newberry edition, and the volumes were shaped by contributions from such prominent Melville scholars as Alma A. MacDougall, Lynn Horth, Walter Bezanson, Brian Higgins, Donald Yannella, Robert C. Ryan, Mary K. Bercaw, Patricia L. Ward, R. D. Madison, and Richard Colles Johnson. The textual scholarship of the Newberry editors has at times reoriented critics' understanding of crucial passages in Melville's works, a fact strikingly exemplified by the 1988 Northwestern-Newberry edition of *Moby-Dick*'s reassigning of the poignant monologue at the heart of "The Gilder" to Captain Ahab, which continues to complicate critics' readings of the novel in productive ways.[6]

While *Billy Budd* has always been the Melville text most in need of textual scholarship and interpretation, two other Melville texts have been the subject of considerable debate among textual scholars looking to ascertain Melville's intentions and the shape of his artistic development: *Typee* and *Pierre*. In addition to being Melville's definitive biographer and an editor for the Northwestern-Newberry Edition, Hershel Parker also contributed one of the more contentious strands of textual criticism on Melville with his insistent argument that the version of *Pierre* that Melville actually published should not be seen as constituting Melville's true intention for the novel. Parker argued that Melville had built a brilliant psychological novel when he was writing *Pierre*, but as a result of his arguments with his publishers, had deliberately sabotaged the novel by inserting passages that existed only to revile and satirize his perfidious publishers. So convinced was Parker that the published version of *Pierre* was inadequate, that he produced his own edition of the novel, which he called the "Kraken Edition," so named because of Melville's reference in a letter to Hawthorne to a work that would be to *Moby-Dick* as a kraken (giant squid) is to a whale. Although the originally published text is still the one most commonly used, Parker's intervention had the salutary effect of pushing all Melville scholars to consider carefully their grounds for their views of Melville's final intent in writing *Pierre*.[7]

Many of Melville's biographers and textual scholars have been resistant to literary theory as a concept, and literary critics and theorists, as we shall see in the chapters which follow, have been too often ignorant of the labors of biographical and textual scholars. John Bryant's work on *Typee* from the 1980s through the first decade of the twenty-first century had the effect of reinvigorating the exchange among theory, criticism, and scholarship in Melville studies. Bryant's work was spurred by the discovery in 1983 in a barn in upstate New York of early manuscript versions of parts of *Typee* that highlighted the ways in which Melville's vision for the novel[8] had changed over the course of his writing and revision of the piece. Bryant's work with the *Typee* manuscript fragments produced a full-length critical study, *Melville Unfolding: Sexuality, Politics, and Versions of Typee* (2008) and an electronic edition of *Typee* that allows readers to navigate Melville's process of revision based on the available manuscript documents. *Melville Unfolding* was a careful reconstruction, based on both the manuscript fragments and the divergent English and American editions, of Melville's writing process in researching and composing *Typee*, and in transmuting both his research and his personal experience into art. The effect of the study was to bring biographical and textual criticism into close conversation with questions of both artistic creation and the pressure that Melville's cultural moment exerted on the text.[9]

On the borderline between biographical and textual criticism is the work that has been done over the decades on Melville's reading and marginalia. Merton M. Sealts, Jr. contributed powerfully to our understanding of Melville's mind and his relationship to both his literary contemporaries and his literary forbears with *Melville's Reading*, a volume that evolved over the entire course of Sealts's scholarly life, with versions appearing in book form in 1966 and 1988, and a cumulative supplement appearing in the Melville Society journal *Leviathan* in 2005. In 1957, Sealts also helped establish the content of the lectures that Melville gave during his brief career as a public lecturer in *Melville as Lecturer*, and thus brought to light a body of Melville's work that cast light backwards on his sea novels and forward on his poetry.

Steven Olsen-Smith brought textual and biographical scholarship on Melville to the attention of academia broadly construed when *The Chronicle of Higher Education* published a profile of his work on *Melville's Marginalia Online* entitled "Call Me Digital" in its February 17, 2006 issue (J. Howard). Olsen-Smith, a student of Parker and a collaborator with Sealts, continued Sealts's work on Melville's reading and picked up where Walker Cowen had left off with his transcription of Melville's marginalia to books that Melville was known to have owned and borrowed. Cowen had laboriously transcribed all the marginalia from books that Melville had owned or borrowed and annotated and had written a general introduction to the marginalia that highlighted what he regarded as central trends in Melville's markings of books ranging from copies of Shakespeare and the Bible to copies of books by contemporaries of Melville like Emerson and Matthew Arnold. Cowen's study had taken the form of a 1965 Harvard doctoral dissertation, which by the early years of the twenty-first century was not widely available and moreover was in need of updating. Olsen-Smith demonstrated just how stimulating such an updating of Melville's marginalia could be with his electronic edition of Melville's marginalia to Thomas Beale's *Natural History of the Sperm Whale*. Using technology made available by the Fogg Art Museum (J. Howard, A14), Olsen-Smith recovered marginalia that had previously been deemed lost forever, including most sensationally an annotation that showed that Melville had at one point in the writing of *Moby-Dick* planned to allow Ahab to triumph and kill off the whale at last. Olsen-Smith's endeavors with the Beale edition, and more broadly with his collaboration with other scholars to create a comprehensive, annotated electronic edition of the marginalia to the public, clearly indicated that in the early years of the twenty-first century, the heroic era of Melville scholarship was not yet at an end.

The prominent position that biographical and textual scholarship plays in Melville studies is in itself deeply revealing of the nature of the critical reaction to Melville over the decades. It is by no means obvious that textual and biographical studies would play such a major role in the criticism on any author, much less one who has left such meager traces in both the public and private spheres outside his fiction and poetry. As Charles Roberts Anderson argued mournfully in 1939 and Melville critics and biographers have reiterated ever since, "No other major American author has left such scanty literary remains" (i). Although we now have many more "literary remains" with which to deal than Anderson did, his premise is still largely valid. And yet, biographies of Melville have not only been numerous, they have been influential.

Perhaps this fact need not be wholly mysterious. One of the most defining features of Melville's works, from *Typee* to *Billy Budd*, is the way that they blur the boundaries between life and art, travel and imagination, impersonal speculation and personal faith. If many scholars have found the lure of Melville's life story irresistible, it surely has something to do with Melville's own tendency to weave his life into his work and to express within his work reflections that seem, at least, to be the upwelling of his own soul. Throughout Melville's fiction and poetry he creates compelling first-person narrators like Tommo and Ishmael and characters like Pierre, Clarel, and Rolfe who can easily be identified with Melville himself, and with whom readers not infrequently feel a profound sense of spiritual and intellectual kinship. It is thus no accident that the story of Melville's recovery begins with a scholar who finds parallels in Melville to the crucifixion of Jesus and Socrates' death by hemlock. Melville's readers find in works as disparate as *Typee* and *Clarel*, *Moby-Dick* and *Battle-Pieces*, *The Confidence Man* and *Billy Budd*, an authorial consciousness with which they feel a deep sense of identification, and nothing could be more natural than a desire to get at the source of this intimately familiar, yet uncannily transcendent consciousness. One of Melville's own most frequently quoted passages can serve as a gloss on both this desire and its frustration:

> And still deeper the meaning of that story of Narcissus, who because he could not grasp the tormenting, mild image he saw in the fountain, plunged into it and was drowned. But that same image we see in all rivers and oceans. It is the image of the ungraspable phantom of life, and this is the key to it all. (*Moby-Dick*, 5)

Readers of the voluminous biographical interpretations of Melville may find that the effect of pursuing Melville from Weaver to Parker and beyond is to make the man himself all the more irresistibly "ungraspable." Indeed, no small portion of the pleasure that may be derived from reading and rereading these biographical studies is that they illuminate powerfully the elusiveness of the figure they attempt so heroically to comprehend.

Notes

[1] Unless otherwise noted, all the early references are to be found in Higgins and Parker.

[2] A common misperception in this regard is that Weaver "discovered" the manuscript. As Wyn Kelley recently pointed out in her article "Out of the Breadbox" (2011), the story of the Billy Budd manuscript is not the story of a solitary scholar's

heroic discovery of lost work, but rather of the preservation of Melville's work carried out specifically by the women in the Melville family, from Elizabeth Shaw Melville to Eleanor Melville Metcalf, who ultimately made the manuscript available to Weaver.

³ Anderson's researches in the South Seas continue to resonate in discussions of the relationship between Melville's life and art. In 2006, *ESQ: A Journal of the American Renaissance* published a special triple issue entitled "Melville in the Marquesas: Actuality of Place in *Typee* and Other Island Writings," edited and with a title essay by G. R. Thompson. The issue contains a spirited debate between John Bryant and Robert C. Suggs on the likelihood that Melville actually had the experiences that he narrated in *Typee*, with Bryant arguing that he did, and Suggs arguing that he did not. Other scholars, including G. R. Thompson, Geoffrey Sanborn, and Samuel Otter, contributed essays dealing with both the substance and the significance of the debate between Bryant and Suggs. In a 2009 special issue of *Leviathan: A Journal of Melville Studies* entitled "Melville in the Marquesas" and edited by Henry Hughes, Mary K. Bercaw Edwards made the startling case that Melville may never have entered Taipivai (Typee Valley in the novel) and may simply have remained near the port and drawn his narrative from other sources.

⁴ An exception to the silence of Melville's biographers during this period was Alan Lebowitz's *Progress into Silence: A Study of Melville's Heroes* (1970), which sought to compose an intellectual biography of Melville built around the characterization of the heroes in his novels.

⁵ The blending of Melville's personal, family, and intellectual history came to the fore as well in the most important biographically oriented work dedicated to Melville in the 1980s, Michael Paul Rogin's *Subversive Genealogy: The Politics and Art of Herman Melville* (1985). Due to its focus on political considerations, I will discuss Rogin's work primarily in chapter 5.

⁶ See the explanatory notes on page 804 of the Northwestern Newberry edition of *Moby-Dick, or the Whale* (1988) for a discussion of this change.

⁷ Parker's theory of textual editing is spelled out in *Flawed Texts and Verbal Icons* (1984), which, while not directly focused on Melville, did spell out the basic premises that guided Parker's approach to editing Melville.

⁸ I use the term "novel" to refer to *Typee* in keeping with convention, but it is worth noting that Bryant himself has rejected the idea that *Typee* can adequately be described as a novel, including in his 1995 introduction to the Penguin edition of *Typee* the declaration "This book is not a novel" (xi), which he follows by emphasizing *Typee*'s status as autobiography, travelogue, an anthropological treatise. While acknowledging the force of Bryant's objection that *Typee* does not fit comfortably within the generic conventions of the novel, I retain the more common designation for *Typee* for clarity's sake.

⁹ Bryant also coedited a fluid text teaching edition of *Moby-Dick* for Longman (2006) in order to allow instructors to track the relationship between the American edition of *Moby-Dick* and the British edition of *The Whale* in their teaching. Bryant expounded his theory of the fluid text in his 2002 book *The Fluid Text: A Theory of Revision and Editing for Book and Screen*.

2: Literary Aesthetics and the Visual Arts

THE THREAD OF EXPERIENCE that runs through biographical and textual studies of Melville serves also to connect these studies with criticism and scholarship that are more explicitly aesthetic in their orientation. If the biographical critics emphasized the importance of comprehending the experiences and reading out of which Melville developed his literary art, more formally oriented critics wrestled with the methods by which Melville transmuted experience, both personal and vicarious, into enduring works of literary art. It has become a commonplace in Melville studies to bemoan the insufficient attention paid to aesthetics in discussions of Melville's work, but the direness of the situation is belied by the incredibly rich and varied work that has been done on Melville as a consummate verbal artist and by the upsurge of work in recent decades on the relationship between Melville's verbal artistry and the visual arts.

There are a few recurring strands in the efforts of critics to engage with Melville's artistic qualities. First, and earliest chronologically, there is a tradition of examining Melville's craft as a writer — his appropriation of sources, his process of writing, the genesis of each of his works, particularly of *Moby-Dick*. Second, there is a tradition of formalist criticism of Melville, which examines what R. P. Blackmur referred to as Melville's tendency to "use words greatly" and what Warner Berthoff summed up in a brilliant chapter as Melville's use of "words, sentences, paragraphs, chapters." Third, there is an approach to Melville that seeks to take his measure among the giants of world literature. This tendency connects Melville to the great British and German Romantics of his own era and to earlier figures in British and Continental literature like Shakespeare, Milton, and Dante, who are regarded as central figures of Western culture. A fourth tendency is to find in Melville a peculiarly American aesthetic, one which does not so much connect Melville to Shakespeare, Dante, and Goethe as to make him their rival on the basis of his membership in an emerging democratic literature that could challenge the masterpieces of the Old World. A thread that runs across all of these strands is an intuition on the part of many critics that it is precisely the visual qualities of Melville's work that most essentially constitute his artistic greatness. This intuition is never absent from aesthetically based criticism of Melville, but it became most explicit in the last decades of the twentieth century, when an increasing number of scholars examined closely both Melville's use of the visual arts and the analogies between his work and that of painters and photographers.

F. O. Matthiessen's magisterial study of mid-nineteenth-century American literature, *American Renaissance: Art and Expression in the Age of Emerson and Whitman* (1941) exemplified both the promises and the perils of reading Melville primarily as a self-conscious verbal artist. By positioning the portion of *American Renaissance* that dealt with Melville near the conclusion of the study, Matthiessen suggested that Melville's work represented a culmination of many of the elements of the American Renaissance that he had identified as occurring in the 1850s. For Matthiessen, American literature came of age during the 1850s, and the distinguishing feature of the works of Emerson, Hawthorne, Thoreau, Melville, and Whitman was "a devotion to the possibilities of democracy" (xiv). Melville became a perfect example of the union between faith in democracy and faith in art because of his combination of verbal artistry, imaginative gusto, and working class themes. Matthiessen's influence in both Melville studies and American literary studies more generally is so broad that I will be considering *American Renaissance* in chapters 3, 5, and 6 as well as in the present chapter, but even in the tradition of specifically aesthetic responses to Melville, Matthiessen's stature is immense.

Matthiessen's influence on later Melville critics derives from several central elements in his argument. First, Matthiessen anticipated Richard Chase and Charles Feidelson, Jr. in seeing the romance and symbolism as the characteristic artistic modes in antebellum American literature, and thus helped initiate a strand of criticism that allowed Melville's aesthetic to be compared favorably to the more realistic aesthetic of English Victorian novelists. Second, as Matthiessen's title *American Renaissance* hints, Matthiessen saw Melville and his American contemporaries as counterparts to the explosion of literary activity that characterized late sixteenth- and early seventeenth-century England, and Matthiessen was particularly astute in tracing lines of influence from Shakespeare, Sir Thomas Browne, and Sir Robert Burton on the development of Melville's prose fiction.[1] Third, and partially as a result of his sensitivity to Melville's sources in the English literary Renaissance, Matthiessen paid closer attention than any previous critic to Melville's use of language (although at least at one point, Matthiessen's enthusiasm here led to a major misstep). Finally, and perhaps less obviously than the first three elements, Matthiessen understood the visual qualities of the major American writers of the mid-nineteenth century, and thus forecast the interest in Melville's relation to the visual arts that has flowered in the last thirty years.

One of the most notorious moments in *American Renaissance* came in the midst of what was otherwise a careful and subtle reading of *White-Jacket*. Matthiessen singled out for particular praise the expression "soiled fishes of the deep," exclaiming over the way in which the phrase combined cleanliness and filth in one complex image. The problem with this, as John W. Nichol pointed out in 1949, was that the phrase was actually a printer's error in the Constable edition of *White-Jacket* that Matthiessen was using: the passage should have read "coiled fishes of the deep" (50) — a rather less startling formulation, and one which would not have invited a rhapsody on the juxtaposition of filth and cleanliness. Matthiessen's unfortunate gaffe did not really diminish the depth of insight in his reading of Melville, but it did illustrate that even in literary criticism, sometimes brute facts intrude.

One of the enduring conflicts that have shaped Melville criticism over the decades has been the tension between Melville as the great literary outsider of his own century and his status as the ultimate literary insider since. R. P. Blackmur's reading of *Moby-Dick* and *Pierre* in "The Craft of Herman Melville: A Putative Statement" (1938) reflected the need that critics were already feeling in the 1930s to offer a more measured response to Melville's artistry than the ecstatic encomiums of the 1920s. Blackmur, who was among the most influential of American Formalist critics, found that Melville's greatness emphatically did not consist in his being a master of the novelistic form. Blackmur began by suggesting that Melville's reputation was sufficiently sturdy to endure a candid analysis of his faults as a writer, and then proceeded to draw up a seemingly damning indictment of Melville as a novelist. Melville, Blackmur noted, had "added nothing to the novel as a form, and . . . nowhere showed conspicuous mastery of the formal devices of fiction" (75). Moreover, following early biographers like Raymond Weaver, Blackmur asserted that Melville's last forty years had been largely empty of literary accomplishment — like so many critics before and after him, Blackmur discounted *The Confidence Man* and *Billy Budd*, and spurned Melville's poetry altogether. Blackmur's consideration of the Gothic elements is Melville's fiction was also distinctly uncomplimentary, and seemed to take for granted that Gothicism was itself a taint.

One might expect that Blackmur's conclusion would be that Melville was an overrated blight on American literary history after this beginning, but Blackmur worked his way back into an apology of sorts for Melville's eminence. Melville, it turned out, was not at heart a novelist at all according to Blackmur. He was, however, something more characteristic of the American literary sphere in the nineteenth century: a preacher. Blackmur staked his evaluation of Melville's literary significance particular on Melville's capacity for manipulating language, and he suggested that this capacity manifested itself most clearly in Melville's use of what Blackmur dubbed the "putative statement." A "putative statement" in Blackmur's lexicon was a verbal construction that "passes for description" but is actually "primarily the *assertion* of an emotional relation" (87). This sort of assertion, Blackmur contended, was the primary aesthetic mode of the sermon, but given the heterodoxy of Melville's religious views, no sermon that Melville could have preached could have been published and circulated. Melville's artistic accomplishment, then, was to find room in the novel for the sorts of emotionally compelling statements that were found in sermons, and *Moby-Dick*, in this view, becomes a great work of art insofar as it is the delivered text of Melville's undeliverable sermon.

Despite Blackmur's own association with poetry, he did not devote much analysis to Melville's poetry. Indeed, an enduring problem of Melville scholarship has been how to account for the relationship between Melville's renowned prose fiction and his often seemingly invisible poetry. Two of the earliest efforts to incorporate a consideration of Melville's poetry into his larger body of work appeared in the 1940s: William Ellery Sedgwick's book-length study *Herman Melville: The Tragedy of Mind* (1944) and Robert Penn Warren's essay "Melville the Poet" (1946). In Sedgwick's case, the consideration of Melville's poetry was built into a thoroughgoing interpretation of Melville's entire career, and focused especially on *Clarel*. The reason that Sedgwick made a defense of *Clarel* a major part of his study becomes apparent once we consider that his posthumously published study as a whole focuses on the development of Melville's religious and philosophical thought. As a result, the bulk of my discussion of Sedgwick's work will follow in chapter 3. Sedgwick's discussion of *Clarel*, however, is noteworthy for its contribution to our understanding of Melville's aesthetics, for he was among the first critics to discern a design in Melville's poetry. Sedgwick accounted for the starkness of much of Melville's prosody, and the choice to use rhymed tetrameter as the metrical scheme for *Clarel*, by positing that the form of *Clarel* is a visible sign of a transformation in Melville's basic philosophy: Sedgwick averred that by the time he wrote *Clarel*, Melville had so advanced beyond the youthful self that had composed *Moby-Dick* that he had achieved a "new state of consciousness, in which his spontaneous ego or self-consciousness no longer played an all-commanding role" (202). *Clarel*'s form thus becomes, not a sign of Melville's technical incompetence as a poet, but rather of a "counter revolution in his consciousness" (203). As will be seen in chapter 3, *Clarel*'s religious and philosophical explorations would become important to many critics. Where Sedgwick broke new ground was in refusing to dismiss the form of *Clarel*, and by extension Melville's poetry as a whole, as literary art.

Robert Penn Warren, himself both a major Modernist poet and a scholar of poetry, provided a particularly powerful endorsement for the idea that Melville's poetry should not always be relegated to the shadows of his monumental prose fictions. Because of his theological and philosophical emphases, and perhaps because of his untimely death as well, Sedgwick had restricted his discussion of Melville's poetry almost exclusively to *Clarel* — and it was only in the service of interpreting *Clarel* that Sedgwick acknowledged the existence of *Battle-Pieces*, Melville's best-known collection of poetry, or the later verse of *John Marr and Other Sailors* or *Timoleon*. Warren, by contrast, began his evaluation of

Melville's poetry with a reading of "In a Bye-Canal" from *Timoleon* and drew most of his examples of Melville's poetic craft from *Battle-Pieces*. Warren admitted at the outset the case against Melville's poetry, acknowledging that "he is a poet of shreds and patches" (144). Warren's reading of "In a Bye-Canal" attends to both the passages from the poem that represent a competent performance of the poetic norms of the late nineteenth century and those in which "the metrical pattern is sorely tried and wrenched" (145). This tension between the smooth and the rough in Melville's prosody thus became an outgrowth of Melville's philosophical concern with duality, and so for Warren, as for Sedgwick, what had been regarded as irredeemable flaws in Melville's poetry became instead an indication of his ability to match the structure of the poem to the subject matter at hand — a trait that made him an eminently suitable subject for New Critical close reading. As major discussions of Melville's artistry in his prose appeared in increasing volume in the 1940s and 1950s, Sedgwick and Warren helped to keep the discussion of Melville's poetic craft alive as well.

In *Call Me Ishmael* (1947) Charles Olson, another poet-critic, provided one of the most idiosyncratic and influential readings of Melville in the history of Melville scholarship. Olson's reading of *Moby-Dick* was itself written in the manner of a prose poem, and clearly echoed the style of D. H. Lawrence's *Studies in Classic American Literature*. Olson's model for literary criticism related to Melville reached back further than Lawrence, however. The critical precursor most important to Olson was none other than Melville himself. In "Hawthorne and His Mosses," Melville had constructed his review of Hawthorne around two central ideas: the potential for originality in American literature, and the importance of Shakespeare as a model for Americans aspiring to literary greatness. Olson followed Melville's cue with a book that began with what was unique about America as a source of artistic inspiration and continued into a richly textured discussion of Shakespeare's role in shaping *Moby-Dick*. These elements had already been touched upon by Matthiessen, but in Olson's hands they took on a furious urgency that seldom appears in literary criticism.[2] After reviewing the story of the sinking of the whaleship *Essex* by a sperm whale in his prologue, Olson began the body of his argument by asserting bluntly that "I take SPACE to be the central fact to man born in America," and he followed this assertion with a dizzying array of facts relating to the size of the North American continent and the specific import of whaling for the industrialization of the young American nation (11). Olson found space, movement, and industrialization to be crucial to the shaping of Melville's literary forms, and he found these aspects of American life to be particularly determinative for the form which Melville's appropriations of Shakespeare took. Olson argued that it was space that made America a fitter topic for the novel than the drama, and he suggested that Melville had accomplished successfully the feat of transmuting the qualities that he revered in Shakespeare into an American idiom in *Moby-Dick*. Ultimately, Olson's most important success in *Call Me Ishmael* was in his ability to demonstrate how Melville had transmuted the unpoetic substance of industrialization and economic expansion into high art. Meanwhile, his emphasis on geographical expansion forecast the debates over Melville and imperialism that would emerge in the 1980s and 1990s.

The case of F. O. Matthiessen demonstrated both the degree to which formalist criticism could enhance Melville studies and the necessity for formalist criticism to remain grounded in textual and biographical evidence. Howard P. Vincent's *The Trying Out of Moby-Dick* (1949), William Gilman's *Melville's Early Life and Redburn* (1951), and Merrell Davis's *Mardi: A Chartless Voyage* (1952) formed the leading edge of a tradition of getting at Melville's artistry through precisely this sort of evidence. In each of these works, Melville's art is seen as developing from a range of sources in Melville's reading and his experience, and like Charles R. Anderson, these critics revealed that Melville relied substantially more on other written sources, and with less acknowledgment, than would be countenanced in the twentieth century. Vincent's concern with analyzing the sources of Melville's craft proved to be a defining feature of his career. He revisited the methods that he used in his study of *Moby-Dick* in his 1970 study of *White-Jacket*.

The impulse towards reading Melville as an artist gained impetus in a particularly elegant form with Walter Bezanson's article "*Moby-Dick*: A Work of Art." Bezanson established a multistep framework for reading the artistic qualities in *Moby-Dick* that was to set the tone for many better-known treatments of Melville's artistry. As with his later treatment of *Clarel*, Bezanson quietly laid the groundwork for much of the criticism that followed, and there are few figures whose work is more justly revered by those who have dedicated their careers to Melville studies. Bezanson's argument proceeded from the material objects that defined the shape of *Moby-Dick* outward toward more abstract concerns. The first cluster of features of Melville's art that Bezanson identified he classified as "matter," identifying the overarching matter of the novel as whaling, and subdividing whaling into its implications for the natural world, the historical world, artifacts, techniques, and the object of the voyage, which of course was to kill and process whales. Bezanson briskly identified Melville's sources regarding these elements of whaling as including logbooks, histories, and personal narratives, and suggested that these rather mundane elements become art in *Moby-Dick* through the agency of his next two categories: a dynamic and a structure. Bezanson found that the dynamic of *Moby-Dick*, the source of the action and tension in the novel, was neither Captain Ahab nor the white whale, as might commonly be supposed, but rather the narrator, Ishmael. Having placed narration firmly in the center of his discussion of the novel's artistry, he proceeded to what may be the most influential part of his argument, the suggestion that there is not one Ishmael in *Moby-Dick*, but two. The second Ishmael, Bezanson wrote, is the engaging and imaginative young man we meet in the opening chapters. The first, and more pervasive Ishmael, however, is the narrator who creates the story of the Pequod out of the materials of memory and imagination. This distinction remains particularly useful for anyone who is teaching the novel to undergraduates, and it is the sort of illuminating insight that once pointed out seems as if it has been perfectly evident all along. The consciousness of the two Ishmaels became for Bezanson the central artistic force in Melville's novel. Bezanson's final category was the structure of *Moby-Dick*. He argued that the novel was not formless, as Blackmur, among others, had hinted, but rather stunningly intricate in its design. Bezanson carefully categorized the rhetorical modes of Melville's novel (expository and poetic), the use of natural objects and characters as symbols of metaphysical concepts, and the use of dramatic and sermonic forms as means of commenting on the text. He noted as well that the arrangement of chapters takes the form of clusters that are united by a particular event or idea. In explaining the relationship of these clusters to one another, Bezanson suggested that what ties the components of matter, dynamism, and structure together in *Moby-Dick* is Melville's use of "free organic form" — a means of structuring the novel that allows the ideas and events that Melville discusses to create their own form, rather than imposing a prearranged structure onto them. The influence of the New Criticism, with its theories of the organic nature of poetry, is evident in Bezanson's essay, but what makes Bezanson's work remarkable is his ability to adapt New Critical organicism to a novel that clearly defies the idea that the best art is the compact, "well-wrought" (to use Cleanth Brooks's metaphor) object.

Charles Feidelson, Jr.'s *Symbolism and American Literature* (1953) engaged head-on with the question of why Melville's writing, and particularly *Moby-Dick*, felt so contemporary to critics in the mid-twentieth century. Feidelson suggested that Melville's use of a complex and ambivalent form of symbolism was what best explained the tremendous sense of kinship that mid-century critics and artists felt for Melville. Like Matthiessen, Feidelson engaged a variety of major mid-nineteenth-century American writers, and like Matthiessen he gave Melville a particularly prominent place among them. Feidelson acknowledged that Melville seemed to be uninterested in matters of genre and form as it was understood in the mid-nineteenth century, summing up this view of Melville's aesthetics elegantly at the start of his section on Melville:

> [Melville] would seem a prime example of the demonic writer, carrying all before him by what he *is* rather than what he can *do*. He is often indifferent to the details of structure; his speculations are seldom profound and sometimes juvenile; he offers little variety of fictional character or situation. His greatest gift is a sense of tone and attitude, behind which we cannot help looking for an individual speaker; and this speaker, as it happens, can be taken as a very modern personality. (163)

Having made this concession, Feidelson argued, however, that the symbol, a device inherited from the religious typology of the Puritans, was essential to understanding Melville's art, and that even our sense of "an individual speaker" behind Melville's work, which nudges us toward biographical criticism, is a product of Melville's symbol-making imagination. Feidelson defined symbolism as being "autonomous in the sense that it is quite distinct both from the personality of its author and from any world of pure objects, and creative in the sense that it brings into existence its own meaning" (49). By emphasizing the theological roots of some of Melville's most important verbal effects, Feidelson carried on the tradition inaugurated by R. P. Blackmur of regarding Melville as a preacher without a church, and the sermon as his most important rhetorical mode, and indeed, Feidelson frequently cited Blackmur as one of his most important authorities. Feidelson's reading of Melville emphasized the ways in which Melville created images (most notably the doubloon Ahab nails to the masthead in *Moby-Dick*), and self-consciously examined the ways in which the symbols create their own meanings.

Given the high seriousness that Melville's fiction was accorded by the 1950s, Edward Rosenberry's *Melville and the Comic Spirit* (1955) was a welcome change, starting as it did with the image of a woman from the Marquesas showing her "most intimate tattooing" to the French Navy (1). Rosenberry noted particularly the bawdy humor of *Typee* and *Omoo*, and he also found the use of self-deflating humor by Melville's early narrators to be particularly worthy of comment. In a chapter dealing most directly with the formal aspects of Melville's humor, Rosenberry summed up Melville's "comic manner" as consisting in exaggeration, understatement, and "his brilliant selection and placement of *le mot juste*" (35), along with irony and puns. Rosenberry deftly connected elements of Melville's humor that might seem frivolous or self-indulgent to Melville's profoundest philosophical concerns: puns, for example, are illustrations of Melville's "understanding of a fundamental principle of semantics: 'that words are but algebraic signs, conveying what they please' [*Mardi* 89:222]" (77). Rosenberry found that the philosophical comedy of Rabelais provided a source of Melville's artistic strategies comparable to the influences of the great writers of Renaissance England traced by Olson and Matthiessen.

Melville's status as a writer of romances was secure by the late 1950s, but his short fiction had been considerably less visible in book-length studies of Melville's artistry. This would change with the publication in 1960 of Richard Harter Fogle's unpretentiously titled *Melville's Shorter Tales*. Astonishing as it may seem, given the eminence that "Bartleby, the Scrivener" enjoys in the present literary canon, Fogle was able to casually observe in a footnote in 1960, forty years after the beginning of the Melville Revival, that Leo Marx's 1953 essay "Melville's Parable of the Walls" was "the only full-scale treatment of the story I have seen" (27). Fogle found much more than earlier critics had found in "Bartleby" and throughout Melville's short fiction. He observed that Melville's interest in multiple perspectives as the only avenue to a complex truth was embodied in the form of much of his short fiction, both through the use of the "diptych, or two paneled structure" form (a concept Fogle borrowed from Jay Leyda) and through the tension between "the march of fate and the quest for truth" and a "leisurely digressiveness" that seems to undercut the earnestness of the quest for truth (5). Fogle analyzed each of Melville's tales and sketches from the *Piazza Tales*, and he suggested that the most representative of the group was the one he saved for last, *Benito Cereno*. Melville's artistry in *Benito Cereno*, Fogle argued, took the form of a maze, a patterned structure of trust and doubt experienced by a mind in a state of delusion. Like so many of the other tales, it set up alternative vantage points from which to view the world (Delano's, Don Benito's, Babo's), and it employed symbols that were both complexly resonant and self-critical (126). What makes *Benito Cereno* the most important example of Melville's artistry, alongside *Moby-Dick*, Fogle ultimately asserted, was its status as "the realization of mystery, the effective presentment of complexity" (143). Fogle's work on the short fiction laid a foundation for what would become a major strand in Melville scholarship by the 1970s and 1980s.

Daniel Hoffman's *Form and Fable in American Fiction* (1961) considered Melville's artistry in the context of a wider exploration of the formal characteristics peculiar to American imaginative literature as it emerged in the nineteenth century. Like his predecessors, Hoffman found Melville central to the development of a specifically American literary canon, and he also embraced the by-then familiar trope of Melville's career as a trajectory upward to *Moby-Dick* and downward in the whale's wake, asserting that "*Moby-Dick* was the book that Melville was born to write; his earlier books are but a making ready for it, his later ones a falling-off from its singular and forever after inaccessible achievement" (221–22). This familiar trajectory took on a new significance in Hoffman's hands, however. More than any of his predecessors, Hoffman turned to the oral tradition in America rather than to the Greek and Roman Classics, the English Renaissance, or the Continental Rabelais for the source of Melville's artistic prowess. Hoffman especially emphasized the developing genre of frontier fiction as a source for Melville's work, regarding Thomas Bangs Thorpe's "The Big Bear of Arkansas" (1841) as a precursor to *Moby-Dick*. Hoffman's insight into the connection between folklore and Melville's craft allowed him to expand on the work that Rosenberry had done on Melville's humor and engage with those elements of Melville's art that were distinctively American.[3] Hoffman's interest in humor and American folklore, along with his lifelong interest in the fiction of Edgar Allan Poe, meant that he was peculiarly well-equipped to comment on *The Confidence-Man*. Following Richard Chase (discussed in chapter 5), Hoffman found folklore and humor to be central to *The Confidence-Man*'s continuity with *Moby-Dick*, while he saw the more corrosive satire, irony, and skepticism in the later novel as diminishing the scope and power that Melville attained in his masterpiece. For Hoffman, *The Confidence-Man* translates the form of the picaresque, most closely associated in world literature with *Don Quixote*, into American terms. Hoffman concluded, however, that it was the failure of the optimism associated with much of American folklore in *The Confidence-Man* that caused it to fall short of the work of the master of American picaresque, Mark Twain.

Warner Berthoff's *The Example of Melville* took aesthetically oriented criticism of Melville's body of work away from the nationalist and philosophical paradigms of Matthiessen and Feidelson, and back towards an analysis of Melville's work as willed artistic production. Like Blackmur, Berthoff found the locus of Melville's significance in his use of language; unlike Blackmur, he felt little need to deplore Melville's structural departures from novelistic conventions. Rather, Berthoff's study meticulously explored the artistic structure of Melville's work, working from Melville's larger artistic effects in his creation of landscape and character down to matters of diction and sentence structure. This emphasis on the structure of Melville's work as it appeared in print, meant that Berthoff also departed from the tradition of source criticism associated with Vincent, Gilman, and Davis.

Berthoff's analysis of Melville's formal strategies is worth reviewing at length, as it is still among the most comprehensive and arrestingly insightful approaches to questions of form in Melville's prose fiction. After devoting the first two chapters to an incisive overview of Melville's career, Berthoff begins his consideration of Melvillean aesthetics with a chapter entitled "The Melvillean Setting." From *Typee* onward, Melville's work is characterized by a vivid pictorial quality. Berthoff then draws a connection between *Typee*'s success and the conventions of nineteenth-century landscape painting. Berthoff considers the pictorial effects in *Omoo*, *Israel Potter*, and *The Encantadas* as well, emphasizing the interplay of the human and natural worlds in Melville's verbal pictures before moving on to the heart of the chapter, a discussion of the artistry of the setting of *Moby-Dick*. Berthoff identifies four "worlds" that he regards as shaping the narrative of *Moby-Dick*: the human society ashore that provides the comic opening to the novel, the "virtual city of the races and talents of men" that emerges on shipboard (81), the "non-human world of the sea and the indifferent elements" against which the sailors strive (84), and the mythological world developed by the whalemen in response to their inhospitable surroundings. For Berthoff, each of these worlds serves to amplify Melville's project of comprehending, in distinctly human terms, a cosmos that dwarfs the human figure. The interplay between human puniness and nobility and natural brutality and grace constitutes the dramatic interest of a novel that, Berthoff suggests, can be read as a massive verbal painting.

From the large canvas of Melville's settings, Berthoff moves in for an examination of Melville's most memorable characters. The most distinguishing features in their development he finds to be Melville's "imaginative fidelity . . . to the observable conditions of [human]existence" and his inexhaustible curiosity about his characters (91–92). While acknowledging that Melville's novels do not feature the complexly layered characters of later realist novels, Berthoff makes the counterintuitive argument that characterization is crucial to Melville's art, suggesting that Melville was able to create memorable characters because of his fascination with the quirks, the oddities, and the unexpected traits that make up human beings, and he repeatedly finds evidence of Melville's twin traits of imaginative vigor and unremitting curiosity in his construction of character.

Berthoff's next step is to move through more conventionally formal elements: narrative framing, plotting, and the construction, as the title of chapter 7 indicates, of "words, sentences, paragraphs, chapters." In each of these cases, Berthoff finds Melville's idiosyncrasy, curiosity, and sheer imaginative vitality to be the traits that render his work artistically compelling. In terms of narration, Berthoff finds Melville's most distinctive contribution to narrative art in "the prolonged conspiracy between 'I' and 'you'" that appears in his best work (119). This observation goes a long way toward explaining the powerful sense of identification with Melville that many of his readers have felt: if readers view Ishmael as both a stand-in for Melville himself and as a friend who shares their deepest intuitions about the nature of life, it is small wonder that many of Melville's readers, scholars and general readers alike, tend to see themselves in him. In relation to Melville's storytelling, meanwhile, Berthoff quarrels with R. P. Blackmur's earlier assertions that Melville had made no substantial contributions to the form of the novel. Contra Blackmur, Berthoff suggests that Melville's use of the "told story" — a tale that, like "The Town-Ho's Story" in *Moby-Dick*, is recounted retrospectively as part of a larger work — represented a true formal innovation in the structure of the novel (139). Drawing on the French distinction between *recit* and *roman*, Berthoff argues that Melville was a master of the *recit*, the recounting of events that have already taken place without the illusion of dramatic immediacy, to a degree that marked a substantial advance in the craft of the novel. Moreover, Berthoff suggests that the prominence of the "told story" in Melville's work demonstrates the pressure exerted by the conventions of magazine fiction in antebellum America — thus making Melville's use of this form a specifically American contribution to the form of the novel (134).

In his analysis of "words, sentences, paragraphs, chapters," Berthoff followed not only Blackmur's admiration for Melville's use of language on the micro-level, but also Newton Arvin's detailed analysis of Melville's linguistic ingenuity. Where Berthoff excelled even these estimable precursors, however, was in his ability to move seamlessly from the level of diction to sentence structure to paragraphing to the shape of Melville's chapters, demonstrating beautifully how each of these structural elements contributes to the edifice of Melville's fiction. Berthoff's analysis here defies summary, but a few key elements can stand in for his subtle discussion of Melville's effects. Berthoff finds Melville's diction to be characterized by an interplay of luminous imagery with a sure command of the grammatical and linguistic roots of words and a potent sense of rhetorical purpose. Melville's sentences, meanwhile, function most effectively "at the level of ordinary workmanship" in *Moby-Dick*, where each sentence, whether terse or ornate, seems to fulfill its function in the novel perfectly — with the exception, Berthoff concedes, of some over-wrought dialogue (167). In Melville's later work, however, Berthoff sees a falling away from Melville's mastery of the sentence, resulting in sentences that are stuffed with information rather than serving to illuminate realities.

The enduring significance of Berthoff's work can be seen in part in the major projects that have grown out of hints that appear in *The Example of Melville*. Central late-twentieth and twenty-first century Melvilleans like John Bryant, Robert K. Wallace, and Samuel Otter have expanded on Berthoff's insights into, respectively, the centrality of humor to Melville's work, the relationship of Melville's work to Romantic landscape painting, and the relationship of Melville's work to the seventeenth-century genre of the "anatomy." The fecundity of Berthoff's insights, the precision of his analysis, and the gracefulness of his expression all ensure that *The Example of Melville* continues to be one of the most essential texts for any student of Melville's aesthetics.

Berthoff's rigorous engagement with the artistic qualities of Melville's work was joined by powerfully innovative discussions of Melville's aesthetics in the late 1960s and the early 1970s. For Edgar Dryden, the paradox of telling the truth through fiction, which Melville himself identified as central to the works of Shakespeare, became the guiding principle for a subtle and erudite study of Melville's work. Indeed, the paradox of telling the truth through fiction becomes doubly, perhaps even infinitely, paradoxical in Dryden's hands: for Dryden, the hard-won truth towards which Melville's fiction tends is that of the fictiveness of truth. If Berthoff's study circled around *Moby-Dick* as the centerpiece of the Melville canon, Dryden vigorously demonstrated that Melville's artistry developed both before and after his most famous work, going so far as to make *The Confidence-Man* rather than *Moby-Dick* the teleological culmination of Melville's literary career.

Dryden grounded his study in his consideration of the philosophical underpinnings of the theory of the novel, finding Melville's embrace of the subjective, the "I" in his narratives, to be the key to understanding the most characteristic elements of his art. Thus, Melville's earlier novels became "Portraits of the Artist as a Young Man" for Dryden, and each of Melville's early narrators became illustrative of a way of being an artist in Melville's world (*Melville's Thematics*, 37). In keeping with Berthoff's identification of the recollection, or "told story," as Melville's crucial formal innovation, Dryden also found memory to be central to Melville's artistic practice. In Melville's early novels, Dryden viewed Melville's protagonists as artists intending to represent the truth of the world as it is and in search of education through experience. By the time of *The Confidence-Man*, Dryden maintained, Melville had lost all faith in the capacity of experience to educate, and of fiction to represent experience. *Moby-Dick* is thus defined artistically by its occupying the crucial and artistically felicitous moment between Melville's faith in experience and representation and the collapse of that faith. *The Confidence-Man* represented the logical end point of Melville's artistic quest, but it also constituted a medicine too bitter for most of Melville's readers, even in the twentieth century, to swallow (*Melville's Thematics*, 151–95).

It is readily apparent that the major aesthetically oriented readings of Melville's work from the 1960s — Fogle, Hoffman, Berthoff, Dryden — tended overwhelmingly to focus on his prose. Walter Bezanson, one of the pioneers in analyzing the artistry of Melville's prose, provided an important reminder of the significance of Melville's poetry in his introduction to the Hendricks House edition of Melville's long poem *Clarel*. Picking up where Sedgwick and Warren left off in the 1940s, Bezanson argued that *Clarel* represented a high point in Melville's later career comparable to *Moby-Dick* in the early (and better known) portion of Melville's career. In much the same way that Bezanson consolidated an aesthetic reading of *Moby-Dick* that proved so compelling as almost to seem like common sense, he set the terms for future considerations of *Clarel* (which, needless to say, have proved rather less numerous than the critical analyses and invocations of *Moby-Dick*). Perhaps the clearest signal that Bezanson had revitalized the discussion of Melville's poetry appeared later in the 1960s, when Robert Penn Warren revisited Melville's poetry, with much more attention to *Clarel* than he had paid in his 1946 essay, and explicitly praised Bezanson's introduction for illuminating the importance of *Clarel*. By the time of his 1967 introduction to the *Selected Poems of Herman Melville*, Warren was prepared to grant Melville more credit as a poet than he had in the 1940s. Meanwhile, Hennig Cohen had also contributed to the preservation of Melville's poetic legacy by editing scholarly editions of *Battle-Pieces* and Melville's *Selected Poems*.

Even more neglected than *Battle-Pieces* and *Clarel*, however, had been Melville's collections of poetry published during the last three years of his life or left unpublished after his death. William Bysshe Stein sought to remedy this curious critical omission with his 1970 study *The Poetry of Melville's Late Years*. Stein argued that Melville's later poetry represented a substantial development of Melville's poetic talent that had taken place after the publication of *Clarel* in 1876. In fact, Stein dismissed *Battle-Pieces* and *Clarel* as being unworthy to be compared with the sophistication of Melville's last poems, and thus left them out of his study entirely. Subsequent work on Melville's history as a poet, particularly Hershel Parker's *Melville: The Making of the Poet* (2007) casts doubt on Stein's chronology: it would appear that at least some of the poems from the later collections actually antedate *Clarel* (1876) and even *Battle-Pieces* (1866) as they were initially written for an 1860 volume that was ultimately never published. Nonetheless, Stein's readings of the poems, the majority of which were certainly written in Melville's last years, remain compelling. Stein saw the later Melville as an artist who had achieved something new in relation to his earlier work because he had freed himself from the residual Christianity that haunts his earlier fiction and poetry. Like the proponents of the "testament of acceptance" reading of *Billy Budd* (for a discussion of which see chapter 3), Stein saw Melville as having resolved his central anxieties late in life; unlike those scholars, Stein believed he had become reconciled, not to God, but to the absence of God, thus allowing himself new latitude in his artistic expression, and allowing for a playfulness and freedom in the later poems that did not appear in the (relatively) better-known poetry.

At a time when Melville's fiction had been the subject of protracted discussion and his poetry was becoming an increasingly respectable topic for literary debate, John Seelye's *Melville: The Ironic Diagram* (1970) sought to propound a theory of Melville's creativity that would account for the entire scope of Melville's body of work in poetry and prose. The "ironic diagram" that Seelye found in Melville's work was "a diagrammatic opposition of forces, expressive of Melville's own conflict of belief" (6). This opposition of forces was given shape by the model of the symposium throughout Melville's career, Seelye argued. Thus, wherever one finds oneself in Melville's long and varied career, one is always in the midst of a conversation among multiple points of view, and this, to borrow a phrase from Ishmael in the opening chapter of *Moby-Dick*, is "the key to it all." The weakness of Seelye's argument was its tendency to flatten out a career that after all was more diverse in its approaches to form than most authors'; the strength of the argument was that it appeared (and still does appear) largely to be true. Surely if there is one quality about Melville's work that any teacher will want students to bear in mind, it is Melville's remarkable ability to hold divergent understandings of the world in a state of suspense. Seelye thus provided an elegant and persuasive genesis for the most salient qualities in Melville's art.

Melville's poetry had attracted its partisans over the years, and the numbers were growing by the early 1970s, but prior to William Shurr's *The Mystery of Iniquity* (1972), there had been no thorough-going exploration of all of Melville's poetry from *Battle-Pieces* to his last works. Shurr devoted generous chapters to discussions of *Battle-Pieces*, *Clarel*, *John Marr and Other Sailors*, *Timoleon*, *Weeds and Wildings*, and even *The Burgundy Club Sketches*, about which Shurr's predecessors had been silent. He concluded with a reading of *Billy Budd* that emphasized its roots in Melville's poetic career. Shurr's work proved an important precursor to the in its consideration of Melville's concern with imagery and visual descriptions of objects as well as in its focus on Melville's poetry. Shurr devoted two chapters to static images in *Clarel* and to the ways in which these static images acquire dynamism, respectively. Particularly important to the growing body of scholarship on Melville's poetry was Shurr's inclusion of *Weeds and Wildings* and *The Burgundy Club Sketches* and his demonstration that, even in these lesser-known, and (in the case of *Weeds and Wildings*), seemingly lighter works, we find Melville's formal concern with representing visual objects and his philosophical trepidation that behind these objects lay a malign cosmos. Shurr's inclusion of *The Burgundy Club Sketches* meant that he was able to engage more directly than previous critics with Melville's evolving viewpoints on the visual arts as these viewpoints were expressed in poetry.[4]

As Melville's poetry increasingly began to claim space for itself in the canon of nineteenth-century American literature, his short fiction continued to move at a markedly uneven pace toward the center of the American literary canon. "Bartleby, the Scrivener" was increasingly the subject of brief studies and had by the mid-1970s emerged as a major text in both critical and classroom contexts. Melville's other works of short fiction lagged behind, but the 1970s produced three important books dealing solely with Melville's short fiction: R. Bruce Bickley's *The Method of Melville's Short Fiction* (1975), Marvin Fisher's *Going Under: Melville's Short Fiction and the American 1850s* (1977), and William Dillingham's *Melville's Short Fiction: 1853–1856* (1977). Dillingham will be discussed in the next chapter due to his interest in Melville's religious and philosophical proclivities, and Fisher will be discussed in chapter 5. Bickley's study, however, featured aesthetically oriented readings of Melville's short fiction, both building on Richard Harter Fogle's earlier work and extending it. Bickley focused on the ways in which narrative structure and voice, rhetorical constructions, and varieties of irony developed throughout Melville's short fiction. Bickley also used Melville's juvenilia, the framed stories within stories, and the abortive "Agatha" narrative that Melville had suggested to Hawthorne to put the development of Melville's short fiction in context. What was missing in previous studies of the short fiction was Melville's ability to develop both character and concealed philosophical and even "ribaldly comic" messages through a variety of "ironic personae" (22–23). In keeping with Melville's task of writing for the popular magazine market when composing short fiction, he created pieces that were on the surface sentimental confessions, but which contained layers of subversive ironies.

Harrison Hayford, a central figure in the development of Melville studies because of his extensive editorial work with the Northwestern-Newberry edition of Melville's work, brought aesthetics together with textual criticism in a pair of important essays from this period: "'Loomings': Yarns and Figures in the Fabric" (1975) and "Unnecessary Duplicates: A Key to the Writing of Moby-Dick" (1978). George R. Stewart's "The Two *Moby-Dicks*" (1954) had already put forward the idea that the form of *Moby-Dick* had been shaped, not by some grand design, but by the merging of two distinct novels. Hayford, however, lent texture to this argument in "Unnecessary Duplicates," suggesting a method of reading *Moby-Dick* that could separate out multiple stages in Melville's compositional process as a means to understanding Melville's literary craft. In "Loomings," meanwhile, Hayford examined the ways in which the first chapter of *Moby-Dick* brought together the most central formal motifs of Melville's wider career.

Nina Baym's 1978 article, "Melville's Quarrel with Fiction" made Melville's concerns about the expressive capacity of language itself the center of a highly influential reinterpretation of the arc of his career. Baym argued that in fact Melville should not be regarded primarily as a writer of fiction at any point in his literary career and that in fact Melville's most distinctive formal trait was his hostility toward fiction and toward all established literary form. Baym believed *Redburn* to be the work in which Melville best created a shapely fictional narrative, yet showed that Melville had expressed scorn for his own accomplishment in *Redburn* specifically because it was fiction and because it adhered to a recognizable literary form. When she turned to *Moby-Dick*, Baym found that its frequently scorned early reviewers had been more reliable interpreters of the book's strangeness and generic multiplicity than the twentieth-century scholars who scorned them. Ultimately, Baym's most important contribution to

Melville scholarship in "Melville's Quarrel with Fiction" was her recognition that all of Melville's work fit only loosely into conventional generic categories, a fact that has often helped to explain why Melville's artistry has been obscured in critical discussions.

The 1980s were a decade that, while rich in Melville criticism generally, did not produce many aesthetically oriented analyses of Melville's work. Exceptions to this tendency are found in a pair of essays by Shirley Dettlaff and a monograph by Richard S. Moore, both of which forecast a vigorous revival of interest in Melville's aesthetics in the 1990s and beyond. In "Ionian Form and Esau's Waste" (1982) and "Melville's Aesthetics" (1986), Dettlaff examined Melville's engagement with the visual arts and art criticism, particularly that of Matthew Arnold. Moore, meanwhile, found in Melville's interest in the sublime in nature room for a rereading of most of Melville's fictional canon, and through this interest came to focus as well on the intersection of Melville's work and the visual arts. Moore showed that American artist Thomas Cole's use of the natural sublime in his landscape paintings mirror the landscape descriptions that appear frequently in Melville's work from *Typee* in 1846 through the short fiction of the mid 1850s, particularly "The Piazza." The contrast between a circumscribed beauty and a boundless sublime that appears so often in *Moby-Dick* was both analogous to Cole's work and also connected to the intersection of nationalism and American expansionism with the natural sublime that was becoming increasingly important in the 1830s and 1840s. Moreover, Moore demonstrated that Melville used such divergent sources as the illustrations of whales drawn from Thomas Beale and others that Ishmael analyzes and criticizes in the cetological chapters of *Moby-Dick* and the drawings of the Italian artist Giambattista Piranesi (1720–78) to create a Kantian aesthetic of the dynamic and the mathematical sublime in his work (138–50). Although Moore's study is not now so well known as it deserves to be, it provided an important preview of the movement from text to image in aesthetically oriented Melville criticism in the last decade of the twentieth century and the first decade of the twenty-first.

If Melville's differences with his contemporaries have been the subject of most explorations of his works' formal qualities, there has also frequently been a countervailing tendency to place him firmly in the context of nineteenth-century American literary culture. David Reynolds's *Beneath the American Renaissance* envisioned Melville, like Poe, Emerson, Whitman, Thoreau, and Dickinson, as a figure who both used popular forms and strove to transcend them. If this was not an entirely unprecedented argument in regards to Melville (see for example Hoffman and Bickley above), it still served to make this fusing of the popular and the cerebral a characteristic that tied Melville closely to his most important contemporaries, and Reynolds's reading of Melville's short fiction in particular suggested an approach to Melville's work that could acknowledge both its conventional aspects and its startling revisions of convention.

Reynolds looked to American popular literature for the sources of Melville's artistry; Leon Chai, meanwhile, turned to the transatlantic development of Romanticism in his study *The Romantic Foundations of the American Renaissance* (1987). Chai meticulously tracked the ways in which theories of symbolism, science, pantheism, subjectivity, and representation drawn from such European Romantics as Goethe, Coleridge, and Carlyle are acted out in Melville's work, particularly in *Moby-Dick* and *Pierre*. Like Reynolds, Chai showed that the characteristic of Melville's work that he chose to explore made him a representative figure for his time period.

Chai and Reynolds had both placed Melville near the center of a major reinterpretation of American literary culture. In a more focused vein, Mary K. Bercaw's *Melville's Sources* (1987) provided another point of connection with biographical and critical studies of Melville by tracking relentlessly the materials out of which Melville created his art. Bercaw's work was notable not so much for introducing a new theory of Melville's methods of literary production as for providing the kind of groundwork on which any theory must rest.

The impulse toward concrete, verifiable literary scholarship about Melville's craft that Bercaw's work represents appeared in another form with Dan McCall's 1989 study *The Silence of Bartleby*. McCall's book was the sort of happy paradox to which any scholar might aspire: a stunningly erudite review of the criticism on "Bartleby the Scrivener" that at the same time cast substantial new light on Melville's artistry in the story, and did both in a volume of 154 pages with wide margins. McCall developed his reading of "Bartleby" in tension with what he referred to as "the Bartleby industry" — the mass of scholarship surrounding "Bartleby" that had emerged from the mid-1960s to the late 1980s. Though McCall found much to praise in some readings of Melville's story, he expressed skepticism about whether "the Bartleby industry" as a whole served to elucidate or to obscure the phenomenon presented by Melville's greatest short story. Much of *The Silence of Bartleby* was a polemical refutation of attempts to abstract a hidden meaning from the text, and McCall was especially concerned to defend the narrator of "Bartleby" against the charges of bad faith that numerous critics had leveled against him. McCall summarized and critiqued readings of Bartleby as Hawthorne, Thoreau, or Melville himself, and of the narrator as either an oppressive capitalist "master" to Bartleby or as a fool devoid of moral self-awareness. The polemics, however, should not obscure what was most crucial about McCall's book: McCall wished to appreciate "Bartleby" on its own terms, and he viewed this task primarily in aesthetic terms. Moreover, McCall's approach to aesthetic questions was, like so many of the best formalist readings of Melville, heavily informed by historical, biographical, and textual scholarship. If McCall rejected what he deemed overly politicized readings of Melville, he was also sharply critical of formalist readings that ignored concrete evidence from Melville's own life and reading. McCall demonstrated that aesthetically oriented readings of Melville could thrive in the late 1980s, a time associated with the heyday of "High Theory," and that they could do so by drawing on the rich tradition of Melville scholarship that had been flourishing for decades. By defending the lawyer who narrated the story against his detractors, meanwhile, McCall made Melville's creation of a rich and distinctive narrative voice the crucial element in his craft.

John Bryant's *Melville and Repose* (1993) also found narrative voice to be at the center of Melville's artistry. In taking up the question of humor in Melville's work, Bryant reopening a vein of inquiry initially explored by Edward Rosenberry (1957) and Daniel Hoffman (1960).[5] Bryant's discussion of Melville's humor, however, was informed by a more detailed analysis of predecessors like Washington Irving, Edgar Allan Poe, and Thomas Bangs Thorpe, a more substantial knowledge of the textual history of Melville's work, and a more current engagement with literary theory than was possible for the earlier scholars. Bryant built his discussion of Melville's humor around three major works: *Typee*, *Moby-Dick*, and *The Confidence-Man*. His analysis of the humorous aspects of *Typee* was rendered especially groundbreaking by his using the fragments of the manuscript for *Typee* that had been discovered in the 1980s in order to gain a clearer sense of Melville's process of revision in creating his first major work. Bryant found Tommo's "rhetoric of deceit" — his tendency toward hoaxing and bad faith — to be crucial to the early development of Melville's humor. In *Moby-Dick*, he showed that Ishmael's humorous persona as narrator teeters between melancholy narcissism and cosmopolitan good humor. Indeed, Bryant suggested that Ishmael's humorous alternation between extremes ultimately gives *Moby-Dick* its artistic shape: "Ishmael finds voice through lyric meditation. Its tone is genial despair; its structure, the circle; its vocabulary, picturesque" (204). Tommo's "rhetoric of deceit" evolves into Ishmael's "tense repose" (204), as a means of holding together Melville's discordant artistic impulses. As in his reading of *Typee*, Bryant used textual criticism to make an important aesthetic point: that Harrison Hayford and Hershel Parker's identification of Ahab rather than Ishmael as the speaker of the central monologue in chapter 114 of *Moby-Dick*, "The Gilder," is essential to understanding how Ishmael's voice comes to shape every part of the text, even the character of Ahab. Finally, in his reading of *The Confidence-Man* Bryant discovered Melville's development of a "voiceless voice" (231), that leaves readers themselves at sea, seeking to find meaning when there is no distinctive narrative voice to provide it. In this regard, Bryant's study also represented an advance over Rosenberry's earlier work on Melville's humor. For Rosenberry, *The Confidence-Man* was where Melville's humor went to die; for Bryant, this last full-length novel by Melville represented a legitimate development in the evolution of Melville's narrative theory and in Melville's use of humor as a crucial structural element in his narratives.

After Bryant's study, discussions of Melville's artistry turned rather decisively from the aural metaphor of voice toward visual metaphors and actualities. Christopher Sten contributed to a major new direction in the discussion of Melville's aesthetics with an edited collection of essays that would add immensely to the gathering momentum of studies of Melville and the visual arts. *Savage Eye: Melville and the Visual Arts* (1991) brought together the critics who would open up Melville studies to considerations of Melville's interactions with paintings, sculptures, imprints, sketches, and daguerreotypes over the following decade. Shirley Dettlaff's 1982 essay "Ionian Form and Esau's Waste: Melville's View of Art in *Clarel*" had offered a premonition that a substantial body of work on Melville's relation to the visual arts would emerge, and it had also illuminated the degree to which Melville's interaction with the visual arts was shaped by his reading of art critics, particularly Matthew Arnold. *Savage Eye* had the effect, however, of making the topic central rather than peripheral to Melville studies: in 1982, Dettlaff's work had had an unusual focus for a study of Melville; after *Savage Eye* was published, considerations of Melville and the visual arts appeared steadily throughout the next two decades. Sten's introduction provided a sweeping overview of both Melville's personal encounters with famous paintings, sculptures, and works of architecture and his recurrent tendency to use both works he had seen and works about which he had read as important symbols in his fiction and poetry. The essays in the collection provide an anatomy of Melville's interaction with the visual arts: his reading in art criticism (Douglas Robillard), analogues between Melville and J. M. W. Turner (Robert K. Wallace), religious art (Sanford Marovitz), architecture (Bryan Short), the picturesque (John Bryant), Dutch genre painting (Dennis Berthold), and classical aesthetics (Gail Coffler), among others.

In the wake of *Savage Eye*, which ensured that Melville's relation to painting and sculpture could never be ignored by critics hoping to understand his artistry, came a series of books that built upon that collection's promise. None was more expansive in its scope that Robert K. Wallace's 1993 study *Melville & Turner: Spheres of Love and Fright*. For Wallace, it was the great British Romantic painter J. M. W. Turner's "powerful aesthetic of the indistinct" that enabled Melville to achieve the effects for which *Moby-Dick* is revered (1). Wallace's study does not lend itself easily to summary, because he combined readings of paintings by Turner and others with close readings of *Moby-Dick* in such a way that the entire book is filled with moments that illuminate the visual qualities of Melville's literary imagination. Wallace's ability to correlate Turner's visual effects with Melville's verbal effects truly alters the way that even someone with a long acquaintance with Melville reads *Moby-Dick*. After reading Wallace, it is impossible not to see *Moby-Dick* as much as a gallery of images derived from Melville's art collecting and viewing as it is a compendium of Melville's indefatigable reading.

The recovery of visual analogues and sources for Melville's work in the 1990s was paralleled by a gathering movement toward the recovery of his poetry. A surprising source of this recuperation of Melville as poet appeared in the *New Republic* in Helen Vendler's 1992 essay "Desert Storm." Vendler had long been revered as the dean of academic criticism of poetry, and as a scholar who had immersed herself in such "poet's poets" as John Keats and Wallace Stevens, she could not easily be dismissed as a mere partisan of Melville and his obscurer works. The argument that she made, however, amounted to a thoroughgoing vindication of Melville's status as a major American poet. Against critics who had found the metrics of the poem clumsy, Vendler admires the "driving momentum" of the lines (40). Beyond a defense of the metrics of the poem, moreover, she describes Melville's use of language in *Clarel* in terms reminiscent of earlier critics' delighted rediscovery of the artfulness of Melville's verbal strategies in *Moby-Dick*, describing Melville's language in *Clarel* as "idiomatic, fearless, and torrential" (42). Because of her critical distance from the world of Melville studies and her eminence as a scholar of poetic form, Vendler's observations in this relatively short piece have had the effect of heartening scholars of *Clarel* when they have doubted that their own unusual passion for the poem is justified.

Bryan Short's *Cast by Means of Figures* (1992) showed how attention to form in Melville's works could connect usefully with one of the most rapidly expanding sub-disciplines within English studies: the history and theory of rhetoric. Fueled also by the rhetorical emphases of deconstructive thinkers like Jacques Derrida and Paul de Man, *Cast by Means of Figures* had the effect of extending R. P. Blackmur's insight that the sermon was one of Melville's most characteristic literary modes. Short took as his starting point the influence of Hugh Blair's (1718–1800) revision of classical rhetorical theory (so as to ally rhetoric more closely with figurative language and the sublime than with logic and formal argument) on Melville's frequently extravagant rhetorical constructions. Meanwhile, Melville struggled to move beyond Blair in one central aspect of his work: unlike Blair, he believed that imagination could play an important role in creating knowledge, and not merely in embellishing knowledge with external figures. Even in Melville's juvenilia, there was a tendency toward using figurative language as a means of suggesting "the promise of imaginative gratification that demands verbal participation" (21). This promise was expressed ever more insistently through the rhetorical tropes of Melville's major novels. In *Typee*, he uses literary language to create knowledge in the form of a dialectic between the naïve character Tommo and the more self-conscious authorial perspective represented by Tommo as the narrator. Short identified a variety of rhetorical devices that Melville used in *Typee* as vital to the form of his works, from hyperbole to "complex apostrophe," which by shifting its addressee wildly creates both a playful persona and an "intimacy between author and reader" (34). Short tracked Melville's rhetorical development through each of his early novels, culminating in the imaginative achievement of *Moby-Dick*, which for Short bridged the divide between an early period in Melville's fiction characterized by an increasingly audacious and subtle use of figurative tropes, and a later period that rejected figurative language and its capacity for truth and turned toward iconoclasm, taking the form of a rhetoric of silence in *Pierre* and Melville's short fiction and the form of "radical irony" in *The Confidence-Man* (137). Short eloquently sums up the capacity of *Moby-Dick* to bring together the image-making Melville of the novels preceding it and the image-breaking Melville of the fiction that follow it:

> *Moby-Dick* writes the final chapter of a story exemplary in pre-twentieth-century literature — the story of an author uncovering, exploring, and judging, with unsurpassed boldness and insight, a dizzying range of rhetorical structures — figures of speech and thought — central to persuasive *ethopoeia* of his day. Melville's courage and intellectual impatience leave him, like Ishmael, the "orphan" of his own success. (108)

For Short, then, as for Edgar Dryden two and a half decades earlier, the post-*Moby-Dick* phase of Melville's career became not a falling away from greatness, but the unavoidable consequence of the depth of Melville's vision. The defense of *The Confidence-Man* as a central piece in Melville's body of work that characterized readings of Melville's career by Short, Dryden, and (as we shall see in chapter 3) H. Bruce Franklin, was taken up thirteen years after Short's study by Sianne Ngai's *Ugly Feelings* (2005), in which Ngai argues that "Bartleby, the Scrivener" and *The Confidence-Man* are the crucial texts for understanding the role of affect throughout Melville's career. As it did for her predecessors, for Ngai *The Confidence-Man* matters because of what it rejects: it is the "Bartlebyan refusal of empathy" in the tone of Melville's last full-length novel that makes *The Confidence-Man* a crucial moment in Melville's varied career (50). Ngai also offers a provocative reading of *Pierre* as an expression of negative affect in Melville, drawing on Priscilla Wald's argument in "Hearing Narrative Voices in Melville's *Pierre*" (1990) that *Pierre* could be read as a successful formal experiment that "frustrates narrative expectations" (Wald, 100).

Sheila Post-Lauria's *Correspondent Colorings: Melville in the Marketplace* (1996) also recognized Melville's status as a rhetorician in that he was concerned throughout his career with the question of multiple audiences. Post-Lauria found that Melville had interacted with popular literary conventions from the start of his career, thus belying the common portrayal of a writer who resisted the tides of popular culture in creating high art that was utterly different from the work of his contemporaries. Post-Lauria began with Melville's adaptations of the conventions of travel literature in *Typee* and *Omoo*, and moved to a counterintuitive identification of Melville's initial audience for *Typee* as the group of readers who had made the sentimental fiction of the nineteenth century so popular. She established this through a close reading of passages in the manuscript version of *Typee* that emphasized the narrator's emotional responses to his experiences. She further noted that in the British edition of *Typee*, these sorts of responses had been downplayed, leading her to conclude that Melville shaped his books carefully in relation to his audiences. Subsequent readings of each of Melville's full-length novels confirmed that Melville had indeed constructed his works using nineteenth-century conventions at each step of the way, while revising these conventions to make them fit his own preoccupations. Post-Lauria argued that Melville thus could not be seen merely as "an alienated, frustrated artist who felt frustrated and superior to his culture" but rather as "a writer who ingeniously colored his works with topical forms, themes, and styles" (xv). In this way, Post-Lauria both confirmed David S. Reynolds's earlier arguments for the popular roots of the American Renaissance and expanded a long-standing body of work (dating back at least to Howard Vincent, William Gilman, and Merrell Davis in the late 1940s and early 1950s) that explored the motley origins of Melville's craft.

In addition to portending a revived interest in Melville's poetry and an intensified interest in Melville's relation to the visual arts, the 1990s saw a return to the sort of ambitious attempts to define the contours of Melville's artistic achievement that had appeared throughout the 1960s. Christopher Sten's *The Weaver-God, He Weaves: Melville and the Poetics of the Novel* (1996), constituted one of the most comprehensive attempts to define Melville's prose artistry ever undertaken. Sten's use of genre as a means of defining the contours of Melville's career was reminiscent of John Seelye's 1970 study *Melville: The Ironic Diagram*, but unlike Seelye, Sten attempted to attend more to the differences among Melville's works than the similarities. Moreover, Sten challenged a consensus about Melville's lack of interest in novelistic forms and genres that had included such luminaries as Charles Feidelson and Nina Baym. Sten argued that Melville had made a concerted effort to adapt a variety of forms that represented a cross-section of the available literary modes of the mid-nineteenth century and anticipated the development of new modes in the twentieth, from the romance to the experimental novel.

Douglas Robillard, like Robert K. Wallace, followed his contribution to *Savage Eye* with a book-length study of Melville's relation to the visual arts, *Melville and the Visual Arts: Ionian Form, Venetian Tint* (1997). Building on Wallace and on Merton M. Sealts's *Melville's Reading*, Robillard presented a taxonomy of how the visual arts appeared in Melville's fiction and poetry throughout his career. Robillard argued that *ekphrasis*, the act of writing about an art object and deriving one's inspirations for writing from art objects, was one of the most central and consistent elements in Melville's oeuvre, and he mapped Melville's career in terms of movements to or away from *ekphrasis*. As with so much Melville scholarship, Robillard began with Melville's reading and moved to Melville's own novels, highlighting his immersion in poetry filled with art objects by Homer, Shakespeare, Dryden, Byron, and Keats, before setting Melville in the American context of the ekphrastic practices in the fiction of Washington Irving, Nathaniel Hawthorne, and Edgar Allan Poe and the nonfiction of Richard Henry Dana, Jr. and Washington Allston. Robillard further intimated that the later Melville owed much to the ekphrastic models found in German writing, and particularly the poetry of Heinrich Heine. Melville's reading was supplemented by the Dutch and Italian paintings that Melville viewed with his own eyes while traveling in Europe.

For Robillard, *Redburn*, *Moby-Dick*, *Pierre*, and *Clarel* became the most important way-stations through Melville's career because each of these books turns insistently toward ekphrasis when dealing directly with painting and sculpture as well as architecture and even furniture. Robillard examined the use of the visual arts in each of these major works, and found that Melville's use of images had shaped the themes and narrative of each work. Robert K. Wallace's remarkable appreciation of *Moby-Dick* as the apex of Melville's efforts to make language from images can be seen in Robillard's work as consistent with the wider arc of Melville's career.[6]

Elizabeth Schultz took a complementary tack to the directions explored by Sten, Wallace, and Robillard in *Unpainted to the Last* (1995). Schultz dedicated the first six chapters of her study to a discussion of the illustrators of *Moby-Dick*, including most notably the Rockwell Kent engravings in the 1930 Lakeside Press edition, the Boardman Robinson paintings in the 1943 Limited Editions Club edition, and Barry Moser's 1979 illustrations to the Arion Press edition. In the final four chapters, she moved from between the covers of editions of *Moby-Dick* to the visual productions of painters and sculptors who were inspired by the book. She placed especial emphasis on the acknowledged importance of Melville to the emergence of abstract expressionism in the 1940s. She began with a reading of two of Jackson Pollock's paintings in light of *Moby-Dick*: *Pasiphae* and *(Blue (Moby-Dick)* both from 1943, identifying Ishmael's expression "the ungraspable phantom of life" as being at the heart of what Pollock sought to accomplish in *Pasiphae* (133). She moved from Pollock to discussions of numerous abstract expressionist painters and sculptors, focusing particularly on Frank Stella's metal-relief paintings associated with *Moby-Dick* from the 1980s and 1990s. Schultz demonstrated that the influence of the visual arts on Melville was paralleled by Melville's profound influence on the visual arts. Moreover, Schultz's exploration of twentieth-century artists' use of Melville indicated that the artists who found a model for their work in *Moby-Dick* shared the resistance to strict generic conventions that Nina Baym had found to be so fundamental to Melville's approach to his major prose works.

The alternating dismissal and defense of Melville's poetry has been a constant in Melville criticism from the 1940s on, and from the late 1990s on, the question of Melville's poetry moved to center stage. Lawrence Buell's essay "Melville the Poet" (1998) argued that Melville turned toward poetry as a result of his "quarrel with fiction" described by Baym in 1978 — for Buell, Melville's turn toward poetry was a natural development for a writer obsessed with communicating Truth. Following William Ellery Sedgwick, Walter Bezanson, Robert Penn Warren, and Helen Vendler, Buell suggested that many of the apparent stylistic infelicities of Melville's poetry were the result of self-conscious design. Buell was especially effective in taking the long view of Melville's poetic achievement, moving from brief lyrics embedded in *Mardi* up to the last poems Melville published before his death. In 1999, William C. Spengemann produced his own apologia for Melville's poetry, also entitled "Melville the Poet." Unfortunately, Spengemann suggested that Melville's poetry was universally presumed to be of inferior quality (a suggestion that the material in this chapter, for example, does not bear out) and that Melvilleans were responsible for the neglect of Melville's poetry because of their literary nationalism. This drew a rebuke from Elizabeth Renker in a 2000 letter to *American Literary History*, the journal in which Spengemann's initial piece was published. Despite this flaw, Spengemann's essay performed an important service by both acknowledging the extent of Melville's poetic production and placing this production in an international context alongside Browning, Hardy, and Hopkins, as well as the major Modernist poets of the twentieth century. Spengemann located the importance of Melville's poetry in its refusal to reproduce the poetic voice of *Moby-Dick*, or indeed any consistent voice at all, and related this tendency to the "knowing irony" in which Melville's poetry is "bathed" (601). Thus, though Spengemann underestimated the lively tradition of engagement with Melville's poetry among Melvilleans, and though he did not note the renaissance of interest in Melville's poetry that was in process as he wrote his essay, he nonetheless contributed mightily and insightfully to this very revival.

Samuel Otter's 2006 article, "How *Clarel* Works" had the effect of continuing a tradition of delighted and insightful reverie on Melville's use of language that dated back to Blackmur. With the possible exception of Shirley Dettlaff, Otter did more to draw attention to Melville's poetic craft in *Clarel* than any piece of criticism since Bezanson's introduction to the Hendrick's House edition of *Clarel* in 1960. Otter focused his analysis of *Clarel* on Melville's use of stones and language associated with stones as a dominant literary trope in his discussion of Jerusalem and its environs, comparing the role of stones in *Clarel* to Whitman's "leaves of grass." Otter also found hardness to have metaphorical and literal significance when Melville's use of the visual arts in *Clarel* was taken into account. He examined Melville's discussion of Piranesi's *Carceri* in Canto 2 of *Clarel*, finding that Melville modeled his verse on Piranesi's subterranean mazes, while reflecting on the complexities of human identity and sexuality: for Melville, Otter argued, Piranesi's prints and Melville's own complex and elusive style of versification in *Clarel* both become icons of the human heart.

In concentrating on the meaning of Melville's formal choices in writing poetry, Otter was not alone. Indeed, the early years of the twenty-first century saw the formal aspects of Melville's poetry become the subject of more vigorous discussion and debate than had appeared at any previous time in the history of Melville studies.[7] In the same *Companion to Herman Melville* that featured Otter's essay on *Clarel*, Elizabeth Renker contributed a bracing argument for Melville's eminence as a realist poet. Renker contended that "Melville was a realist poet writing in the age of realist prose" ("Realist Poet," 482). This position allowed Renker to contend that Melville's poetry was as much misunderstood and underrated through the twentieth century as was his prose throughout the years leading up to the Melville Revival.[8] Renker's most important contribution in the essay was her observation that Melville's late poetry, because it so often explored the relationship between prose narratives and poems, was actually entirely consistent with the history of the development of *Billy Budd*, which began as the poem "Billy in the Darbies," and developed into a prose narrative. Thus, as Renker demonstrated, *Billy Budd* was not a shocking anomaly in the career of a man who had long given up on fiction altogether, but rather the product of years of writing along the boundaries of fiction and poetry (487). This line of thinking regarding *Billy Budd* had been suggested by William Shurr in 1972, but Renker's framework of "realist poetry" had the particularly salutary effect of explaining the shift in *Billy Budd*'s prose style from that of Melville's earlier fiction.

Like Walter Bezanson, Edgar Dryden began his career as a Melvillean with an influential study of Melville's fiction, only to return later in his career to a powerfully reasoned defense of Melville's poetry. In *Monumental Melville: The Formation of a Literary Career* (2004), Dryden shifted the focus of Melville's career from its fictional first act to its poetic second act, arguing that Melville's turn to poetry constituted a rejection of the demands of verisimilitude imposed by fiction, and allowed Melville to "give full rein to the trickeries and subversive goings-on that occur within [literature's] boundaries" (65). In his earlier work, Dryden had shifted the center of Melville's career from *Moby-Dick* to *The Confidence-Man* based the movement toward subversion and trickery throughout Melville's fictional career; in *Monumental Melville*, he found that this movement explained Melville's devotion to poetry rather than fiction in his later years. Thus Dryden offered a counterpoint to Renker's view of Melville as a realist poet: rather than representing a turn to literary realism, the poetry for Dryden represented an intensification of Romantic irony in Melville's work.

What made *Monumental Melville* such a representative piece of aesthetically oriented Melville scholarship for the opening years of the twenty-first century was Dryden's explicit linkage of Melville's turn to poetry with his turn to the visual arts as a metaphor for the kind of literary production to which he aspired.[9] Citing Sten and Robillard, Dryden defined Melville's method of writing poetry as the production of "speaking pictures" as part of a proto-Modernist attempt to "apprehend past and present spatially" (67). Dryden located the "monumental" aspect of *Battle-Pieces* in the collection's attempt to bring past, present, and future together by means of image and allusion; in *Clarel* and the later poetry, he found Melville constructing monuments to the inevitability of death. As in Dryden's earlier *Melville's Thematics of Form* (1968), *Monumental Melville* showed that Melville was at heart an author who created brilliantly illusory artifices out of disillusionment with the potential of art to represent reality.

Virginia Jackson brought Melville's poetry onto a much broader stage within the field of English studies in general than it had previously occupied with her 2008 essay on *Battle-Pieces* in *PMLA*. Jackson had made her name with a highly praised study of Emily Dickinson's poetry in 2005, and in her article "Who Reads Poetry?" Jackson built her argument around a reading of Melville's short poem "The Portent" from *Battle-Pieces and Aspects of War*, the volume of Civil War poetry that Melville published in 1866. Jackson saw "The Portent" as being entangled in a larger move in American literary culture toward the "lyricization" of poetry — the reimagining of poetry in general as being defined by the lyric mode, and she enlisted a careful reading of the poem to make her larger literary-historical point. "The Portent," Jackson suggested, is a lyric that resists the idea that literature could be identified exclusively with the lyric form. She read the material contained within parentheses in the poem as exemplifying a characteristically lyrical approach to subjectivity. The material not enclosed in parentheses contains a critique of seemingly unified lyric form contained in the parentheses through its mixing of radically different forms and genres. The multigeneric quality of Melville's most ambitious long fiction had long been recognized; Jackson suggestively brought to the attention of critics the multigeneric qualities of even Melville's briefest poems.

Studies of Melville's verbal artistry and its connection to other modes of art have proved to be as diverse and unpredictable as Melville's own body of work. In some ways, this category of Melville criticism is the most slippery and difficult to define of all. In another sense, however, it is the approach that best mirrors Melville's own subtle and elusive array of texts. If accounts of Melville's artistry struggle to contain the complexities of his effects, they also serve to illuminate the reasons that reading Melville can be so exhilarating. Moreover, Melville's own tendency to blend the aesthetic the philosophical and the cultural has meant that many discussions of Melville's aesthetics have proved surprisingly durable through changing academic fashions because they have reflected a similar tendency to engage with cultural issues.

There is nonetheless a discernable trajectory for discussions of Melville's artistry over the years. A focus on words, ideas, and erudite allusions in Melville's published work was the dominant mode of aesthetically based scholarship from the 1940s through the 1970s. During this period Melville was seen as an artistic rebel estranged from his culture, and with a few exceptions (such as Walter Bezanson, Robert Penn Warren, and Hennig Cohen), critics emphasized his prose works in general at the expense of his poetry. Also during this period, however, the range of Melville's prose works regarded as aesthetically significant increased: in the early years, the focus is on *Moby-Dick*, with Melville's earlier novels being considered largely as precursors to his masterpiece, and *Pierre* being considered as a symptom of the collapse of his artistic gift and perhaps even his sanity. The short fiction and *The Confidence-Man*, meanwhile, merited little consideration at all. By the early 1960s, an increasing number of critics became engaged by the short fiction, and by the end of the 1960s, *The Confidence-Man* had emerged as a crucial part of the Melville canon. The 1990s and the first decade of the twenty-first century, a period when aesthetic studies of Melville might have been expected to be eclipsed by cultural studies, remained a vibrant period for artistic considerations of Melville because of an increased interest in Melville's sources, analogues, and influence in the visual arts and in his poetry, which was increasingly seen as mirroring the visual arts in its form.

The prospect for future aesthetically based criticisms of Melville as of this writing lies, then, in these two distinct directions: the first, and the path most likely to be crowded during the second decade of the twenty-first century, is the ongoing discussion of Melville's relation to the visual arts. Robert K. Wallace and Dennis Berthold in particular continue to produce important work on the sources of Melville's imagery in paintings, sculptures, and imprints to which he had access, and the current wave of interest in the meaning of the daguerreotype for nineteenth-century American literature promises to be productive of further scholarship. Matthew Cordova Frankel's recent essay, "Tattoo Art: The Composition of Text, Race, and Voice in Melville's *Moby-Dick*" (2007) has suggested the potential that considerations of body art have for extending discussions of Melville's aesthetics.

The path that is currently less well traveled but which may offer an even more extensive prospect in the long run is the exploration of Melville's poetry. Much has been done to establish Melville's eminence among nineteenth-century American poets, but much remains if the full implications of Melville's years as a poet are to be comprehended. In particular, despite William Bysshe Stein's efforts in 1970 and William Shurr's in 1972, Melville's late collections, *John Marr and Other Sailors*, *Timoleon* and *Weeds and Wildings* have only begun to receive the scholarly consideration that is their due, much of it courtesy of the indefatigable editorial and critical efforts of Douglas Robillard, who edited both a new selected edition of *The Poems of Herman Melville* (2000) and a facsimile edition of *John Marr and Other Sailors* (2006). The publication of the Northwestern-Newberry Edition of Melville's *Published Poems* in 2009 means that there is finally a standard scholarly edition for this important segment of Melville's career. Ninety years after the Melville Revival, the full scope of Melville's artistic achievement remains to be explored.[10]

Notes

[1] For a superb extension of Matthiessen's work on Browne, see Brian Foley's "Herman Melville and the Example of Sir Thomas Browne."

[2] It should be noted that Olson preceded even Matthiessen in discussing Shakespearean echoes in Melville with his 1938 article "Lear and Moby-Dick." Indeed, Merton M. Sealts reported in *Pursuing Melville* (1982) that Olson was angered by Matthiessen's work on the Shakespeare connection, arguing that it was derivative of Olson's own work (109).

[3] Kevin Hayes's study *Melville's Folk Roots* (1999) is a more recent consideration of the influence of folklore on Melville's work.

[4] Also in 1972, A. Carl Bredahl, Jr., published a brief work entitled *Melville's Angles of Vision*, which began to make the case for understanding Melville in light of the visual aspects of his work.

[5] Jane Mushabac's *Melville's Humor: A Critical Study* (1981) is the other book-length treatment of the issue of humor in Melville.

[6] Hsuan L. Hsu extended Robillard's discussion of Melville's use of ekphrasis to *Battle-Pieces and Aspects of War* in his 2002 article "War, Ekphrasis, and Elliptical Form in Melville's *Battle-Pieces*." Hsu argued that Melville undermined totalizing images of the Civil War in the visual arts in order to develop multiple perspectives on the war in his poetry.

[7] Elizabeth Renker had predicted just such a revival in an exchange with William Spengemann in *American Literary History* at the turn of the millennium. Spengemann had called for more attention to Melville's poetry in his article "Melville the Poet" (1999) but had alleged that prospects were bleak due to the literary nationalism of Melvilleans. Renker took issue with this assertion, and argued that indeed an upsurge in scholarship on Melville's poetry was already under way. Renker contributed to the fulfillment of her own prophecy with several articles on Melville's poetry in addition to a coedited special issue of *Leviathan* on Melville's poetry in 2006.

[8] One objection to Renker's argument that she did not really address was that Melville's two contemporaries who wrote poetry at the same time that he did and who are almost ubiquitously recognized as canonical poets, Walt Whitman and Emily Dickinson, could also be described as "realist poets in an age of realist prose." Renker's larger argument about the realist qualities of Melville's poetry seems persuasive, however (although not incontestable in light of Edgar Dryden's reading of Melville's poetry as characterized by his skepticism toward representation) and perhaps the gap between Melville's reputation and those of Dickinson and Whitman has much to do with the fact that Melville's poetry is handicapped by being attached to a much better-known body of prose.

[9] Two other studies that link Melville to monuments and architecture are Shawn Thomson's *The Romantic Architecture of Herman Melville's Moby-Dick* (2001) and Ian S. Maloney's *Melville's Monumental Imagination* (2006).

[10] Not yet published as of this writing, but promising to set the tone for future discussions in this area, is the collection *Melville and Aesthetics* (2011), edited by Samuel Otter and Geoffrey Sanborn.

3: Melville's Beard I: Religion, Ethics, and Epistemology

NEITHER BIOGRAPHICAL EXAMINATIONS of Melville the artist nor aesthetic inspections of his portraits have been able to dispense with the category of criticism that deals with Melville as a thinker. Indeed, this has been a source of anxiety for both biographical and aesthetically oriented critics: in 1938, Charles R. Anderson, one of Melville's most influential biographical critics, complained humorously about Melville's beard and the wisdom it was taken to imply, suggesting that reading Melville for evidence of his philosophical or religious thought was squeezing out considerations of his life and experiences. Warner Berthoff, one of Melville's most insightful aesthetically oriented critics, began his superb study *The Example of Melville* (1964), by stating that he would not be dealing with Melville's work as "a provider of 'scripture'" (3), thus acknowledging the degree to which Melville has been regarded as precisely a "provider of scripture" by admirers over the years. The pages that follow discuss critics who have approached Melville in religious or philosophical terms as a prophet, sage, or both.[1]

The debates that have grown up around Melville as thinker have tended in two directions: one set of discussions has sought to define the contours of Melville's religious thought in terms of both his works and what one can reasonably surmise about his personal belief system, and the other major set of discussions has attempted to situate Melville in relation to the major American philosophical movement of Melville's time, Transcendentalism, and its precursors in European and Asian philosophical thought. Since these two strands are so closely interwoven with each other, I consider them as a unit, although I will be pointing out the varying emphases on religious or philosophical thought that appear along the way. Just how interconnected these emphases can be is apparent in the efforts of numerous mid-twentieth-century critics to claim Melville as a proto-existentialist. The combination of the religious and the philosophical in so much of Melville criticism reflects a leading characteristic of Melville's work, in that he approaches religious questions with an irreverently analytical eye, and philosophical issues with an emotional and ethical intensity often associated with religious belief. The scriptures that Melville provides in his writings, to use Berthoff's analogy, are both religious and secular, and like all scriptures, have proved widely variable in the range of interpretations they inspire.

Writers for many religious journals in the mid-nineteenth century believed they knew exactly what sort of alternative scripture Melville was providing, and they emphatically did not approve. In one of the more scathing responses to Melville's first novel *Typee*, a reviewer in *The Christian Parlor Magazine* (July 1846) described the novel as "An apotheosis of barbarism! A panegyric on cannibal delights! An apostrophe to the spirit of savage felicity!" (Higgins and Parker, 52). The reviewer proceeded to describe Melville himself as a "traducer of missions" (53) motivated by hatred of the missionary enterprise, and in some danger of damnation for the content of his book. Melville, the reviewer suggested, was most hostile to Christianity and besotted with religious alternatives to Christianity, and was therefore an untrustworthy witness as to the activities of missionaries. A year later, *The Christian Observatory* (May 1847) included a similar blast against Melville's infidelity and "low thoughts of the Gospel" (Higgins and Parker, 69–72). If the Protestant religious press was wrathful in its condemnation of *Typee*, the Catholic press seemed altogether too pleased by the comeuppance received by Protestant missionaries in the text. A reviewer in the *United States Catholic Magazine and Monthly Review* (November 1847), was thrilled to find that a self-acknowledged Protestant like Melville could confirm that Protestant missions tended toward the "temporal destruction" of Polynesian peoples (Higgins and Parker, 78). Indeed, some Protestants were able to hint darkly that Melville's critique of Protestant missions only revealed a secret loyalty to the Catholic Church lurking below the surface of his writing. Nineteenth-century reviewers continued to grapple with the question of Melville's religious loyalties throughout his career, and Ishmael's religious relativism in *Moby-Dick* became grounds for condemnation for some reviewers. The almost unanimously negative reception that greeted *Pierre* also reflected anxiety about what appeared to be anti-religious elements in the plot, and so far as it was reviewed at all, *The Confidence-Man* was viewed with suspicion as a nihilistic tract of despair.[2]

As might be expected, Nathaniel Hawthorne put forward a view of Melville's religious and philosophical proclivities that was at once more nuanced and more sympathetic than those in the popular religious press. After Melville had visited Hawthorne in Liverpool, where Hawthorne was stationed as the American Consul, Hawthorne wrote what is still the single most famous and influential account of Melville's religious proclivities:

> Melville, as he always does, began to reason of Providence and futurity, and of everything that lies beyond human ken, and informed me that he had "pretty much made up his mind to be annihilated"; but still he does not seem to rest in that anticipation; and, I think, will never rest until he gets hold of a definite belief. It is strange how he persists and has persisted ever since I knew him, and probably long

before — in wondering to-and-fro over these deserts, as dismal and monotonous as the sand hills amid which we were sitting. He can neither believe, nor be comfortable in his unbelief; and he is too honest and courageous not to try to do one or the other. If he were a religious man, he would be one of the most truly religious and reverential; he has a very high and noble nature, and better worth immortality than most of us. (from the Northwestern-Newberry edition of Melville's *Journals*, 628)

Hawthorne found Melville to be an ambivalent spiritual seeker, wandering between faith and doubt without finding either to be an adequate resting place for Melville's uncertainties. There seems to be little reason to question Hawthorne's description of where Melville's religious inclinations stood in 1856, but it is worth noting that nearly half of Melville's life, and much of his work, lay ahead of him at that point. One of the questions that has continued to fascinate students of Melville's thought is whether the "desert wonderings" Hawthorne described ever reached a conclusion.

Melville's critics have often sought to give the writer the happy ending that they, like Hawthorne, have felt that he deserved. The texts that have figured most largely in this endeavor have been Melville's long poem *Clarel* and his posthumously published novella *Billy Budd*. What that happy ending consists of has differed, depending on the perspective of the critic. One of the most famous of these efforts came very early indeed in the story of Melville criticism. E. L. Grant Watson coined the phrase "testament of acceptance" to refer to what he, drawing on Lewis Mumford's 1929 biography of Melville, saw as Melville's final reconciliation to the religious faith that he had lost as a younger man. Watson argues that "Melville is no longer a rebel" at the close of *Billy Budd* (322), but, rather, has created an allegory of his own journey toward the solution to the moral and psychological problems posed in *Moby-Dick* and *Pierre*. Billy Budd becomes an allegorical type of Christ; Captain Vere becomes Pontius Pilate — but a Pilate who has accepted responsibility for his sin and thus been redeemed; Billy's final words, "God bless Captain Vere!" become both an act of Christ-like forgiveness and an indication of the mystical union of the souls of Billy and Vere, who represent for Watson two central elements of the human personality, finally in harmony with each other. This conclusion made *Billy Budd* a quasi-sacred text for Watson, and it also had the effect of baptizing Melville's entire body of work. If Melville had been an unbeliever throughout his life, Watson averred, the end result was a beautiful "testament of acceptance" that represented a final triumph of faith.

Not surprisingly, the happy death that Watson envisioned for both Billy and Melville has not always seemed happy at all to other readers. F. Barron Freeman's introduction to *Melville's Billy Budd* (1948) argued that what Melville experienced in life and represented in *Billy Budd* was not so much acceptance as resignation. Joseph Schiffman went a step further in his 1950 article "Melville's Final Stage," suggesting that the novella should be read as a sign of Melville's movement towards irony in his later work. Conceding that Charles Weir, Jr. in "Malice Reconciled" (1944), William Ellery Sedgwick in *Herman Melville: The Tragedy of Mind* (1945), and Willard Thorp in the *Literary History of the United States* (1948) had all followed Watson's argument, Schiffman still regarded the story as an ironic celebration of the ultimate triumph of an expanded version of human rights in the British Navy as an indirect result of the unjust executions of sailors like Billy.[3] Thus *Billy Budd* became for Schiffman a story of change, not acceptance, about not God, but human society. A more polemical response to the "testament of acceptance" theory was Phil Withim's 1959 article "*Billy Budd*: A Testament of Resistance." For Withim *Billy Budd* is actually a critique of Billy's failure to resist his own unjust hanging and the failure of everyone else aboard the ship to resist an unjust legal system. Withim thus concluded that Melville's final testament is a call for courage, not piety.

With controversy already underway regarding the religious import of specific texts from Melville's career, William Braswell's *Melville's Religious Thought* (1943) attempted a broad interpretation of Melville's attitude toward Christianity throughout his career, and has remained fundamental for anyone engaging with Melville's representations of religion. Braswell started with the biographical data of Melville's personal contact with religious communities: the Calvinist past of both the Melvills on his father's side and the Gansevoorts on his mother's, Allan Melvill's emphasis on moral instruction in child-rearing, the close ties of the Melville family to the Dutch Reformed Church after Allan Melvill's death, the connection with Unitarianism forged by Melville's marriage to Elizabeth Shaw, and Melville's close friendship with the Episcopalian Duyckincks and Morewoods. He proceeded from there into a survey of Melville's wide-ranging reading, both in the Bible and in numerous religious and secular figures. The bulk of Braswell's study, however, was devoted to an exploration of how Melville's represented religious belief in his published books. Braswell emphasized that in both published works like *Mardi* and *Pierre* and in his marginalia to the works of others, Melville expressed a strong preference for a religion of the heart over rationalism and doctrinal precision. He also stressed Melville's interest in the divine qualities of humanity as expressed in the Hebrew and Christian scriptures and elsewhere. Seeing these religious tendencies as antithetical to Melville's inherited Calvinism, Braswell led the way in developing a portrait of Melville as a conflicted Romantic rebel against Calvinist orthodoxy.

Having established Melville's credentials as a religious outsider, Braswell then confronted potential contradictions in Melville's work. In

White-Jacket, for example, Melville produced prose that "gives to the cursory reader the impression that its author was a fundamentalist Christian" (50). Braswell rightly rejected this impression on the grounds that *Mardi*, written shortly before *White-Jacket*, and *Moby-Dick*, written shortly after *White-Jacket*, both exhibit a more ambivalent attitude toward Christianity. His explanation for this apparent contradiction was that Melville was both acting as a propagandist in his critique of flogging in *White-Jacket* and thus attempting to appeal to an audience more orthodox than himself and giving expression to a genuine affinity for the ideal of Christian charity. When Braswell turned to *Moby-Dick*, he found that Melville's tendency toward heart-religion and his skepticism had fused to make him an "accuser of the deity" (57). Melville's protest against a Calvinist God in *Moby-Dick* became a more doctrinally specific critique of Christian thought in *Pierre*, according to Braswell. He concluded with a brief chapter on Melville's "long search for peace" (107) — a clear allusion to Raymond Weaver's depiction of the last four decades of Melville's literary career as "the long quietus." The brevity of Braswell's consideration of this portion of Melville's career is unfortunate, since Melville addresses matters of faith extensively in *The Confidence-Man, Battle-Pieces, Clarel, John Marr and Other Sailors, Timoleon,* and *Billy Budd*. Moreover, the fact that Braswell devoted little attention to *Typee* and *Omoo* meant that there was little opportunity to discuss the ways in which Melville's thought might have evolved over the course of his life. Thus, Braswell's Melville was ultimately Hawthorne's Melville, and Melville scholars were left to search for the elusive shape of the development of Melville's religious thought throughout his career.

William Ellery Sedgwick's *Herman Melville: The Tragedy of Mind* (1944) was built around the image of Melville as a disillusioned spiritual seeker who ultimately transcended his doubts, and he both reinforced the "testament of acceptance" school of thought and extended Braswell's discussion of Melville's religious development considerably. He dealt with Melville's career from *Typee* to *Billy Budd*, albeit with some important omissions in that the magazine fiction and *Battle-Pieces* are crammed together in one twenty-five-page chapter, and *Omoo* at the beginning of Melville's career and the post-*Clarel* collections of poetry towards the end are omitted altogether. In addition to the scope of Sedgwick's study, it was also an important advance in its carefully crafted portrayal of Melville as a religious thinker. Sedgwick's summary of Melville's importance as a religious thinker is worth quoting at length:

> To Melville, as to [Milton's] angels, the ultimate truth presented itself in the form of the age-old questions of Christian theology. Like them, too, he "found no end, in wand'ring mazes lost." If it be urged that these questions were antiquated and could lead nowhere,

and that the mind that occupied itself with them could only find itself in a void, the objection is to be brushed aside as trivial. For, to go no further, not the forms in which the truth seemed to present itself, but his mind's urge out of its own deepest and universal nature to get at the truth was the source of vital interest. (9)

For Sedgwick, Melville's engagement with Christian theology was more than either the Romantic rebellion against Calvinism that Braswell saw and that Geoffrey Stone was soon to see or the use of Christian tropes for propagandistic purposes that Braswell found in *White-Jacket*. Theology provided a conceptual counterpoint to the world of Melville's experience, and Melville judged the world of experience by conceptual measures derived from theology, and theological concepts by the data of his real-world experiences. This schema served to connect works from across Melville's career, and Sedgwick saw that trajectory moving toward an acceptance of necessity in *Clarel*, and an ultimate reconciliation with the world in *Billy Budd*. He states the "testament of acceptance" school's case beautifully, concluding "Melville has been restored to the radiant visage of life, whose shining secret is, it has its salvation in its own keeping" (249). Sedgwick's words only become more poignant when we consider that his study of Melville was published posthumously, and his reflection on Melville's last work was among the last things that Sedgwick himself wrote.

Merton M. Sealts found Melville's use of Plato to be more significant than questions of religious faith and doubt to understanding his most important work. In a series of articles in the early 1940s, Sealts dug into the philosophical underpinnings of Melville's work, particularly in regard to questions of knowledge. Sealts's essays "The World of Mind: Melville's Theory of Knowledge" (1940), "Melville's 'I and My Chimney'" (1941), and "Melville and the Philosophers" (1942) all explore Melville's engagement with questions of epistemology. Later in his career, Sealts's essays "Melville and Emerson's Rainbow" (1980) and "Melville and the Platonic Tradition" (1980) continued his investigation of Melville's philosophical leanings, while "Melville's Geniality" (1967) was a crucial discussion of the persona that Melville developed throughout his work. In the first two 1940s essays, Sealts argued that Melville resisted both common-sense empiricism and speculative rationalism in favor of a careful exploration of the irrational elements in human consciousness, with the chimney in "I and My Chimney" standing in for Melville's own struggle with irrationality. In "Melville and the Philosophers," Sealts surveyed Melville's engagement with philosophy, emphasizing Pierre Bayle's dictionary as source for much of Melville philosophical knowledge, and concluded that by the time of *Billy Budd*, Melville had found a satisfying philosophical synthesis: "Socratic wisdom, stoic serenity, and Christian love" ("Philosophers,"

30). In his later work from 1980, Sealts looked at Emerson and Plato as coordinated influences on Melville: it was Emerson's Platonism that alternately drew and repelled Melville, and Plato become alive to Melville through Emerson. Sealts made the important point, at times neglected, that at no time in his career was Melville's attitude toward Plato or Emerson static. Melville may have mocked Transcendentalism and Platonism in his major novels of the 1850s, but he also returned to both Emerson and Plato later in his career. Perhaps no more succinct summing up of Melville's troubled relation to these two figures has been produced than Sealts's formulation near the conclusion of "Melville and the Platonic Tradition": Melville was, writes Sealts, "an idealist who mistrusted idealism" ("Platonic Tradition," 336). These essays, representing the arc of one of the most important careers in Melville studies, have all been collected in *Pursuing Melville, 1940–1980*, thus allowing Melvilleans to trace the development of Sealts's scholarship on Melville.

Millicent Bell's "Pierre Bayle and *Moby-Dick*" (1951) marked one of those frequent breakthroughs in Melville scholarship that occur as the result of careful attention to his reading and allusions, and Bell highlighted both the idealism and the mistrust of idealism that Sealts found in Melville's work. Sealts and Howard P. Vincent had both referred to Melville's use of Pierre Bayle's dictionary already, but Bell was the first to explore Melville's reading of the work in detail, pointing out that Melville's lack of training in languages other than English meant that he relied heavily on translated encyclopedic works like Bayle's *Dictionnaire historique and critique*, which he read in 1849. This meant that Bayle provided Melville with a great deal of his exposure to non-Anglophone philosophy and theology, which in turn afforded Bell a significant angle into Melville's thought. Bell saw Bayle as being a particularly important influence on Melville in relation to the problem of evil and philosophic and religious dualism, introducing him to dualist religious traditions like Zoroastrianism, Gnosticism, and Manicheanism that exerted such a powerful influence on the construction of, among other characters, Ahab and Fedallah in *Moby-Dick*. Bayle, like Melville, was brought up in the intellectual traditions of Calvinism, and like Bayle, Melville found that the inconsistency between a benevolent and all-powerful deity and a cruel world was intolerable — and the presence of a force for evil in the world that could act as a counterpoise to goodness seemed almost inescapable for both men. Bell was thus able to provide a source for the mysterious "Descartian vortices" to which Melville has Ishmael refer in the chapter "The Masthead" in *Moby-Dick*: Descartes's philosophical dualism, like Zoroastrian religious dualism, suggested a comprehension of the universe in which evil could be understood. Bell also noted that Bayle was important to Melville as an early historical critic of the Bible, and many of Melville's skeptical references to the Book of Jonah were influenced by

Bayle.[4] Bell's article remains an important milestone in Melville scholarship because it opened up the question of Melville's skepticism and his engagement with religious traditions other than Protestantism.

By the late 1940s, the question of Melville's religious thought was being discussed in considerably more complex ways than the straightforward continuum of faith and doubt. A complicating factor in discussions of Melville's faith was that, quite simply, Melville dealt with more than one variety of faith in his body of work, and he was being read attentively by adherents of multiple religious traditions. In *Melville* (1949), Geoffrey Stone approached Melville's religious thought from a specifically Catholic vantage point without claiming Melville for Catholicism — indeed, rather the reverse. Stone saw the sense of tragic conflict that formed the heart of Melville's work as derivative of both the Romanticism that was his artistic creed and the Calvinism that had been the faith of many of his forbears. Stone argued that unlike European Romanticism, American Romanticism was a rebellion against Calvinism, itself a rebellion against Catholicism. He traced what he regarded as a combination of Calvinistic pessimism about human nature and Romantic insistence on self-assertion through Melville's work, arguing that he never escaped the burdens of determinism and egotism at any point in his career. *Billy Budd* became for Stone neither a "testament of acceptance" nor a "testament of resistance," but rather a precarious acknowledgment of reality. Moreover, Stone contended that Melville was neither "the mystic [n]or metaphysician he has been called" (162). Melville's tragedy was that he was an artist of the "heart's obstinacy" never able to find a source of answers outside the "sovereign self" (162). Stone concluded that Melville's beliefs never rose to the level of sophistication found in his verbal artistry, but nevertheless informed that artistry. For Stone, Melville's Romanticism is ultimately incompatible with his religious intuitions, and his residual Calvinism prevented his Romanticism from tending toward optimism about the human condition.

Few studies of Melville have worn as well over time as Nathalia Wright's *Melville's Use of the Bible* (1949), which tracked Melville's use of biblical allusions and explored Melville's use of biblical commentaries as source material for his representations of religion. Perhaps because of Melville's passion for reading and crafting his art out of materials derived from his reading, source studies have always been an effective means of approaching Melville, and there are few if any sources more important to Melville than the English Bible. Wright argued that the emphasis on subjectivity that pervades Melville's work was the direct consequence of his exposure to and affinity for ancient Hebrew thought in the Bible, and that the irregularities of his style were biblical in that they served a subjectivity similar to that of the Hebrew prophets. Like Stone and Braswell, Wright ultimately saw Melville as a Romantic rebel, but she illuminated the degree to which he expressed his rebellion in biblical terms. According to Wright, Melville used the Bible not as a source of answers to his spiritual conundrums, but rather as a source of metaphors for speaking about "symbolic and fragmentary manifestations of the one absolute, which is in the last analysis inviolable" (188). The Bible thus became for Melville a source of form and the approximation of an endlessly elusive truth.[5]

W. H. Auden's *The Enchafed Flood* (1950), found a place for Melville amid such then-contemporary movements as existential philosophy and neo-orthodox theology. Pairing *Moby-Dick* with *Don Quixote*, Auden suggested that Ishmael and Don Quixote constituted the most important models for the ideal Romantic hero in Western literature. Following the classifications established by the Danish philosopher Søren Kierkegaard in *Fear and Trembling* (himself a hero to Auden), Auden defined heroes as being aesthetic (distinguished by "exceptional gifts"), ethical (distinguished by wisdom), or religious (distinguished by "absolute passion") in their orientation (91–94). Auden's Romantic hero, of whom Ishmael and Don Quixote are emblematic, combines something of all three qualities in the person of the literary artist, and Ishmael is distinguished from Don Quixote by his self-consciousness (102). Ishmael thus became for Auden a peculiarly modern hero: complex, self-conscious, self-pitying, and self-congratulatory. Captain Ahab, by contrast, represented the religious hero in a state of daemonic defiance. Auden thus found in Melville a religious thinker who combined romantic Prometheanism with a proto-existential sense of the absurd. Small wonder, then, that Auden would not have been alone in embracing Melville as an artistic model in the post–World War II era, and small wonder that the leading existential novelist and thinker Albert Camus would be among Melville's most enthusiastic readers during this disillusioned era.

It should come as no surprise that Melville would resonate powerfully with a writer who combined literature and philosophy in his body of work, and who obsessively revisited themes like rebellion and suicide throughout his career. Like Auden, Camus saw Melville as having profound resonances for twentieth-century existentialism. Camus's brief 1952 essay on Melville illustrated his sense of kinship with the central religious and philosophical questions raised by Melville's work. Although his summary of Melville's career was inaccurate, suggesting that Melville's prodigiously active years as a poet between *The Confidence-Man* and his death only produced "a few infrequent poems" (288) — the "long quietus" view introduced by Raymond Weaver taken to its most absurd extreme — Camus's sense that Melville was a preeminent student of the absurd as understood by mid-twentieth-century existentialists is expressed beautifully and persuasively. Camus aptly notes that "in judging Melville's genius, if nothing else, it must be recognized that his works trace a spiritual experience of unequaled intensity, and that they are to some extent symbolic" (289). For Camus, the religious significance of Melville's work was derived primarily neither from Melville's own religious beliefs or doubts nor from his representations of religious faith and practice, but rather from his potent abilities as a "creator of myths" (290). Especially in *Moby-Dick*, *Benito Cereno*, and *Billy Budd*, Melville had indeed created his own scriptures interpreting the universal qualities of the human condition. Like Camus, Henry A. Murray in "In Nomine Diaboli" (1951) considered *Moby-Dick* in relation to psychology and mythology, regarding Melville as a kind of architect of a new religious thought thoroughly informed by the science of his day. Murray particularly emphasized the degree to which the religious elements in *Moby-Dick*, especially those which tended toward blasphemy, constituted a blast against middle-class society in Melville's day, suggesting that "Melville's clear intention was not to bring rest, but unrest, to intrepid minds (451).

At the same time that existential thinkers were recovering Melville for the post-war era, Ronald Mason's *The Spirit Above the Dust* (1951) demonstrated something of the reach that enthusiasm for Melville could have. When Mason died in 2001, he was best known as a writer about the popular British sport of cricket, and not as a literary critic. Before cricket, however, there was Melville. Mason's study covered Melville's entire career, and while Mason made strong claims for Melville's artistry, his primary focus was on the development of Melville's mind and thought. The early chapters trace a fairly conventional arc for Melville's career from innocence in *Typee* through imaginative ambitiousness in *Mardi* and *Moby-Dick* to bitter disillusionment in the magazine fiction and *The Confidence-Man*. The later chapters, however, mark an advance in extending Sedgwick's observations on the importance of understanding Melville's poetry, and particularly *Clarel*, for any critic wishing to present a rounded picture of Melville's thought. Mason considered *Clarel* an "act of faith" on Melville's part (242), the faith being Catholic in its sympathies, even though he had established no formal religious connection with the Roman Catholic Church. For the Melville who wrote *Clarel*, Catholicism provided "just that necessary blend of regulation and rapture that could illuminate an individual without rendering him either unsuitable for modern society or too readily corruptible by its compromises" (241). This embrace of spiritual discipline in Melville's later work complemented a parallel development: Mason made the epilogue to *Clarel*, with its ambiguous suggestions of hope in the resurrection of the dead, into an acknowledgment by Melville of the primacy of the heart over the objections to faith made by the mind. *Clarel* thus became a crucial premonition of Melville's ultimate religious reconciliation in *Billy Budd*. Following the "testament of acceptance" school of thought, Mason regarded *Billy Budd* as representing a "state of assured resolution," and believed that the simplicity of the structure of Melville's posthumous novella was determined by this mental and spiritual state.

It would be hard to imagine a more antithetical reading of Melville's religious thought to Mason's than Lawrance Thompson's *Melville's Quarrel with God* (1952). Thompson rejected the idea that Melville had become reconciled to Christian theology in his later days. Taking issue with both the "testament of acceptance" school of thought on *Billy Budd* and the view that Braswell, Sedgwick, and Mason put forward that Melville's career was a quest for faith, Thompson argued with scathing wit and intensity that Melville's literary career was devoted to mockery:

> The gist of it is simple. [Melville] spent his life not merely in sneering at the gullibility of human beings who disagreed with him but also in sneering at God, accusing God, upbraiding God, blaming God, and (as he thought) quarreling with God. The turn which his life had taken translated him from a transcendentalist and a mystic into a inverted transcendentalist, an inverted mystic. To this extent, then, he was consistent, in spite of all his concomitant inconsistencies, to the very end of his life. Like his own Captain Ahab, he remained a defiant rebel, even in the face of death. (425)

Thompson's Melville was, like Geoffrey Stone's, a disillusioned Romantic. Unlike Stone, Thompson saw little evidence of change and development over the course of Melville's career. After an early ambivalence toward religious belief, expressed in Melville's first novel *Typee* and arising out of an unhappy childhood in which he lost his father and experience a tense relationship with his mother and her Calvinistic faith, Melville moved to ever-deepening levels of disillusionment in his succeeding books. By the publication of *Moby-Dick* in 1851, he was an out-and-out rebel against the Calvinist God with whom he had grappled in his youth, and throughout the remainder of his career and life he devoted himself to ridiculing orthodox Christian readers by means of an elaborate "triple talk" that would deceive those foolish enough to take him as anything other than a ferocious critic of Christianity (424). *Billy Budd* was thus the culmination of a career-long indictment of the Christian God's "divine depravity," with Captain Vere playing the role of a treacherous and sadistic deity. Therefore, according to Thompson, the "testament of acceptance" school of *Billy Budd* had fallen into Melville's trap, and attempts to regard Melville as a man of faith were folly. Thompson's argument is paralleled and anticipated by William S. Gleim's 1938 study, *The Meaning of Moby-Dick*, which suggested that "the book may be regarded as a giant hoax, in which [Melville] satirized all man-made religions and challenged the perspicacity of his contemporaries" (3). As the following pages will indicate, the hypothesis of "bad faith" associated with Thompson and Gleim has cast a long shadow in Melville criticism.

Thompson's work provided a valuable note of dissent to the standard view of Melville's religious development, and has remained an important and substantial minority position. Moreover, Thompson presented his arguments against an ultimately reconciled Melville with a high degree of eloquence and clarity. What emerges for an informed reader today is that Thompson's reading of Melville is highly persuasive precisely so long as one grants his assertions about Melville's intentions in creating specific narrators. For example, the narrator in *Billy Budd* is said to be held up for ridicule by Melville. As long as one accepts this premise, *Billy Budd* does indeed fall into line as a satire on "divine depravity." If, however, one returns to *Billy Budd* looking for indisputable proof of the narrator's untrustworthiness and folly, disappointment is likely to be the result. Thompson also suffered from the problem associated with any analysis that depends heavily on tone: one reader's sly sarcasm can easily become another's soulful sincerity, and in the absence of extensive biographical research, the nuances of tone can be as dependent on the observer as on the observed. The other crucial, and nearly inexplicable, omission in Thompson's study was a consideration of the poetry. Thompson probed Melville's fiction carefully, but gave at best cursory attention to the poetry in general and *Clarel* in particular. Given the length and scope of *Clarel* and its relentless focus on religious questions, this omission is truly odd. Thompson's study, impressive and subtle as it was, thus became, not the final word on Melville's position on Christian doctrine, but rather one more contribution to a debate unresolved in his time and ours.[6]

The Confidence-Man looms large in any consideration of belief in Melville's work. Elizabeth Foster's pioneering work in bringing Melville's last full-length novel into a modern scholarly edition in 1954 also provided a landmark in religious and philosophical discussions of Melville's work in the form of its introduction. Foster read *The Confidence-Man* as a scathing satire on the lack of charity among Christians, so that in her view the novel fit nicely with Thompson's reading of *Moby-Dick* as a deliberate yet covert mocker of Melville's Christian readers. Like Thompson, moreover, Foster read Melville as deliberately obscuring his true meanings. Therefore, the combination of Foster's edition of Melville's last full-length novel in 1954 with Thompson's 1952 study of Melville's career meant that the tide was turning away from readings that portrayed Melville's religious trajectory as heading toward redemption. Unlike Thompson, however, Foster thought that even if Melville's faith in God seemed strained, his faith in humanity, however attenuated, abided. Melville concluded, Foster writes, that "One cannot trust God; one cannot trust nature; but one must cling to some faith in man, for the alternative is too frightful" (lxxxix). This "last-ditch humanism" was for Foster Melville's closest approach to redemption (lxxxix).

Milton R. Stern's *The Fine Hammered Steel of Herman Melville* (1957) exemplified the beginning of a turn from straightforward positioning of Melville on a faith-doubt tradition in relation to either Christianity or

Platonism and towards an approach that would follow some of the less obvious clues in Melville's work where they might lead. Stern centered his study on the complex nature of Melville's relationship to the ideas of Transcendentalist contemporaries like Emerson and Thoreau. Stern chose to omit an extended analysis of *Moby-Dick* from his study, preferring instead to use *Typee*, *Mardi*, *Pierre*, and *Billy Budd* to illuminate the progress of Melville's thought. He argued that what distinguished Melville from his Transcendentalist contemporaries was his resistance to both anthropocentrism (the tendency to make humanity the measure of all things in the universe) and individualism, which was a pillar both of literary transcendentalism and of American public culture more generally. Melville thus became for Stern a Naturalist in Romantic's clothing, using the symbolism and rhetorical devices typical of his time period, but in the service of non-anthropocentric and communal ideals that meshed better with the Naturalist movement of the later nineteenth century. Particularly telling was Stern's reading of *Billy Budd*. Unlike critics who saw Billy's death as either a redemptive moment or as a sign of Melville's final disillusionment with the Christian deity, Stern focused instead on the reported death of Captain Vere in the last pages of *Billy Budd*. Vere's death meant that the man who attempted to shape society into conformity with justice and reason ultimately failed, and while Vere's courage and decency provide grounds for hope, his defeat reflects the persistence of obstacles to human fulfillment of both natural and social varieties. The ending of Melville's great posthumous novella thus took takes on a conceptual richness and subtlety denied it by even its most enthusiastic earlier advocates. For Stern, *Billy Budd* exemplifies the clash between aspiration and its frustration at the heart of Melville's work:

> The furious hopefulness of the work is the indestructibility of human aspiration. The furious hopelessness of the work is that nothing but the wrong channels for that aspiration remain. So the human heart will continue to be the trap of the lure, the primitive perfection, the chronometrical Adam-Christ, who still exists in the deeps of history and experience, mired by the oozy weeds and events of the man-of-war world. (238)

Stern's Melville is thus ultimately concerned, not only with his own spiritual reconciliation and resistance, but with the deepest promptings and misgivings of the human heart.[7]

James Baird's *Ishmael* (1956) was the first study to take seriously Melville's interest in religious traditions other than Christianity. Baird's study was a mix of Jungian archetypal criticism seeking universal figures in the midst of Melville's fiction and (more interestingly, from the standpoint of a twenty-first century reader) cross-cultural criticism exploring Melville's interest in primitivism early in his career and the religious possibilities associated with Asia later in his career. Baird's early chapters on primitivism located Melville's interest in the South Pacific in the Romantic-era crisis of cultural authority associated with the decline of Christian orthodoxies in the nineteenth century. Baird then moved beyond the internal crises of Christianity in his consideration of how Asian religions, and particularly the figure of the avatar from Hinduism, figured in Melville's understanding of divinity. The combination of Melville's reflections on the indigenous faiths of the Pacific and his reflections on Hinduism caused him to place a particular emphasis on the concept of escape from the self and from linear time in his major works (174). Baird's emphasis on Pacific religious traditions also led him to draw close parallels between Melville and Gauguin, another Western artist who had declared his independence in Polynesia. Unlike some later scholars, however, Baird did not credit Melville with an extensive knowledge of Eastern religious traditions, suggesting that although Melville referred to numerous religious traditions in his work, these references were "encyclopedic," rather than having been integrated into Melville's own thought. The importance of multi-religious references lay in the "feeling which informs the symbol" (177) — the emotional resonances suggested by these references. Melville could afford to be nonspecific and unrigorous in these allusions to comparative religion because his ultimate goals were not conceptual but affective. Thus Baird was less interested in explicating Melville's thought in relation to religion than in examining the particular symbols — whiteness, the cross, the monstrous whale — that recur in his body of work.

Like Baird, Merlin Bowen was concerned to shift the conversation about Melville from a diagnosis of his presumed faith or lack thereof to an inductive consideration of the data of Melville's thought that could be extrapolated from his work. In *The Long Encounter* (1960), Bowen found Melville caught not so much between the Christian deity and the Christian devil as between "the unknown self" and "the opposing other" (4). Indeed, the search for a philosophical Melville was defined precisely by Melville's elusiveness: "The ideas are there as part of the very substance of his art. But any attempt to fix or systematize them only ends up in a weakening of one's sense of the dynamic complexity of Melville's attitude toward life" (8). In order to understand the "dynamic complexity" of Melville's thought, Bowen presented a series of responses in Melville's work to the problem of the unknowability of the self and the resistance of the other, defining them broadly as "Defiance," "Submission," and "Armed Neutrality." One important implication of this schema was that Bowen's description of the trajectory of Melville's career was quite distinctive: unlike those among his predecessors who saw *Billy Budd* as Melville's final word on matters of faith, Bowen took the (to my mind more sensible) view that *Clarel*, as Melville's last sustained meditation on the relation of self and other, should be seen as his most mature and developed statement on the matter. *Clarel* was for Bowen Melville's great statement in favor of an "armed neutrality" between submission and defiance — the Melville of *Clarel* was neither Ahab nor Bartleby, but a thoroughly developed version of Ishmael, the ambivalent narrator of *Moby-Dick*. If *Moby-Dick* is "Ahab's story, not . . . Ishmael's," *Clarel* represents the culmination of the question Ishmael begins in "Loomings," the first chapter of *Moby-Dick* (252–53). Bowen's Melville resides in the tensions between opposites that provide all of his works with their energy, rather than in an identifiable choice of a specific religious or philosophical position.

Baird had suggested that considerations of Melville's religious thought could go beyond his relationship to Christianity. H. Bruce Franklin's *The Wake of the Gods* (1963) focused on Melville's use of comparative mythology, primarily in *Mardi*, *Moby-Dick*, and *The Confidence-Man*. Franklin argued that Melville's reading in comparative mythology and religion and his attempts to reinterpret religious and mythological motifs offered a key to Melville's entire career. Curiously, Franklin did not devote much space to *Clarel*, the long poem that is the most concerned with religion and mythology of any of Melville's work, or indeed to any of Melville's later poetry, choosing instead to cite snippets from the poem in the service of his readings of other texts. The portions of *The Wake of the Gods* devoted to *Pierre* and the short fiction of the 1850s, moreover, feel a bit strained in their attempts to make these texts fit into the larger mythological framework, especially because Franklin himself acknowledged that the core of these texts was ethical rather than mythological.

Franklin's readings of *Mardi*, *Moby-Dick*, *The Confidence-Man*, and *Billy Budd* were a revelation, however, and remain among the finest readings of Melville's work in relation to world religions. Franklin found that the mythic universe that Melville developed in *Mardi* was deeply indebted to the Hindu religious traditions about which Melville read in *Indian Antiquities* (1793–1800) and *The History of Hindustan* (1795–98) by Thomas Maurice. In *Moby-Dick*, by contrast, Franklin regarded the references to Indian mythology to be secondary to the overwhelming influence of Egyptian mythology in the representation of both the whale and Captain Ahab. He suggested that *Moby-Dick* is a retelling of the Osiris myth, in which Captain Ahab becomes Osiris and the whale is the monster Typhon (81). Franklin's meticulous reading of *Moby-Dick* in light of Egyptian thought is still compelling today, and remains essential reading for anyone considering the role of religion in *Moby-Dick*. His dismissal of the significance of the Hindu references in *Moby-Dick* is less persuasive today, particularly since it seems not to acknowledge fully Melville's ability to juggle a variety of religious traditions at one time in his best work.

This tendency is not overlooked in Franklin's discussion of Melville's last full-length novel, and indeed, Franklin reserved his most audacious claims for *The Confidence-Man*, claiming that it "is Melville's most nearly perfect work. . . . Not a word is wasted or misplaced" (153). Franklin found in *The Confidence-Man* a rejuvenation of the interest in Hinduism Melville displayed in *Mardi*, concluding that the April Fool's Day setting for the novel revealed its roots in then-recent publications on the Indian festival Huli. Starting from Huli, Franklin traced concrete correspondences between the various incarnations of *The Confidence-Man* and the avatars of the central Hindu deities. He argued that the April Fool's joke around which *The Confidence-Man* circulates is thus complexly multi-religious: Melville uses multiple avatars, in the Hindu sense, for Christ, thus creating a text that is an inversion of Melville's previous treatments of mythology in *Mardi* and *Moby-Dick*. Franklin suggested that in the earlier novels, Melville built his story around complex jokes by creating false avatars; in *The Confidence-Man* the joke is precisely that the double-dealing title figure is a true avatar of Christ — and of other central figures in world religions like Vishnu and the Buddha. As Franklin tersely sums up his argument: "In this universe man's Savior — Manco Capac, Vishnu, Christ, Apollo, the Buddhist's Buddha — is embodied in the Confidence Man, who is also man's Destroyer — Satan, Siva, the Hindus' Buddha. Melville's mythology converts all gods into the Confidence Man" (187). Like Edgar Dryden's reading of Melville's theory of fiction later in the decade, Franklin's reading of Melville's use of mythology places *The Confidence-Man* at the climax of Melville's achievement rather than dismissing it as an ill-conceived denouement to Melville's career as a writer of fiction.

Finally, Franklin's reading of *Billy Budd* portrayed Melville as revisiting his obsession with both mythology and Asian religious thought at the end of his life and career. Once again, symbolism associated with Christ and Christianity blends with the multiple avatars of divinity in Hindu religious thought to emphasize the illusory nature of the physical and moral worlds. By taking this tack, Franklin largely avoided the "testament of acceptance" debate in order to track the ways in which Melville created a mythical treatment of the human condition with global religious resonances. As with *The Confidence-Man*, the ultimate implication of Melville's mythology is tragic, representing a world in which self-preservation is ultimately dependent on injustice — a sorrowful conclusion to a lifetime of grappling with the intricacies of human answers to life's ultimate questions. In fact Franklin's own career took a rather dramatic turn after *The Wake of the Gods*. Rather than continuing to pursue the multi-religious approaches to Melville that he had so successfully pioneered, he turned toward political activism, and his future engagement with Melville was to be precisely with the questions of social justice, injustice, and war with which he concluded his discussion of *Billy Budd*. That phase of Franklin's career, however, remains to be discussed in chapter 5.

Franklin's strategy of using comparative mythology as a way into Melville's art and thought enjoyed a vogue in the later 1960s and early 1970s. M. O. Percival's *A Reading of Moby-Dick* (1967) discussed Melville as a philosopher and employed Jungian myth criticism alongside comparative mythology in analyzing the parallels between New England Calvinism and fatalistic elements in Hinduism and Zoroastrianism, finding parallels to Ahab's rhetoric in the *Bhagavad-Gita*. Percival's reading also showed the influence of existential philosophy as employed in 1950-era discussions of Melville by W. H. Auden and Albert Camus in that he sought to read Melville in the light of the philosophical works of Soren Kierkegaard and Martin Buber.[8] In 1970, H. L. Kulkarni sought explicitly to contradict Franklin's dismissal of Hinduism as a central source for *Moby-Dick* in his aptly named study *Moby-Dick: A Hindu Avatar.* Kulkarni argued (rightly, in my view) that the passages that Franklin had taken as mockery of Hinduism are more accurately read as a mockery of the failure of any artistic representation of the whale (9). Kulkarni saw *Moby-Dick* as centrally concerned with the reconciliation and integration of opposites, making it an essentially Hindu book. This feature explained even Melville's famous description of the novel in a letter to Hawthorne as a "wicked book":

> [*Moby-Dick*'s] wickedness perhaps lies in its departure from Christian theology and Western tradition, which may be described as either/ or, where good and evil are regarded as exclusive entities. The special claim to distinction of Hindu thought is the reconciliation of good and evil, love and hate in the highest existence of the spirit. It is on the foundation of this mystic harmony and truth of unity that *Moby-Dick* firmly stands. It is this spiritual character of the novel that makes Melville feel "spotless as the lamb." (66)

It is unfortunate that to this point Kulkarni's intuitions regarding *Moby-Dick* have not been followed by more extensive studies of Melville's engagement with South Asian religious thought, but it is a mark of the fecundity of Melville's imagination that such promising intellectual landscapes remain to be explored.

Paul Brodtkorb's *Ishmael's White World* (1965) addressed the epistemological questions posed by *Moby-Dick* using philosophical methods drawn from phenomenology. Brodtkorb found Ishmael's consciousness as narrator to be the central fact of *Moby-Dick*, and he meticulously examined the contours of Ishmael's world. Ishmael's consciousness of the material world, his shipmates aboard the *Pequod*, time, and his own evanescent moods became the organizing principle of Brodtkorb's phenomenological reading. Given Melville's ambivalent attraction to the Romantic exaltation of selfhood, Brodtkorb's reading was very much in tune with some of Melville's own most significant emphases. By seeing Ishmael as the key to the novel, Brodtkorb was able to show how Ishmael's "boredom, dread, and despair" shape everything the reader encounters in *Moby-Dick* (148). He left for other scholars, however, the question of how Ishmael's mental universe and the external world of experience might intersect with each other, for Brodtkorb's *Moby-Dick* was defined exclusively by the contours of Ishmael's mind. This approach had the important virtue of allowing Brodtkorb to cast a skeptical eye on assertions of satirical intent (such as those by Lawrance Thompson) that seemed to read Melville's mind based on relatively scanty evidence. Brodtkorb's rigorous bracketing out of matters on which certainty is not possible gave his work particular authority.

Brodtkorb's decision to take an Ishmael's-eye view of *Moby-Dick* found significant parallels in the Melville criticism of the early 1970s. In an inspired exploration of the meaning of mental experience in Melville's work, William B. Dillingham made the remarkable contribution to Melville scholarship of publishing, over the course of three decades, a comprehensive account of Melville's intellectual development. In *An Artist in the Rigging* (1972), a study of Melville's novels from the pre-*Moby-Dick* period, Dillingham found that Melville's early novels had been obsessed with the nature of experience and the role of the human mind in interpreting experience. Over the next quarter century, Dillingham published three more books on Melville, which taken as a group told the entire story of Melville's career: *Melville's Short Fiction* (1977), *Melville's Later Novels* (1986), and *Melville and His Circle* (1996). Dillingham's investigation of Melville's artistry took as its axiom the idea that Melville's form was not careless, as some even of Melville's aesthetically oriented admirers, like Blackmur and Feidelson, had suggested, but rather organic. For Dillingham, Melville's formal strategies grew out of his own intellectual quest to understand his world, and thus the form of Melville's work was determined by patterns based on his intellectual biography. The result of this theory was that Dillingham tracked Melville's form with a great deal of sensitivity and acuity. He also provided perhaps the most extensive development of the approach that Howard Vincent, Merrell Davis, and William Gilman had developed a generation earlier in showing how Melville transmuted both his readings in his books and his experiences into art. Although it is impossible in this space to do justice to the prodigious scope of Dillingham's work, its implications for understanding Melville's philosophical and religious development can be summarized briefly as follows. Dillingham showed that the power of Melville's work is dependent on a tension among the raw data of nature and experience, the shaping imagination of the observer, and the pressures exerted on Melville's development as an artistic observer by his own extensive reading and consumption of visual art. In *Melville and His Circle* in particular, Dillingham revealed the depth of Melville's engagement with philosophic contemporaries like Arthur Schopenhauer, but from the beginning of *An Artist in the Rigging*, the intersection of art and philosophy was always central to Dillingham's reading of Melville.

Melville had by this time frequently been discussed as an acerbic critic of a variety of religious and philosophical traditions as well as an ultimately reconciled believer in some of these same traditions. In *Melville's Drive to Humanism* (1971), Ray B. Browne extended Lawrance Thompson's reading of Melville as a critic standing against religious orthodoxy by attempting to define the contours of the humanism that Browne believed Melville was *for*. Browne argued that critics who had read *Billy Budd*, for example, as a fundamentally affirmative work, were right — they were just wrong about what it affirmed. Browne saw *Billy Budd* as a ringing endorsement of Thomas Paine's religious skepticism and impassioned arguments for *The Rights of Man* (both the title of one of Paine's most important pamphlets and the name of the ship from which Billy is impressed) and a rejection of the conservatism of Edmund Burke as represented by Captain Vere. The "single most powerful sinew in all Melville's works" for Browne, was humanism, understood as solidarity with "the common people of the world" (394). Melville's radical gesture of acceptance, in *Billy Budd* and throughout his career, was directed toward his fellow human beings, not towards a non- or super human deity.

Even as Browne sought to depict Melville as a figure in the vanguard of the critique of religious orthodoxy in nineteenth-century America, some scholars sought to indicate how Melville's work drew on earlier orthodoxies and preserved at least their formal properties. One such study, Ursula Brumm's *American Thought and Religious Typology* (1970) both situated Melville within the broader context of American religious and intellectual culture and helped to infuse theological rigor into Americanist readings of Melville's work. Brumm found that Melville's art and thought were structured by the Hebrew and Christian scriptures, and particularly by Melville's habit of reading the world around him typologically, far more than earlier critics had recognized. "Typology" as Brumm used it referred both to the ancient Christian exegetical practice of joining the Old and New Testaments by finding prophetic "types" in the Old Testament that would be fulfilled by corresponding "antitypes" in the New Testament and to the New England Puritan practice of reading the natural world typologically by finding spiritual correspondences to events in the physical world. Brumm tracked Melville's use of typology backwards through his career, using *Billy Budd*'s narrator's phrase "the lexicon of Holy Writ" as a way of defining Melville's wider use of scripture, classical allusions, and natural symbolism. For Brumm, Melville constructed a language out of the materials of scripture, history, myth, and nature that could explain the phenomena of the world in which he lived and his own intellectual engagement with these phenomena. When taken up by Sacvan Bercovitch in the later 1970s, Brumm's insistence on the importance of typology to Melville would have far-reaching effects that I will take up in chapter 5.

Brumm's exploration of Melville as a wide-ranging typologist was paralleled by Robert Zoellner's reading of Melville's use of metaphor in *The Salt-Sea Mastodon* (1973). Zoellner followed Brodtkorb in regarding Ishmael as the presiding consciousness of *Moby-Dick* and in seeing all the philosophical content of the novel as having been filtered through Ishmael's moods and experiences. Like Brumm, Zoellner found the figurative nature of Melville's work to be charged with significance for the understanding of his thought, and Ahab's figurative language to be especially central. Ultimately, Zoellner proposed, *Moby-Dick* is a novel that asks readers to pass judgment on and decide between the philosophy of existence and knowledge propounded by Captain Ahab and that propounded by Ishmael. Using the quarter-deck scene where Ahab first informs the crew of his intention to pursue vengeance on Moby Dick, Zoellner argues that Ahab's reading of the universe as a blank wall that is ultimately meaningless indicates the crudeness of his epistemology. Ahab sees only the apparent absurdity of the world of sensation in its own terms, and is thus moved to rage and hatred. Ishmael's more sophisticated epistemology is shown in his acknowledgment of the ways in which the perceiving human mind shapes the very world that it observes, an acknowledgment that leads him toward empathy and acceptance. The overall arc of Zoellner's argument was compelling: that Melville's use of metaphor demonstrates the power of the observing mind in shaping the world it perceives and thus shows us the importance to his thought of the philosophical idealism associated with Immanuel Kant. But Zoellner's work also illustrated the problems that even well-conceived philosophically or aesthetically oriented scholarship can encounter when matters related to textual criticism are taken for granted: Zoellner made the fifth paragraph of chapter 114 of *Moby-Dick*, "The Gilder," the centerpiece of his exposition of Ishmael's epistemological stance (9). This was an unfortunate choice, given that Harrison Hayford and Hershel Parker had already raised the suggestion in the 1967 Norton Critical Edition of *Moby-Dick* that Ahab, not Ishmael, is the speaker in this paragraph, which, as they drily noted in an understated footnote in the 2002 edition, "has implications for any critical argument that takes Ishmael and Ahab as embodying opposing values" (373). Nonetheless, Zoellner made clear something that had been implicit in prior discussions of Melville's thought: the formal devices that he uses are rarely devoid of illumination for those seeking to understand Melville's view of either the natural world or the human mind.[9]

It is perhaps surprising that in a chapter discussing religious and philosophical approaches to Melville, so little has yet been said about the single work in Melville's canon most explicitly engaged with religious and philosophical issues: his long poem *Clarel*. Aside from Walter Bezanson's 1943 dissertation and 1960 notes and introduction to the Hendrick's House Edition of *Clarel*, the poem had largely been slighted in the early decades of Melville criticism. The slights extended to Bezanson himself, as he revealed in the Spring 2010 issue of *Leviathan*, reporting that due to his publisher's financial difficulties at the time, he received no compensation for the labor of love that had brought about the first modern scholarly edition of *Clarel*. It is hard not to see the fate of this edition of Melville's most ambitious poem as mirroring the fate of the poem itself: revered in theory, rarely acknowledged in practice. Nonetheless, Bezanson's work on *Clarel* remains one of the greatest achievements in Melville scholarship. Perhaps the shabby treatment that scholarly discussions of *Clarel* had received in earlier decades prompted the response that Vincent Kenny reported receiving from when he revealed his interest in working with *Clarel* to a mentor: "Kenny, I believe you have greater fortitude than intelligence"! (Kenny, xv).

Nonetheless, the early 1970s saw a cluster of new scholarship surrounding *Clarel*: Joseph G. Knapp's *Tortured Synthesis* (1971), Franklin Walker's *Irreverent Pilgrims* (1974), and Kenny's own *Herman Melville's "Clarel"* (1973). Walker's discussion of Melville was the least probing of the three, and he focused primarily on comparisons and contrasts with J. Ross Browne and Mark Twain. Nevertheless, he provided a valuable service to Melville scholarship by reminding scholars of the popularity of the Holy Land travel narratives with which *Clarel* is engaged. Knapp's argument was more subtle, and it continued a longstanding tradition of Catholic interest in *Clarel*. Knapp maintained that Melville's long poem works its way from doubt driven by a vivid realization of the existence of evil to a kind of faith, not to Knapp's own Catholicism necessarily, but to an endurance of the agonies of life that can lead to hope. Knapp concluded that "With *Clarel*, the vision had come full circle, for from his new perspective Melville saw that if goodness could not exist without evil, neither could evil exist without good. Truth was not to be found in destroying or negating evil, but in accepting the organic intermixture of both" (115). Knapp thus saw *Clarel* as the product of a hard-fought struggle for wisdom, and believed that in writing *Clarel*, Melville had obtained the wisdom that he sought. Like Knapp, Kenny saw *Clarel* as an expression of Melville's own internal struggles, evoking Hawthorne's diagnosis of a perpetually unresolved quest for certainty. For Kenny, the Melville who emerges at the end of *Clarel* is an heroic existentialist in the tradition of Camus, who has learned wisdom from staring into the void. Melville's quest for the meaning remained necessarily unresolved, but what he gained was "the painful wisdom that turns a man into a hero" (226).[10]

T. Walter Herbert's *Moby-Dick and Calvinism* (1977) built his reading of around Melville's struggle with Calvinist dogma. Melville's engagement with Calvinism had been approached earlier — Lawrance Thompson wrote about it in *Melville's Quarrel with God* (1952), and more recently Thomas Werge had addressed the matter in an article, but Herbert was the first to make Calvinism the centerpiece of a full-length study of Melville. Moreover, Herbert's reading marked, in theory at least, a substantial advance over Thompson, because Herbert proposed to address Melville's relation to both Calvinism and its great nineteenth-century rival, Unitarianism. He followed two crucial lines of argument. First, he saw Melville as being truly exceptional in terms of his times in that he was able to look past a "theocentric" view of the universe in which the centrality of God's existence for all human experience was taken for granted. Second, he regarded Melville as a thinker engaged very specifically in questioning the supernaturally oriented Calvinism that had characterized much of earlier American religious thought. In this regard, Melville resembled the Unitarians and other theological liberals of his day. The strength of Herbert's analysis lay in his determination to eschew the ahistorical practice of placing Melville's use of biblical tropes into the context of twentieth-century biblical scholarship rather than the nineteenth-century contexts for biblical reading in which Melville was immersed. Herbert tracked Melville's implicit and explicit references to and arguments with Calvinist orthodoxy brilliantly. But he failed to clarify Melville's relationship to Unitarianism, the faith of his father Allan and his wife, Elizabeth Shaw Melville, which means that the distinction between Melville and his liberal but "theocentric" contemporaries was also not clearly defined, while Melville's relationship to non-Christian religious traditions was largely outside the purview of Herbert's study. Nonetheless, it remains the clearest and most thoughtful explanation of how Melville both rebelled against Calvinist theological models and made use of them in his art.

The focus on experience that characterized William B. Dillingham's work was brought together with T. Walter Herbert's theological emphases and the earlier philosophical emphases of Merton M. Sealts, Jr. in Rowland Sherrill's *The Prophetic Melville* (1979). Sherrill built his study around the poles of experience and transcendence, arguing that Melville's prophetic voice developed out of a need to experience wonder in a brutally utilitarian "man-of-war world." Sherrill saw the early Melville as an oppositional figure, prophetic because of his active detachment from the distorted norms of his culture. *Moby-Dick*, however, pushed Melville's prophecy beyond mere opposition to the flaws of his culture to a visionary sense of wonder and transcendence: "the deeply reformative thrust of [*Moby-Dick*] suggests his convictions that fiction needed to bear accountability to its auditors as well as to its own central vision, that his prophetic speaking in fictive forms could be effectual, and that therefore changes of cultural perception were possible" (3). For Sherrill, *Billy Budd* represented Melvilles's belated discovery that the reformative optimism about communicating prophetic truth to an audience was ultimately an illusion. Melville thus became a prophet of transcendence who was tragically without honor, and whose vision was not only incomprehensible to the nineteenth century, which did not embrace most of his work, but also to the twentieth century, which embraced him without understanding him. Sherrill ends on a hopeful note of his own, however, suggesting that Melville's "image-making capacity" remains essential to human experience (238).

Bainard Cowan's 1982 study *Exiled Waters: "Moby-Dick" and the Crisis of Allegory* also brought questions of knowledge and meaning to the fore. Rather than prophecy, however, Cowan focused on the role of allegory in Melville's writing, and its significance for understanding the philosophical and religious crises of the nineteenth century. Cowan made particular use of the tools of deconstructive, hermeneutic, and Marxist literary theory derived from such figures as Walter Benjamin, Hans-Georg Gadamer, and Paul de Man (indeed, the emphasis on allegory as an organizing principle testified to de Man's broad influence in the field of English studies at the time). Cowan employed one of the most proto-deconstructive passages in all of Melville's work, the chapter "The Journey and the Pamphlet" from *Pierre*, to illustrate "the Romantic crisis of allegory" (32–33). Tying this chapter to Soren Kierkegaard's ironic reflections on un-Christian Christendom in the nineteenth century, Cowan stressed the ways in which Romantic allegory in general and Melville's use of allegory in *Pierre* in particular evinced the anxieties of a society that had lost the internal coherence of its dominant narratives — where Christianity and Christendom, seemingly identical, served instead to disrupt each other. In the midst of this cultural crisis, Cowan claimed, Melville used allegory to highlight evanescent traces of truth and meaning in both nature and human society. Both the natural markings of the sperm whale and the marked pagan body of Queequeg in *Moby-Dick*, then, became traces of potential truths that could not be systematized into earlier Western cultural narratives. Indeed, the bodies of both whales and humans grow increasingly important in the parts of Cowan's study bearing the impress of the Russian thinker Mikhail Bakhtin, who had been seen as a predecessor by many deconstructive thinkers after his work was posthumously translated into English in the 1960s and 1970s. Cowan showed how Melville's approach to the body intersected with what Bakhtin described as the "carnivalesque" in Rabelais, thus providing a more precise formulation of the relation between Melville's work and that of Rabelais that Melville scholars had been noting since the 1950s. Melville's art and thought coincided for Cowan in the weaving together of fragments of disrupted narratives, and it is the epistemological power of memory that Cowan made the fulcrum of Melville's work, concluding that "What Ishmael has learned is that community exists most permanently in remembrance" (180). When cultural narratives are broken, the art of memory, Cowan implied, matters most.[11]

James Duban's *Melville's Major Fiction: Politics, Theology, and Imagination* (1983) dealt primarily with Melville's relation to providential readings of American history. Duban looked at the ways in which Melville's religious thought connected him with the wider cultural currents of his day, finding it imbued with the political and social questions of the mid nineteenth century. Political questions predominate through the first half of Duban's study (for more on which see chapter 5), but he focused increasingly on specifically philosophical and theological issues in the chapters devoted to *Pierre, The Confidence-Man* and *Clarel*, and *Billy Budd*. *Pierre* was Melville's attempt to grapple with the praise of moral intuition found in the writings of major Transcendentalists like Emerson and George Ripley. Pierre's own moral development tracked closely with the development of Transcendentalism from its break with Unitarianism over the Miracles Controversy through its increasing movement toward subjectivism. (The subject of the controversy was whether or not supernatural intervention into the natural world ever actually occurred; the Transcendentalists said no, more orthodox Unitarians said yes.) Duban regarded Melville's authorial stance on Pierre the Transcendentalist character as "closer to Jonathan Edwards's outlook on human nature" than to Emerson's (191), and believed this Edwardsean tendency set the tone for Melville's later writing on religious topics. In relation to *Billy Budd*, Duban's reading resembled that of Lawrance Thompson in that he saw the narrator as an object of criticism — the narrator's moral complacency, in Duban's view, is what Melville ultimately resists in *Billy Budd*.

I began this chapter with Warner Berthoff's reference to Melville as a "provider of scripture." Lawrence Buell's "*Moby-Dick* as Sacred Text" (1984) was devoted to the scriptural and canonical status of Melville's most famous work. Calling the novel "a record of an encounter with the divine" (54), Buell read *Moby-Dick* as both scripture and anti-scripture, "a sort of modern Book of Revelation, yet also a book that casts doubt on the possibility of revelation, yet again in that very act of doubt-casting a work that . . . remains in some measure faithful to a biblical sense of God's elusiveness" (55). For Buell, as for H. Bruce Franklin before him, *Moby-Dick* was a novel that communicated an ungraspable truth by means of comparative religion and mythology, and thus constituted, along with Whitman's *Leaves of Grass*, the most important example of an American secular scripture (69).[12]

The writing of a secular scripture was for Buell a necessary outcome of Melville's being a contemporary of Emerson and the Transcendentalist movement. John B. Williams's *White Fire: The Influence of Emerson on Melville* (1991) devoted itself to exploring Melville's links to and departures from Transcendentalist models. Merton M. Sealts had brought the subject of Melville's relation to Emerson into the scholarly discussion with his 1980 article "Melville and Emerson's Rainbow," which portrayed Melville as a self-conscious interlocutor for Emersonian Transcendentalism. Williams developed this insight into a full-length study, ultimately arguing against the conventional idea that Melville should be seen as a pessimistic critic of Emerson's optimism. Rather, he suggested that Emerson's capacity for pessimism should be noted and that Melville was more receptive to Emersonian idealism than is typically conceded, even in his last work, *Billy Budd*.[13]

Stan Goldman's *Melville's Protest Theism* (1993), perhaps the most theologically precise study of Melville to date, focused exclusively on Melville's late poem *Clarel*, which Goldman regarded as an interrogation of the problem of human suffering in the tradition of the biblical book of Job. Goldman suggested an alternative to both the venerable reading of Melville's career as following a redemptive trajectory culminating in *Billy Budd*'s "testament of acceptance" and the reading of Melville as an irreconcilable Romantic rebel that dated back to Geoffrey Stone and Lawrance Thompson. Goldman managed this by shifting the questions he asked of *Clarel*. Rather than limiting himself to a specifically Christian framework for understanding the poem, as many previous interpreters had done, Goldman examined *Clarel* through the lens of Jewish readings of the Hebrew scriptures. Seen from this vantage point, Melville becomes less a rebel than a sage, giving voice to wisdom that, while not in keeping with Christian supersessionist interpretations of the "Old Testament," is very much in keeping with rabbinic readings of the Hebrew scriptures. As a result, Goldman found a great deal of reverence and faith in *Clarel*, and suggested that Melville's religious stance could best be understood as "protest theism," defined as "the personal, private confrontation between divine hiddenness and the unsatisfied heart" (169). It is a mark of how much this confrontation meant to Goldman that he identified Melville himself as a kind of spiritual teacher in his own right.

Goldman's study marked an important break in Melville scholarship because it showed how Melville could be understood as operating in a Jewish theological framework rather than the Christian frameworks to which he had typically been confined. On a less extensive scale, Jenny Franchot brought the question of Melville's relationship to Catholicism to the fore in a brief section of her massive study *Roads to Rome: The Antebellum Protestant Encounter with Catholicism* (1994). In this study, she situated Melville among a large assembly of American Protestant writers who, to one degree or another, demonstrated an interest in Roman Catholicism. Franchot included a subtle reading of Catholic imagery associated with the Dominican order and the Spanish Inquisition in *Benito Cereno*. Unfortunately, she did not devote significant space to a reading of *Clarel*, the text in which Melville engaged in his most extensive dialogue with Catholicism. Franchot's essay "Melville's Traveling God" (1998) was a more significant contribution to Melville scholarship than her full-length book, because in the essay she tracked Melville's religious thought across his career. In a remarkably subtle and concise argument,

Franchot found that Melville's treatment of Christianity throughout his career was consistently informed by metaphors of travel and displacement — Christianity was not in Melville's work so much a dead faith to be buried or mocked, as Lawrance Thompson would have it, but rather an elusive and fragmentary presence defined precisely by the absence of a fixed, immutable set of doctrines. Franchot's argument reached its climax with a sensitive reading of the epilogue to *Clarel*, which includes "both Christianity and its cancellation" (182).

John Wenke's *Melville's Muse* (1995) tackled the interpenetration of the aesthetic, the philosophical, and the religious in Melville's fiction. As the title suggests, Wenke wanted to trace the sources of Melville's "philosophical fiction," emphasizing the way his philosophical sources blended together in creating his art. Wenke carefully analyzed the tremendous range of philosophical and religious texts that Melville was reading in the late 1840s — indeed his study provided context for much of the fundamental research done by Sealts on Melville's reading. What makes Wenke's study so intellectually exciting for serious students of Melville is the virtuosity of his close readings of passages from *Mardi*, *Moby-Dick*, *Pierre*, and *The Confidence-Man*. Because of his immersion in both Melville's published work and his reading, Wenke was able to take resonant quotations from each of these novels and carefully unpack them, showing, to cite just one example, how Coleridge's philosophical thought regarding matters of epistemology blended with Sir Thomas Browne's diction and sentence structure in a brief quotation from the philosopher Babbalanja in *Mardi*. He elegantly concludes:

> At issue here is not the matter of delineating specific influence. Rather, the presence of related multiple influences highlights the fusing power of Melville's imagination. He brought his own "spontaneous consciousness" — the mind moving in the process of thinking — to the task of reforming his reading materials. (15)

Wenke was further able to show how encounters with intellectuals like the German scholar George J. Adler in his 1849 transatlantic voyage to England had been crucial in shaping the central motifs of *Moby-Dick* (95). Wenke demonstrated that even when an individual Melville character like Babbalanja or Ishmael is speaking, the voice is a subtle synthesis of diverse philosophical influences. In this way, Wenke was able to blend Melville the thinker with Melville the artist to a greater degree than most previous critics.

Walter Kring's *Herman Melville's Religious Journey* (1997) was more biographical than literary-critical in its orientation and discusses Melville's movement toward Unitarianism late in life. It built on Kring's earlier work with Donald Yannella and Hershel Parker that had established both that Melville had been a member of All Soul's Unitarian

Church in New York City at the end of his life and that he had been in the 1860s the subject of an intrigue between the minister at All Soul's, Henry Whitney Bellows, and Melville's brother-in-law Samuel Shaw related to possibly abusive behavior on Melville's part toward his wife, Elizabeth Shaw Melville. (This topic will be discussed at length in chapter 4). Kring, himself a long-time twentieth-century minister at All Soul's, regarded Melville's career as a spiritual search for meaning that resolved itself in the faithful embrace of Unitarian openness to uncertainty and religious pluralism. The fact that Kring was not immersed in Melville's creative work, however, meant that his reading of Melville's life has only been modestly influential among Melville scholars, and Melville criticism still awaits the work that will integrate an understanding of Melville's late admission to membership at All Soul's with an understanding of his creative output.

Jonathan A. Cook's *Satirical Apocalypse* (1996) provided a more comprehensive reading of Melville's last full-length novel than had yet been attempted. Cook's reading of *The Confidence-Man* was built around a careful depiction of the religious culture of mid nineteenth-century America and a thorough exploration of Melville's relationship to that culture. Cook thought R. W. B. Lewis's earlier characterization of *The Confidence-Man* as a "comic apocalypse" was helpful, but regarded the formulation used in his title, "satirical apocalypse," to be a more precise statement of Melville's handling of Christian and other apocalyptic traditions in *The Confidence-Man*. Cook classified *The Confidence-Man* as a "'complex' Mennippean satire" on the apocalyptic tendencies in American thought, identifying the structure of the novel as a dialogue between the pessimism of premillennial religious thought and the optimism of postmillennial religious thought. By focusing on religious thought and Melville's knowledge of religious debates as determinative for *The Confidence-Man*, Cook was able to combine an analysis of the cosmic satire on the universe as a possible empty cipher with a concrete discussion of Melville's specific literary and religious targets in nineteenth-century America. Cook painstakingly identified each character in the novel as being associated with a member of either Melville's person or literary circle. Most strikingly, Charlie Noble is revealed to be a stand-in for Hawthorne, Henry Roberts is Evert Duyckinck, and Melville himself is the Cosmopolitan. Other possibilities are confirmed (Mark Winsome as Emerson) or thrown into doubt (Pitch as James Fenimore Cooper), and many figures (the Man in Cream Colors, Black Guinea, John Ringman, the Man in Gray, John Truman, the Herb Doctor, the P. I. O Man, and Frank Goodman) are shown be variations on Melville himself. Cook's study addressed many of the persistent puzzles of *The Confidence-Man* while at the same time pointing out how indebted the structure of the novel is to a peculiarly American religious and philosophical context.

Alfred Kazin was among the earliest critics to address Melville's parallels with scripture, and his late work *God and the American Writer* (1997) sought to provide a compact version of the religious transformations that took place over the course of Melville's career. Kazin surveyed works from *Moby-Dick* to *Clarel*, finding that Melville's primary religious mode to be ambivalence. Kazin's conclusion reinforced the picture of a divided Melville drawn from Hawthorne's 1856 journal, but perhaps the most important element in Kazin's reading of Melville is the way he linked Melville to broader tendencies toward religious ambivalence in nineteenth- and twentieth-century American literary cultures. Kazin demonstrated that if Melville was not typical of his culture at large in his view of religious belief, he shared many commonalities with his contemporaries and successors in the American literary canon. In a similarly comparative mode, Roger Shattuck revisited the relationship of Melville to Albert Camus and French existentialism in 1997 in the fifth chapter of *Forbidden Knowledge: From Prometheus to Pornography*. Shattuck read *Billy Budd* and Camus's *The Stranger* together as reflections on the meaning — and even the possibility — of justice. As with Kazin, the strength of Shattuck's reading was that it brought Melville into conversation with an author for whom he had profound affinities.

Like Kazin's study, Elisa New's 1998 essay "Bible Leaves! Bibles Leaves!: Hellenism and Hebraism in *Moby-Dick*" pointed toward the resurgence in discussions of Melville's use of the Hebrew and Christian scriptures that appeared in the 2000s, but it also argued strongly for a reading of Melville that saw him as religious rather than philosophical in his primary orientation. *Moby-Dick*, in New's view, was a scathing critique of Hellenic logocentrism from a Hebraic religious standpoint. As her use of the term logocentrism indicates, New used deconstructive literary theory as a way into Melville's religious thought, and she found the crucial opposition in Melville's novel to be that between Hellenic and Christian logocentrism and Hebraic textuality. The character of Ishmael, in New's reading, points toward the open-endedness and historical contingency that she associated with the Hebraic mode and away from the determinism she associated with Christianity. Melville's playful use of John Kitto's *Cyclopedia of Biblical Literature* (1845) to satirize orthodox Christian readings of the story of Jonah was emblematic of his tendency to free biblical accounts from the constriction of logocentric interpretations and open them to a sense of textual play — another important deconstructive concept. Where New's work represented an improvement on, for example, Lawrance Thompson's earlier readings of Melville's humorous approach to scripture in *Moby-Dick* was in the sense of discovering what Melville was for in his readings of scripture rather than simply what he was against. For New, Melville as the author of *Moby-Dick* stood for "historical eclecticism, [the] conviction that the way is *in* rather than through the letter, and . . . a fascination with the syntheses of action and precept in wisdom" (293). New's analysis of *Moby-Dick*, persuasive as it was, could perhaps have benefited from a consideration of Melville's evolving consideration of Hebraism and Hellenism throughout his career, particularly in *Clarel*. And while New did not mention Stan Goldman in her essay, her reading of *Moby-Dick* had important points of contact with his reading of *Clarel*.

Indeed, *Clarel* began to take an increasingly prominent place in considerations of Melville's religious and philosophical development in the years following New's article. Hilton Obenzinger's *American Palestine* (1999) read *Clarel* and Melville's journals from Europe and the Holy Land in terms of their interrogation of providential history, following in the footsteps of James Duban's work on the confluence of politics and theology in Melville's thought from the 1980s. Obenzinger also wrote an important piece on Melville's religious tendencies entitled "Wicked Books: Melville and Religion" (2005), that argued that Melville's religious views remained unsettled and uncertain to the last.

Robin Grey's *Melville and Milton* (2004), which comprised both a major piece of textual scholarship and a collection of essays on connections between Melville and Milton, made a major contribution to the tradition in Melville scholarship of combining biographical, aesthetic, and religious scholarship. Henry Pommer's *Milton and Melville* (1950) had brought together artistic and religious questions decades earlier by considering the influence of Milton's *Paradise Lost* on *Moby-Dick* through a close analysis of the language of both works and the explicit and implicit allusions in Melville's characterization of Captain Ahab to Milton's characterization of Satan. Pommer, however, was not able to draw upon Melville's own annotated copy of Milton, which was not discovered until the 1980s (Grey, xii). Grey provided both a scholarly edition of all Melville's marginalia to his copy of Milton and a careful commentary on the relation of the annotations to Melville's published work produced in collaboration with Douglass Robillard. Meanwhile, Grey extended the work that she had done on Melville's engagement with Milton in her 1997 study *The Complicity of Imagination*, the sixth chapter of which had examined Melville's careful reading of Milton's *Samson Agonistes*. Grey had argued at the time that Melville was especially concerned with the heretical elements in Milton's work, situating Milton as a rebel against Christian orthodoxy. In *Melville and Milton* Grey added an essay on the Miltonic influence on Melville's Civil War collection *Battle-Pieces*, and the collection also included an analysis of Miltonic influences in *Clarel* by John T. Shawcross and David V. Urban and in *Moby-Dick* by Bryan C. Short and Leslie E. Sheldon. The reproduction of the marginalia to Milton was of particular importance to scholars interested in Melville's approach to religion, since Walker Cowen's *Melville's Marginalia* had not included the Milton annotations because they had not yet been discovered when Cowen completed his study. Grey's work remains an important undertaking in textual scholarship, the implications of which for Melville's religious thought remain to be teased out.

William Potter's *Melville's Clarel and the Intersympathy of Creeds* (2004) focused exclusively on *Clarel*, but used comparative religion rather than theology as its lens through which to view the poem. Potter found that *Clarel* served as a sort of encyclopedia of world religions as understood in late nineteenth-century America, and he chose to emphasize the ways in which Asian religious traditions interacted with Judaism and Christianity in *Clarel*, rather than reading the poem as a contest between faith and doubt in the Jewish and Christian traditions. Potter explicitly associated his work with that of H. Bruce Franklin in *The Wake of the Gods* at the outset, and just as Franklin did for Melville's fiction, Potter expanded the frames of reference for understanding religion in Melville's poetry immensely. Potter devoted substantial portions of the extended reading of *Clarel* that opened his study to an exploration of Melville's sympathetic representations of Islam, and he devoted a self-contained chapter to Melville's representations of Islam, Hinduism, and Buddhism in *Clarel*. The portions on Hinduism and Buddhism were particularly significant, because while Islam is inevitably a key point of reference for travel narratives set in the Near East, Melville's invocations of Hinduism and Buddhism make his work unique in the field of mid-to-late nineteenth-century Holy Land writing.[14] Potter thus opened up a rich potential vein by introducing Hinduism and Buddhism into his discussion of *Clarel*, but he limited his reading of these religions in Melville to a few short pages, and, beyond *Clarel*, to an interpretation of Melville's late, short poem "Buddha." Although it is still too early to predict the ultimate effect that Potter's work will have on Melville criticism, it seems fair to suggest that it will be an important influence on further explorations of the multi-religious dimensions to Melville's thought.

Robert Milder's *Exiled Royalties: Melville and the Life We Imagine* (2006) was one of the richest and most comprehensive explorations of Melville's thought ever to appear, and it marked the culmination of several decades worth of influential publications on Melville. Moreover, it bore the impress of a comprehensive knowledge of previous Melville scholarship and a thorough familiarity with Melville's reading — both traits that have consistently marked the best Melville scholarship. The last two chapters, devoted respectively to *Clarel* and to *Billy Budd* and the later poetry are most directly concerned with Melville's relation to religious belief, whereas the second chapter, "The Broken Circle: *Mardi* and (Post) Romanticism," is the most concerned with Melville's philosophy. Here Milder discussed Melville's immersion in German Romanticism, and suggested that the quest for knowledge characteristic of German Romanticism was the main recurring obsession of Melville's career. In the penultimate chapter, "Unworldly Yearners: Agnostic Spirituality in *Clarel*," Milder defines carefully the spiritual tensions at the heart of Melville's most ambitious poetic work, arguing that "Although *Clarel* takes the form of a quest for God, its deepest concern is with the nature and destiny of human beings as they define themselves in the God-less interim" (195). For Milder, the later poetry and *Billy Budd* continued to develop the same sort of ultimately humanistic "agnostic spirituality." He concludes that by the end of his life, Melville found human self-definition to be of paramount moral and religious significance. That Milder pursued Melville's thought throughout the entire span of his career gives this conclusion more authority than the many speculations about Melville's philosophical and religious views based on a brief snapshot of his career.

From the first line of *Moby-Dick* on, an interest in figures associated with Islam permeates Melville's work, and critics from W. H. Auden on have found the connection between Melville's narrator and Islam to be telling. Timothy Marr's *The Cultural Roots of American Islamicism* (2006) was the first study to investigate this strain in Melville's work thoroughly. Marr's discussion was cultural rather than theological in its emphases, but it both extended the earlier work on representations of Islam in Melville's work by Dorothee Metlitsky Finkelstein, Malini Johar Schueller, Hilton Obenzinger, Basem L. Ra'ad, and William Potter, and placed Melville firmly within the context of nineteenth-century American fantasies and debates about Islam. Moreover, Marr did more than his predecessors (with the exception of Finkelstein) to show that Melville's inquisitiveness about Islam is not limited to *Clarel*, but rather permeates his work.[15]

Ilana Pardes's *Melville's Bibles* (2008) took up the idea of Melville as a writer of scripture that Lawrence Buell had discussed in the 1980s and to which Warner Berthoff had alluded in the 1960s. Pardes's work combined her extensive knowledge of theology and biblical exegesis with her engagement with the major cultural issues raised by *Moby-Dick*, thus mirroring to some degree the earlier work of Stan Goldman on *Clarel*. Pardes's approach to Melville's "exegetical imagination" (4), however, was much more topical in its cultural emphases, and she was especially interested in considering the relation of religion to gender and race in Melville's most renowned novel. Adding to a tradition that went back to Lawrance Thompson, Pardes saw Melville as reading biblical texts against the grain, finding artistic sustenance in the rhythms of the Hebrew Bible, but quarreling with its patriarchal and authoritarian aspects. Pardes built her reading around five biblical characters in relation to whom, she argued, Melville had shaped his engagement with the Hebrew and Christian scriptures (although Pardes focused primarily on the Hebrew scriptures): Job, Jonah, Ishmael, Ahab, and Rachel. Pardes read Job's place in

Moby-Dick in relation to Romantic ideas of the Sublime, Jonah's role in relation to German historical criticism of the Bible, Ishmael in relation to Melville's revision of nineteenth-century Orientalism, Ahab in relation to American expansionism and the Mexican-American War, and Rachel in relation to the increasing role of women in the American public sphere. Pardes's analysis of the biblical modes used in *Moby-Dick* is enlightening, but attenuated by the fact that she devoted so little space to Melville's other work of biblical scope and ambition, his long poem *Clarel*.

Pardes's title points to a reemerging interest in the relationship of Melville's work to the Bible in the early twenty-first century. In 2010, Robert Alter's *Pen of Iron: American Prose and the King James Bible* devoted a full chapter to *Moby-Dick*. Alter was particularly acute in pointing out the way in which the parallelism that formed the central structural device in the Hebrew poetry found in the Bible also served as the most important structural device in *Moby-Dick*. Alter also stressed the role of the sermon as an organizing principle throughout the novel, a point that has been made from time to time by Melville critics since R. P. Blackmur in the 1930s, but given life by Alter through his analysis of specific verbal structures like the replication of Levitical blessings and part of Ishmael's monologues throughout the text. Alter classified Melville as a "post-theistic" writer who "no longer believes," but "manifestly still carries the weight of theistic ideas" (56). It is possible to hear echoes here of Lawrance Thompson's idea of a "quarrel with God" and T. Walter Herbert's image of a Melville who lost his audience because he could envision a world that was not "theocentric," but in the subtlety of its details Alter's work extends these earlier analyses. The tension implicit in Melville's status as a "post-theistic" writer also appeared in the relationship Melville developed between the Hebrew and Christian scriptures. Alter suggests that rather than following a conventionally Christian typological reading of the Bible, Melville allowed the Hebrew scriptures to speak powerfully in their own right throughout the novel. This mode of biblical allusion, uncharacteristic for nineteenth-century Christian writers, formed one strand of a general project that both used the Bible constantly and undermined conventional Christian interpretations of the sacred text. As elegant as Alter's reading of the scriptural elements of *Moby-Dick* was, its limitation was that, like Pardes's work, it focused on one moment in Melville's career, and thus left unanswered questions about Melville's post-*Moby-Dick* trajectory.

Michael Colacurcio, one of the world's most distinguished scholars of religion in the work of Nathaniel Hawthorne, turned his attention to the question of Melville's belief in his 2007 essay "Charity and its Discontents." Colacurcio engaged directly with Lawrance Thompson's picture of Melville's adversarial relationship to the deity of monotheism. For Colacurcio, the defining feature of Melville's career was an engagement with the problem of evil: if there is a benevolent power behind the universe, why do innocents suffer? Colacurcio identified the period from *Redburn* to *Pierre* as comprising Melville's most ferocious critique of monotheistic responses to the problem of evil, and suggested that Melville's magazine fiction represented a turn from fiery protest into irony. Colacurcio, perhaps appropriately for a Hawthorne scholar, put Melville's short fiction at the center of his reading of Melville on religion, with a special emphasis on "Bartleby the Scrivener." "Bartleby," "The Piazza," and "Cock-a-Doodle-Doo" each appeared in Colacurcio's essay as illustrations of the ironic gap between human aspirations toward charity and the persistence of evil in the particular form of the suffering caused by poverty. Colacurcio introduced a subtle reading of Melville in relation to Marx, Melville's great contemporary in the cause of political and religious protest in Europe, claiming that although Melville criticizes social and economic injustice with an intensity akin to that of Marx, there is ultimately something left over after one has completed a Marxian reading of Melville, "some structure beyond that of caste and class" (78), which indicates the ultimately determinative role that the problem of evil as addressed by theology has for Melville's philosophy. Colacurcio's summing up is perhaps as clear and nuanced a statement of Melville's attitude toward the divine as has yet appeared. Melville's attitude was "Not quite Job's 'I will love him though he slay me.' More like: I trust he will not destroy me for pursuing without cynicism the moral evidences that call into question our best metaphysical proofs" (79). It is hard to imagine a more succinct or precise statement of the mixture of rebellion and reverence that permeates Melville's body of work.

Like Colacurcio, Branka Arsic found that Melville's short fiction offered a particularly beguiling means of access to Melville's thought, although Arsic's approach emphasized Melville as a philosophic rather than as a religious thinker. *Passive Constitutions, or 7 ½ Times Bartleby* (2007) examined Melville's short fiction as a series of philosophical ruminations on the nature of writing itself. This was not an altogether new tack to take with "Bartleby, the Scrivener": Leo Marx had made a similar argument in 1953 in a brief article entitled "Melville's Parable of the Walls," but Arsic expanded the common practice of making "Bartleby" an allegory for writing to the wider corpus of Melville's short fiction.[16] She found "The Piazza" to be especially telling in this regard. After using a brief discussion of *The Piazza Tales* as a whole to frame her philosophical emphases in regard to "Bartleby," Arsic turned to an intricate series of contemplations of the story itself. In succeeding chapters, Arsic read "Bartleby" as an elaboration of (1) Jonathan Edwards's views on freedom and necessity as outlined in *The Freedom of the Will*, (2) early American physician Benjamin Rush's speculations regarding human psychology, (3) twentieth-century French philosopher Gilles Deleuze's reading of

Bartleby's verbal formulas, (4) Bartleby's resemblance to a chronic user of mind-altering drugs, (5) Bartleby's relationship to both nineteenth-century Transcendentalist thought and deconstructive theories of undecidability,[17] (6) Bartleby's status as a celibate male, (7) the attorney's narrative of Bartleby's life as an "apology to a friend" (154) for the attorney's "being too human himself, but also for the too humanness of all humans" (152), and finally, (7½, in her counting scheme), the formless form of a shapeless cloud. I include the above in a rather breathless list purposefully, because Arsic's study managed not only to make a bewildering number of connections in a very condensed space, but also to command a reader's assent to even those that seemed initially improbable.

Peter Szendy's *Prophecies of Leviathan* (2010) was unique in that it attempted to philosophize about, and indeed with, Melville. Szendy commented specifically on the experience of reading Melville, and in doing so, he tied together, in a relatively brief treatise, a host of interconnected issues related to ethics, aesthetics, epistemology, and religion. Szendy noted the quality in *Moby-Dick* that causes the novel to appear prophetic: he begins, for example, with Ishmael's imagined "grand programme of Providence," with its reference to a "bloody battle in Affghanistan [*sic*]" that seemed all too topical by 2004. This acknowledgment of the prophetic quality of *Moby-Dick* became enmeshed for Szendy with a number of other features of the work: the way in which the bodies of the whales become figures for both books themselves and for the act of reading, the way in which *Moby-Dick* intersects with other Melvillean texts like "The Lightning-Rod Man," "The Apple-Tree Table," and "The Tartarus of Maids" that also combine the appearance of prophecy with the probing of the relation between physical world and text, and the novel's tendency to engage the reader personally in ongoing dialogues about the issues it raises. Although its style showed the influence of French literary theory of the post-structuralist school, *Prophecies of Leviathan* was a deeply engaging study, in part because its playfulness and its concern to establish an interpersonal connection with its reader very much mirrored Melville's own tendency to engage his readers through the construction of a playful if cerebral persona.[18]

The mirror has been a metaphor that has shaped each of the chapters in this study so far, and it seems nowhere so apt as in a consideration of scholars' treatment of Melville's religious and philosophical thought. From *Typee* to *Billy Budd*, and throughout a variety of forms of the novel, the romance, the short story, the sketch, and the poem in between, Melville consistently hints at profound spiritual, ethical, and epistemological meanings, and these hints have elicited powerful responses from his critics, who have often seemed compelled to defend a vision of Melville's faith that resembled their own. Perhaps the clearest explanation of the powerful responses that Melville's works have evoked in this regard appears in Melville's own comments on Shakespeare in "Hawthorne and His Mosses":

> But it is those deep far-away things in him; those occasional flashings-forth of the intuitive Truth in him; those short, quick probings at the very axis of reality; — these are the things that make Shakespeare, Shakespeare. Through the mouths of the dark characters of Hamlet, Timon, Lear, and Iago, he craftily says, or sometimes insinuates the things, which we feel to be so terrifically true, that it were all but madness for any good man, in his own proper character, to utter, or even hint of them. Tormented into desperation, Lear the frantic King tears off the mask, and speaks the sane madness of vital truth. (244)

The "sane madness of vital truth" which generations of scholars have found in Melville's writing has continually drawn them back to the haunting religious and philosophical questions that, implicit or explicit, are never absent from Melville's work.

Notes

[1] Berthoff likely was alluding in this instance to Alfred Kazin's 1950 *Partisan Review* article "On Melville as Scripture."

[2] See Brian Higgins's and Hershel Parker's magisterial collection, *Herman Melville: The Contemporary Reviews* for a cross-section of these responses.

[3] Had Schiffman been writing slightly later, he might have added the distinguished Melville biographer Newton Arvin to this list, as well as Ronald Mason. The tradition of seeing *Billy Budd* as a "testament of acceptance" was embraced recently by Andrew Delbanco in his 2005 biography of Melville (discussed in chapter 1).

[4] As Bell noted, Howard P. Vincent had begun to track references to Bayle in *The Trying-Out of Moby-Dick* (1949), and it was on this foundation that Bell built. James Duban was to continue the tradition of investigating Bayle for sources of Melville's thought in his 1977 article "The Translation of Pierre Bayle's *An Historical and Critical Dictionary* owned by Melville," identifying Bayle as the source for many of Melville's references to tensions between the head and the heart.

[5] For more on Melville's reading of the Bible and appropriation of biblical tropes, see Mark Heidmann's "The Markings in Herman Melville's Bibles" (1990), and my own 2008 essay "One's Own Faith: Melville's Reading of *The New Testament and Psalms*."

[6] The degree to which Thompson's argument lurks in the background even of studies that are diametrically opposed to his in their understanding of Melville's religious thought can be seen in two examples from the years that followed. In 1958, Randall Stewart did not mention Thompson directly in *American Literature and Christian Doctrine*, but he did obliquely criticize Thompson's conclusion, suggesting that "resignation to God's overruling Providence" was the lesson

of *Billy Budd*, and concluding cautiously that "Perhaps [Melville] couldn't have written a book like *Billy Budd* without feeling it" (102). John Frederick was more direct in his 1969 study *The Darkened Sky*, concluding his reading of Melville's late poem "Pontoosuce" with the assertion that "It offers nothing that can be twisted into to the semblance of a petty and lifelong quarrel with God" (122).

[7] Among the scholars who have followed Stern's model and viewed Melville in light of his engagement with the natural world is Brett Zimmerman in *Herman Melville: Stargazer* (1998). Ever since work of Stern and Newton Arvin in the 1950s, scholars had understood that Melville's religious thought was closely connected to his view of the natural world, but Zimmerman moved into new territory by constructing a study of Melville around Melville's understanding of astronomy.

[8] Both Maurice Friedman's *Problematic Rebel: An Image of Modern Man* (1963; revised edition published under the title *Problematic Rebel: Melville, Dostoievsky, Kafka, Camus*, 1970) and Felix S. A. Rysten's *False Prophets in the Fiction of Camus, Dostoevsky, Melville, and Others* (1972) sought to position Melville within the boundaries of an international existentialist tradition as well.

[9] Kim L. Evans's *Whale!* (2002) represented a continuation of the strand of Melville scholarship that paid close attention to Melville's philosophical treatment of the natural world.

[10] Stanley Brodwin's 1971 article "Herman Melville's *Clarel*: An Existential Gospel" had a similar emphasis on the proto-existentialist elements of Melville's long poem.

[11] Like Cowan, John Irwin and Giles Gunn placed matters of interpretation and epistemology at the center of their studies. Irwin's *American Hieroglyphics* (1980) continued the tradition of using comparative religion and mythology to unpack Melville's work and also drew upon the linguistic concerns of poststructuralist criticism. Gunn's *The Interpretation of Otherness* (1978) put Melville in the wider context of the changes in American religious culture that emerged during the nineteenth century.

[12] Buell's argument in this essay was connected to his parallel development of the idea of "literary scripturism" as a central New England literary tradition in *New England Literary Culture: From Revolution through Renaissance* (1986). For Buell's discussion of "literary scripturism," see especially 166–92 in that study.

[13] Michael McLoughlin's *Dead Letters to the New World: Melville, Emerson, and American Transcendentalism* (2003) also sought to trace the contours of Melville's intellectual engagement with Emerson. McLoughlin self-consciously proposed to extend Williams's reading of Emerson's influence on Melville later into Melville's career, and he perform a valuable service by addressing Emersonian elements in *Pierre* and *Benito Cereno*. But his discussion of the other short fiction and *The Confidence-Man* was quite brief, and the lack of a discussion of Melville's poetry meant that a large segment of Melville's career was still unaccounted for by critics seeking traces of Emerson. An important article, Richard Hardack's "Stocks and Bonds: Pantheism and the Chain of Being in the American Renaissance" (1994), took a different tack, arguing that Melville embraced Emersonian pantheism early in his career, only to reject it forcefully in *Pierre* and his subsequent works.

[14] For more on *Clarel's* relationship to other nineteenth-century American representations of the multi-religious nature of the Holy Land, see my 2007 study, *The Romance of the Holy Land in American Travel Writing, 1790–1876*.

[15] I discuss Schueller and Finkelstein at greater length in chapter 6, along with other considerations of Melville's treatment of race, empire, and/or cosmopolitanism.

[16] Bainard Cowan (*Exiled Waters*) had used a similar mode of discussion in his reading of the "Etymology" and "Extracts" portions of *Moby-Dick*. Cowan found writing itself to be the topic Meville alluded to by including these two segments in *Moby-Dick*.

[17] This portion of Arsic's study is influenced especially by Jacques Derrida's cursory but suggestive discussion of Bartleby in *The Gift of Death* (1995). Like many Continental critics before him, Derrida found connections between Melville and Kierkegaard, arguing that "Bartleby" parallels Kierkegaard's impassioned grappling with the story of Abraham and Isaac in *Fear and Trembling*.

[18] Szendy's interest in the philosophical significance of Melville as a writer who dealt with apocalyptic events was anticipated earlier in the decade by Eyal Peretz's *Literature, Disaster, and the Enigma of Power: A Reading of "Moby-Dick"* (2003), which offered a philosophically and psychoanalytically informed reading of the motif of disaster and its relationship to the meaning and moral status of power in *Moby-Dick*.

4: Melville's Beard II: Gender, Sexuality, and the Body

IF MELVILLE'S BEARD HAS BEEN A SIGN for some critics of Melville's sometimes problematic association with wisdom in popular and critical writing alike, for many other critics, the beard portends something else entirely. To some, the stern aspect of Melville's bearded portraits from the 1850s and 1860s associate him not so much with prophecy as with patriarchy, and the resulting body of criticism has delved into Melville's personal life, asking painful questions about misogyny, alcoholism, and physical and emotional abuse. A second approach, which forms a kind of riposte to the first, has looked at Melville's position within a world of writing conventions established in no small part by women, and at his position in a household composed primarily of women, and asked to what degree female sexuality might prove central, rather than peripheral to Melville's project as a writer. A third line of inquiry might be seen as taking the beard as an indication of Melville's concern with masculine experience. This approach to Melville has looked at Melville's representations of manhood and the relationships between men and asked questions both about Melville's own sexuality and the role that his writings play in the history of representations of same-sex desire. Finally, and most recently, some critics have set themselves the question of the meaning of the literal, physical bodies in Melville's texts: female and male, human and nonhuman alike. If the scholars discussed in chapter 3 found their version of Melville in a world of the mind and spirit, the scholars in this chapter have located Melville firmly in the physical, corporeal world of the human body and its natural surroundings.[1]

Domestic Life, Gender, Violence, and Authorship

Melville's own marriage has figured centrally in many of these discussions. From the early days of Melville biography, indeed from Raymond Weaver's pioneering biography of Melville in the 1920s, there was speculation about Melville's relationship to Elizabeth Shaw Melville, his wife. A persistent topic of discussion in biographical studies of Melville has been whether Melville was a bad husband, a bad father, an alcoholic, a verbally abusive man, a physically abusive man, insane, or all of the above. There has been a tendency for Melville critics to divide into defenders and condemners of the man himself in this regard, although the lines between the camps have never been completely clear. Generally, many of Melville's earliest biographers and critics presented him as a misogynist, and suggested that Melville's misogyny reflected badly not on Herman, but rather Elizabeth, Melville — a curious conclusion. More recently, the view of Melville as a misogynist has been used to condemn both him and the masculine bias of the American literary canon. More recently still, biographical critics like Hershel Parker and Laurie Robertson-Lorant have called the entire idea that Melville was a misogynist into question, and scholars of nineteenth-century American literary culture have found that Melville's work was much less divorced from popular nineteenth-century writing by women than had been previously thought. Melville, portrayed as a tortured, individualistic woman-hater by earlier critics, thus becomes a figure who is immersed in an increasingly feminized literary culture in nineteenth-century America, and is not so much an alienated critic as an engaged participant, while Melville the domestic monster becomes a husband and brother who acknowledges his dependence on the many strong and interesting women in his life.

Before the most recent wave of scholarship assessing Melville's personal life, the question of the relation between Melville's work and that of his female contemporaries came up during the 1970s, when women's writing came to occupy an increasingly significant role in interpretations of American literary history. Nina Baym was a pioneer in the field of American women's writing, and her work on Hawthorne and Melville showed the potential of the scholarship informed by investigations of women's writing to transform the scholarship on canonical works by men. Baym's essay on *Clarel*, "The Erotic Motif in Melville's *Clarel*" (1974), marked a departure in criticism of Melville's longest poem because Baym, unlike most of her predecessors, chose to take seriously the idea that the love of Clarel and Ruth was thematically central to the poem. Baym argued that through the tragic failure of the title character to achieve meaning through his relationship with Ruth, *Clarel* espoused fear and suspicion of female sexuality and presented celibacy as the ideal state for a man with spiritual inclinations. The poem's gestures towards homosexuality became for Baym a mere deflection of *Clarel*'s deeper impulse toward male celibacy, with Baym concluding, "So Clarel sees divine love as masculine and earthly love as feminine by nature. The fear of woman is partly a fear of one's own effeminacy, so that homosexuality is seen as a defense *against* feminization rather than an expression of it" (325). *Clarel* thus became a sign of a kind of misogyny on Melville's part that he resisted but could not shake. Ten years later, Warren Rosenberg's "Deeper than Sappho: Melville, Poetry, and the Erotic" (1984) suggested that Melville had managed to achieve "the unification of the erotic and the divine, of earth and heaven" in *Clarel*, demonstrating that the question of Melville's attitude towards the erotic, and indeed toward sexuality in general in *Clarel* continued to be contested.

The question of how Melville might fit into a new American literary history that took full account of women's contributions came up with particular urgency in Ann Douglas's seminal study *The Feminization of American Culture* (1977). Douglas's study was a wide-ranging exploration of the rise of sentiment as an essential component of American literary culture. For Douglas, Melville's work represented a counter-trend to feminization and sentimentalism in American literature, and her reading of Melville's career was reminiscent of the narrative of a proto-modernist Melville rejected by his contemporaries ascendant in the early days of the Melville Revival. Douglas viewed Melville as a critic of sentimentalism, but she also noticed a tension at work in Melville's writing between a sort of "Freudian" emphasis on the personal and the psychological, which she argued appeared primarily in Melville's works that included women, and a "Marxist" emphasis on broader social structures, which she suggested appeared in those of Melville's works that excluded women (298). Douglas also posited Calvinist theology as an important feature of Melville's rejection of sentimentalism, and she regarded Captain Ahab's more Calvinist pronouncements as signs of a masculine revolt against the feminization of the American reading public. *Pierre*, on the other hand, was Melville's concession of defeat in his conflict with sentimentalism. Douglas found *Billy Budd* to be a work that finally transcended Melville's life-long quarrel with his readership, embodying Melville's ability to move beyond sentimental renderings of human experience into pure realism. Like his contemporary Margaret Fuller, Melville was understood by Douglas to be an oppositional figure, resisting the broader impulse toward affect and sentiment in American culture.

Jane Tompkins's *Sensational Designs: The Cultural Work of American Fiction* (1985), also took the tack of treating Melville as an oppositional figure — a man writing in a woman's literary world. Indeed, Tompkins's study was not directly about Melville at all, but Melville was such an important presence in the background of the book, and *Sensational Designs* was so influential among scholars of American literature, that it bears discussing here. Tompkins argued that the popular literature written by women during the nineteenth century, well-regarded in its own time but often patronized in the twentieth century, constituted an important strand in the development of American culture and deserved equal billing with the canonized works of the American Renaissance. Melville ended up standing in for the male authors associated with the American Renaissance who were unpopular in their own time but were lionized as forerunners of the elite literary culture of the first half of the twentieth century. Melville was a useful foil for Tompkins because she was able to find correlations between Melville's work and that of, for example,

Harriet Beecher Stowe or Susan Warner, that justified her claims for the aesthetic importance of women's writing. At the same time, Melville could be seen as an example of the unearned privilege given to culturally marginal nineteenth-century male writers, while influential female authors were neglected by the early generations of American literary scholars. Tompkins both took for granted Melville's canonical status and made his canonization emblematic of the exclusionary practices of many male literary critics. As a result, Melville was never wholly absent from a study that sought to displace him and the other male writers associated with the American Renaissance from the central position they had come to occupy in the nineteenth-century American literary study — and indeed, Tompkins's goal was not to bury Melville, but rather to expand the study of American literature so that a contemporary like Harriet Beecher Stowe could receive the sort of respectful, rigorous consideration that Melville had been receiving since the 1920s.

It is in the context of the recovery of women's importance to understanding nineteenth-century American literature that the discussions of Herman Melville's marriage to Elizabeth Shaw Melville must be understood. Herman Melville's relationship with Elizabeth Shaw Melville had been the subject of conjecture ever since the early days of the Melville Revival. The earliest Melville scholars tended to take the idea that the marriage was troubled as axiomatic, although later scholars would modify this image of the Melville household. Family gossip reported at second hand by the early scholars suggested that Herman might even have been physically abusive toward Elizabeth, and the discoveries by Walter Kring and Jonathan Carey in the mid-1970s of a plot on the part of her brother and pastor to kidnap Elizabeth in order to ease the way for a potential divorce seemed to reinforce the idea.[2] Elizabeth Renker was the first to dwell intensively on the implications of these rumors and conjectures, and as a result, her work served as a focal point for one of the most heated controversies surrounding Melville and gender. In an article in a 1994 special issue of *American Literature* devoted to Melville that was subsequently developed into the chapter that formed the centerpiece of her book *Strike through the Mask: Herman Melville and the Scene of Writing* (1996), Renker marshaled the evidence that Herman had abused Elizabeth at length, and suggested that his likely violence against Elizabeth was connected to his internal artistic demons.

As Renker's discussion illustrated, the spousal abuse case against Melville is built largely out of unproven and (likely) unprovable innuendos and rumors, but the sheer volume of suggestions in this direction make it difficult to dismiss them altogether, as does the fact that some of these suggestions came from very distinguished Melville scholars like Henry Murray and Raymond Weaver. The thrust of Renker's argument, however, was not primarily to convict Melville of spousal abuse (although the way in which she presented the evidence suggested that she found the allegations more plausible than did, for example, the Melville biographer Hershel Parker). Rather, Renker built the image of a violent and impulsive Melville suggested by the hearsay evidence that she examined into a sort of allegory for Melville's relationship to the written word and the empty page. Using surviving Melville manuscripts as visual evidence, Renker argued that a violent effort to remove mental and psychological blocks to Melville's artistic vision led to a violent style of writing that attempts to remove forcibly these blocks from his consciousness. That this blockage was at least in part sexual was suggested by Renker's reading of "The Tartarus of Maids," where an industrial hellscape is described in terms of female sexuality, and the writing process is described in terms of women's fertility (*Strike*, 61–63).

Renker's reading of Melville's manuscript revision, his prose style (she largely ignored his poetry in her early work, although she has since become a leading scholar of Melville's poetry, as chapter 2 indicates), and the biographical evidence that he may have been verbally or even physically abusive as a husband and father constituted an impressive performance that combined psychosexual criticism with close reading and textual materialism. It was not, however, either of the things that it is sometimes glossed as being: a malicious slander on the personal life of a great author, or conclusive proof that Melville was violent and depraved. It was instead a sober look at the possibility that Melville's personal life was characterized by violence joined to some insightful speculations about what this might have meant for his art by a rarefied pun on the word "strike" as an act of physical violence, an act of editorial practice that can seem violent by analogy, and the cosmic violence of Captain Ahab's call in *Moby-Dick* to "strike through the mask." Whether Herman Melville ever either struck Elizabeth Shaw Melville, or as one second-hand anecdote suggested, pushed her down the stairs, remains a disturbing mystery. What is clear is that the evidence is insufficient to convict a living person of such behavior, but adequate to leave unresolved questions about a writer who, along with all eyewitnesses, is long dead.

Elizabeth Schultz and Haskell Springer's *Melville and Women* (2006) was a landmark collection that should put to rest permanently the idea that Melville existed in a wholly masculine world and that women only figure as place-keepers in his fiction. The work on Melville's family life by Renker and Laurie Robertson-Lorant (see chapter 1 for a discussion of Robertson-Lorant's biography of Melville) and the work on Melville's debt to popular literature by Sheila Post-Lauria (for which see chapter 2) set the parameters for the collection. *Melville and Women* included an array of impressive articles that showed that both as family members and as literary influences, women were always very much a part of Melville's social world and intellectual milieu. The collection as a whole represented a significant moment in the history of Melville studies, but several articles were especially important. Laurie Robertson-Lorant, discussed in chapter 1 of this study as a major Melville biographer, contributed a powerfully argued piece decrying the "methodological misogyny" of earlier Melville scholars who had taken the absence of women from leading roles in some of Melville's most renowned texts to indicate a personal distaste for and independence from women on Melville's part (16). Robertson-Lorant explored Melville's relationships with his mother, wife, sisters, and daughter, along with female friends like Sophia Peabody Hawthorne and Sarah Morewood. Moreover, Robertson-Lorant provided an important corrective to common-place views that belittle Elizabeth Shaw Melville, emphasizing instead her intelligence and resourcefulness as well as the profound influence she had on her husband's literary life.

With regard to Melville's textual relationships with women, Charlene Avallone's "Women Reading Melville/Melville Reading Women" and Peter Balaam's "'Piazza to the North': Melville Reading Sedgwick" made clear the extent of Melville's engagement with the writing of his female contemporaries. Avallone dug into Melville's correspondence with Sarah Morewood, among others, to show that Melville acknowledged that women and men in nineteenth-century America belonged to a shared literary culture (99). Avallone also noted Melville's admiring remarks about the writing of Caroline Kirkland and Germaine de Stael, and found lines of influence from Catharine Maria Sedgwick's *The Linwoods* (1835) to *Pierre*.[3] Balaam provided a reading of "The Piazza," the lead story in *The Piazza Tales*, which analyzed the ways in which "The Piazza" commented on Melville's position as an author relative to his celebrated female contemporary Sedgwick. Balaam revealed a wistfulness in Melville's allusions to the work of his more popular contemporary Sedgwick by cleverly using the role that the piazza as an architectural device played in nineteenth-century American understandings of the picturesque.

As Avallone's essay indicated, *Pierre* looms particularly large in discussions of Melville and the writing by women that was so popular during the nineteenth century. Wendy Flory's "Melville and Isabel" argued that the character of Isabel in *Pierre* was symbolic of Melville's own "imagination: a powerfully dynamic, sinisterly coercive creative gift" (121). Flory's reading of Isabel's character and her symbolic role for Melville was rendered particularly effective by Flory's analysis of the numerous echoes of John Keats's odes in some of the more erotically charged portions of *Pierre*. Ellen Weinauer, meanwhile, took a complementary tack in her essay, "Women, Ownership, and Gothic Manhood in *Pierre*," which discussed parallels between Pierre's increasing ghostliness in the novel bearing his name and the legal ghostliness experienced by American women because of the denial of property rights to women under the doctrine of the *femme covert* or "covered woman."[4]

Unlike *Pierre*, *Billy Budd* might seem an unlikely subject for discussion in a collection devoted to Melville and women, given its all-male cast of characters. Wyn Kelley's remarkable essay "'Tender Kinswoman': Gail Hamilton and Gendered Justice in *Billy Budd*" showed that Melville's reading of women's works and his sensitivity to the nuances of gender informed his last work of fiction. As Kelley noted, the idea that the 1889 story by Gail Hamilton (whose real name was Mary Abigail Dodge), "The Murder of Philip Spencer," influenced Melville cannot be conclusively demonstrated to be true, although it had been recognized as a possibility since the 1930s, when Charles R. Anderson had raised the possibility, since there has been no definitive discovery that Melville read Hamilton. Kelley argued that there were, however, points of connection between Hamilton's treatment of the *Somers* Mutiny (the incident that inspired *Billy Budd*, in which Melville's cousin Guert Gansevoort had played an important role) and Melville's treatment of the same incident. Kelley used Melville's invocation of a "tender kinswoman" in *Billy Budd* as a trope for empathy as a way into possible connections between the two texts. Kelley saw Hamilton as a forerunner to the "feminist ethics" of twentieth-century thinker Carol Gilligan, and she argued that Melville was engaged in a philosophical debate on the subject of feminist ethics with Hamilton as he constructed the character of Captain Vere in *Billy Budd*, and particularly when he wrote Vere's response to the presumptive views of the "tender kinswoman." Melville, who as Kelley pointed out may have first been exposed to Gail Hamilton's writing through Elizabeth Shaw Melville's reading, seems likely, Kelley argued, to have incorporated Hamilton's emphasis on female sympathy and intercession into the internal struggles of his male characters. This tendency toward androgyny in Melville's thought was central to the second strand discussed in this chapter, the question of Melville's own sexuality.

Melville's Sexuality

Melville's beard has frequently been understood to represent an aggressive heterosexual masculinity, and it has been understood with equal frequency to conceal androgyny and homoerotic desire. As Hershel Parker has pointed out, Melville began his literary career as a heterosexual sex symbol in the United States, and was, by the end of his life, a kind of gay sex symbol in 1880s and 1890s England.[5] Melville was both praised and attacked for his frank discussions of sexuality during his lifetime, and once his works were recovered during the Melville Revival, it did not take long for critics to recognize that Melville's theological and philosophical reflections were not the only source of the power of his work. Sexuality began to come to the fore in Melville studies in the 1940s and 1950s, when Richard Chase was among the earliest critics to point explicitly to the presence of a homoerotic element in *Billy Budd*, *Moby-Dick*, and *Redburn*. In *Herman Melville: A Critical Study* (1949), Chase noted that in each of these works, attachments between and among men served as a structural principle of the text, and in each of these works, male affection was charged with a strong erotic dimension.

Although Chase and others had acknowledged the homoerotic features of Melville's work, Leslie Fiedler pointed to a truly new dimension in Melville studies with *Love and Death in the American Novel* (1960). After tracking the examples of masculine affection and friendship that appear throughout Melville's career and commenting on the frank depiction of Claggart as a repressed homosexual in *Billy Budd*, Fiedler turned to an extended reading of *Moby-Dick*. Fiedler acknowledged the various artistic and philosophical dimensions that previous critics had seen in *Moby-Dick*, but contended they had missed the degree to which *Moby-Dick* was a love story. Focusing on the initial encounters of Ishmael and Queequeg and the intense if destructive connection between Ahab and Fedallah, Fiedler writes:

> In *Moby-Dick*, the redemptive love of man and man is represented by the tie which binds Ishmael to Queequeg, while the commitment to death is portrayed in the link which joins Ahab to Fedallah, but the two relationships are disturbingly alike: both between males, one white and one colored. . . . Melville is more conscious than he seems at first of the ambiguous nature of the love which he celebrates in *Moby-Dick*, and which, beginning with the encounter of Ishmael and Queequeg, grows ever more general and inclusive, but never less suspect, as the story continues. (531–32)

For Fiedler, *Moby-Dick* was a struggle between love and death, Eros and Thanatos, and it is love that survived in the end. Moreover, the love that Fiedler saw as most important to *Moby-Dick* was the physical love between men celebrated in Plato's *Symposium* and suggested by the biblical story of David and Jonathan, which Melville had scored in his Bible during the year in which he was writing *Moby-Dick*. Fiedler tracked carefully the series of phallic jokes and puns that appear throughout *Moby-Dick*, including the chapters "A Squeeze of the Hand" and "The Cassock," the first of which combines a vision of transcendental comradeship with sly references to masturbation, and the second of which is devoted to a tongue-in-cheek discussion of the whale's penis. Fiedler noted the interweaving of comical and farcical elements in these passages and the description Ishmael and Queequeg's "marriage" at the beginning of *Moby-Dick* with an earnest argument for the primacy of love in human relationships.[6] Fiedler argued convincingly that love and sexuality are not a side-show in *Moby-Dick*, but rather the core of the narrative. Following Fiedler, no account of the meaning of Melville's greatest novel could dispense entirely with the question of physical sexuality, masculine identity, and the human body.

Edwin Haviland Miller's 1975 biography of Melville (discussed at length in chapter 1) served to focus a great deal of attention on the role of sexuality and masculine identity in Melville's work, both by analyzing of the influence of Melville's conflicted relationship to his father on Melville's work and arguing that a homoerotically charged relationship with Nathaniel Hawthorne was central to Melville's artistry. Charles Haberstroh's 1980 study *Melville and Male Identity* showed the influence of Miller's biographical work on Melville's relationships with his family. Haberstroh believed that the figure of the father was the key to understanding Melville's treatment of sexuality in his work, and that Melville's loss of his own father at an early age was determinative for his artistic development. Beginning with a brief overview of Herman Melville's relationships with his father, Allan Melvill, and his mother, Maria Gansevoort Melville, Haberstroh tracked the role of men within families throughout Melville's fiction (ignoring his poetry, however). Haberstroh found "male responsibility" to be thematically central to *Typee* and *Omoo* (51), and *Mardi* and *Pierre* to be representative of Melville's disappointment with his own marriage and indicative of a general suspicion of female sexuality. In *Redburn, White-Jacket*, and *Moby-Dick*, Haberstroh saw Melville engaging the core issue of paternal abandonment and creating alternate sources of masculine affection and affirmation for his narrators: Harry Bolton for Redburn, Jack Chase for White-Jacket, and Queequeg for Ishmael. Ahab, meanwhile, embodied the male self who was unable to come to terms with the experience of paternal loss. Over a decade later, Philip Young's *The Private Melville* (1993) also regarded Melville's family as the key to understanding both his personal development and his literary production. Like Haberstroh, he saw indications of Melville's sense of loss and disillusionment with his father throughout his body of work. Young went beyond Haberstroh, however, in believing that the depiction of Pierre's disillusionment due to his father's marital infidelity was directly drawn from Herman Melville's experiences with his own family, a belief that most recent Melville scholars have been reluctant to endorse.

Robert K. Martin's *Hero, Captain, and Stranger* (1986) was the first study to parse homoerotic elements in Melville's sea fiction vigorously. Martin suggested that the erotically charged male friendships portrayed in the sea novels offered an alternative to the aggressiveness of male sexuality as traditionally understood in North America and Western Europe. What's more, it could even change the way Western civilization understood itself and the cultures with which it was in contact for the better — no small claim. Martin used the schema outlined in his title to explain the shifting patterns of relationships between men in Melville's works. Each of Melville's major sea novels — *Typee, Redburn, White-Jacket, Moby-Dick*, and

Billy Budd (it is not clear why *Omoo* is omitted) — was shaped, Martin claimed, by some combination of the Hero, the Captain, and the Dark Stranger. In Martin's schema, the Captain represents authority, the Dark Stranger represents innocence, and the Hero is the "experiencing self" who must choose between the two (4). The Captain is Faustian, questing, Western man, seeking knowledge, and defined by a narrow view of masculinity, whereas the Dark Stranger represents an "alternative sexuality" that can open up the possibility of an alternative politics to the imperialism that Martin associated with the Captain (6). In Melville's early novels of the South Seas, *Typee* and *Omoo*, the interplay of the Captain, Hero, and Stranger was defined in terms of the confrontation between European and American cultures and the cultures of the Marquesas. Martin noted that the alternative sexual possibilities offered to Tommo, the hero (and in Martin's schema, Hero) of *Typee* in the Marquesas, included both an intimate friendship with Tommo's fellow sailor Toby (who, as Martin noted, was darker in complexion than Tommo) and the sexual allure of the handsome male islander Marnoo, as well as the more conventional infatuation Tommo reported for the female islander Fayaway. *Redburn*, as an account of Atlantic rather than Pacific travel, did not have the exotic cultural possibilities offered by the Marquesas, but Martin found that once again, the male narrator's quest for male companionship was central to the novel as a whole.

In *Moby-Dick*, the marriage of both European and non-European civilizations and of male minds and affections suggested by the earlier novels was consummated in the relationship of Ishmael and Queequeg. Martin found the very form of *Moby-Dick* to be "hermaphroditic," encompassing both the "masculine, productive form" of the novel and the "feminine, non-productive form" of the lyric (67). This was a curious reversal of the conventional distinction many earlier scholars of American literature — and for that matter some of Martin's contemporaries — had made between a "masculine" romance tradition and a "feminine" novelistic tradition in American literature. The overall opposition that Martin created, however, was compelling: Ahab was Faustian, conventionally masculine, and dominant, and therefore dangerous; Ishmael and Queequeg's relationship was androgynous, cross-cultural, and mutual, and therefore an emblem of hope. Thus, in Martin's view, the bearded author who had seemed to some critics to be the embodiment of conventional masculinity was in fact a prophet of new forms of masculinity, encompassing both homosexual desire and a more generalized androgyny.

The final piece in Martin's picture of Melville's sexuality was *Billy Budd*. The homoerotic subtext of Melville's last work had long been noted. Richard Chase, Newton Arvin, and Leslie Fiedler had identified Claggart's obsession with Billy as evidence of repressed homosexual desire, and Martin followed their lead. For Martin, *Billy Budd* was a testament of despair, in which Melville surrendered hope for the alternative sexual possibilities that he imagined in his earlier fiction, and most extensively in *Moby-Dick*. Captain Vere's execution of Billy became for Martin the ultimate triumph of the Captain figure in Melville's work over other possibilities, and thus Martin's study ended on a distinctly doleful note.

Like Martin, Joseph Allen Boone picked up Leslie Fiedler's description of *Moby-Dick* as primarily a love story in *Tradition Counter Tradition: Love and the Form of Fiction* (1987). Boone expanded Fiedler's argument by examining what he called the "polymorphous life force at work in the natural and linguistic worlds of this text" (243). For Boone, Melville was distinctive not so much in the emphasis on masculinity in his work as in his tendency to undermine gender categories. Boone argued that Ishmael's relationship with Queequeg "works to undermine the concepts of sexual polarity and hierarchy embedded in popular definitions of romance" (245). As in Martin's reading of Melville, in Boone's view Melville's treatment of sexuality opened up broadly liberatory political possibilities, and thus had to be understood as the defining feature of Melville's entire project as a writer.[7]

Martin's argument for dissident sexuality as a source of intercultural amity was paralleled closely by Neal Tolchin's argument for sexuality as a source of subversive creativity and social critique in *Mourning, Gender, and Creativity in the Art of Herman Melville* (1988). Tolchin traced the theme of mourning throughout Melville's career, but his argument was most provocative when he addressed the role of mourning in *Pierre*. Tolchin's earlier chapters had argued that Melville's loss at a young age of his father, Allan Melvill, had inspired an ongoing fascination with mourning, in both its personal and sociological aspects, and that the characters of Ahab and Ishmael in *Moby-Dick* derived much of the power from this fascination, while earlier works like *Typee* displayed an anthropological exactness in detailing mourning rituals. In his consideration of *Pierre*, Tolchin found that the personal and social aspects of mourning had come together with sexuality in a particularly explosive combination. Rather than a parody of the conventions of the sentimental novel, *Pierre* was a subversion of the mourning rituals standard in nineteenth-century America. Tolchin noted that Maria Gansevoort Melville (Herman's mother) participated in the gendered cultural rituals surrounding widowhood and mourning by making needlepoint mourning art.

> In *Pierre*, Melville appropriates his mother's mourning art, as he partially models his attempt to authenticate his grief on her personal style of bereavement. However, in his hands mourning art conventions are transformed, and its ideological texture exposed. (142)

Melville accomplished this, Tolchin argued, through the character of Isabel, who was an ironic double for both Pierre's mother and Melville's own, and who embodied a subversive sexuality that undermined socially constructed boundaries for the mourning process. In this way, Isabel's "ability to link creativity and mourning to a sexualized maternal presence" was the ultimate example of Melville's artistic engagement with questions of gender. Tolchin thus extended Robert K. Martin's (and before Martin, Leslie Fiedler's) efforts to place Melville's treatment of gender and sexuality in the wider frame of his literary art.[8]

If subversive female sexuality was at the core of Melville's critique of the conventional aspects of American culture for Tolchin, David Leverenz's *Manhood and the American Renaissance* (1989) examined the implications of masculinity for Melville's art in the context of the wider American Renaissance. Leverenz suggested that representations of masculinity formed a central strand in mid-nineteenth-century American literature. The difference between the ambitiousness of Leverenz's argument and that of say, Charles Haberstroh a decade earlier can be attributed in no small part to the success of feminist criticism in the 1980s. Had Leverenz been writing in the earlier decades of Melville criticism, a focus on masculinity might have seemed redundant, given that the association between masculinity and literary excellence seemed to go without saying. The fact that gender had come to the fore in literary criticism meant that the meaning of masculinity as well as femininity had become a potential subject of discussion. Leverenz focused his analysis of *Moby-Dick* on the terrifying version of masculinity embodied by Captain Ahab. Using psychoanalytic categories to examine Ahab, Leverenz regarded Ahab as a sadomasochistic figure who is tormented most specifically by the demands of manhood in nineteenth-century America. As the title of Leverenz's chapter on *Moby-Dick*, "Ahab's Queenly Personality" suggested, Leverenz was particularly concerned with how gendered language illuminated the ruptures and uncertainties in American manhood. In much of the latter portion of the novel, Leverenz noted, Ahab describes himself in terms that are consistent with nineteenth-century American medical discussions of hysteria, considered to be a particularly feminine disease, associated, as the linguistic roots of the term suggest, with the womb. Leverenz did not see Ahab's use of feminine imagery in talking about himself so much as an expression of androgyny or of a truly feminine element within Ahab's personality as of a wounded masculinity that expressed itself through nineteenth-century conventions of feminine passivity and suffering. Moreover, because Leverenz viewed Ishmael as a sublimated version of Ahab, he saw the suggestions of homosexuality in Ishmael's relationship with Queequeg to be representative of the contradictions and anxieties of nineteenth-century American heterosexual masculinity rather than of a true alternative to this version of masculinity.

The strength of Leverenz's argument in this regard is that it accounts for the many congruencies between Ishmael's character and Ahab's in a particularly elegant fashion; its weakness is that it perhaps fails to take adequate account of the genuine emotion that appears in Ishmael and Queequeg's relationship and in the comradely affection among members of the crew of the *Pequod*. Unquestionably, Leverenz offered a powerful interpretation of the terrors associated with being a man in nineteenth-century America, and he also offered a particularly compelling explanation for Melville's use of King Lear as the primary Shakespearean model for Ahab by stressing the ways in which Lear and Ahab are both representative of wounded masculinity.

Gilles Deleuze's essay "Bartleby, or the Formula" (1989) also demonstrated the continuing attractiveness of readings of Melville that were built around the anguish of masculine psychology and the complex role that the figure of the father can play within this psychology. For Deleuze, tensions between fathers and sons and implications of incest between mothers and sons served as organizing principles of Melville's work from *Redburn* and *Moby-Dick* in Melville's early years, through *Pierre*, "Bartleby," and *The Confidence-Man* in his middle years, all the way to the posthumous *Billy Budd*. The poststructuralist psychoanalyst and philosopher Deleuze concluded that the inadequacy of fathers, from the biological fathers in *Redburn* and *Pierre* to the metaphorical fathers (Captain Ahab, the attorney who employed Bartleby, Captain Vere) in *Moby-Dick*, "Bartleby," and *Billy Budd*, was at the heart of Melville's work: "what Captain Vere and the attorney demonstrate is that there are no good fathers" (84). The anguish of a form of masculinity shaped by the roles of fatherhood and sonship thus became as central to Melville's art for Deleuze as it had been for Miller, Haberstroh, and Leverenz.

James Creech made a forceful argument for the centrality of homosexuality to Melville's literary production in his 1993 study *Closet Writing/ Gay Reading: The Case of Melville's "Pierre."* Creech turned away from Leverenz's tendency to make homosexuality a device for illuminating the terrors of American manhood and back toward Martin's interest in the liberating potential of the alternative sexualities proposed in Melville's work. Whereas Martin had been interested primarily in the all-male environments that Melville depicted at sea and the moments of same-sex attraction that appeared in representations of the Marquesan islanders in *Typee*, Creech found the domestic novel *Pierre* to be a source of illumination regarding Melville's sexuality that both confirmed and exceeded the hints that appeared in the sea novels.

Creech regarded *Pierre* as a text that coded its investment in homosexuality in "the camp epistemology of the wink" (98), and contended that "only willful denial can purge Melville's novels of the yearning gazes and subtle glancings of homoerotic sexuality" (100). Creech found homosexual desire and frustration in the usual places: Claggart's hatred of "the Handsome Sailor" Billy Budd, which Richard Chase had diagnosed in the 1950s as indicating repressed homosexual desire; the villainous Jackson's attraction to and hatred of a young Irish sailor in *Redburn*; and Redburn's intimate friendship with Harry Bolton — although he said surprisingly little about Queequeg and Ishmael's "marriage" in *Moby-Dick* or the descriptions of Marnoo's masculine beauty in *Typee*. *Pierre* was crucial to Chase's argument because he felt that the incest theme in *Pierre* that had proved so unsettling for nineteenth-century readers was actually code for homoerotic desire, and especially for Melville's presumed sexual desire for Nathaniel Hawthorne. Creech did not, however, delve into the Melville-Hawthorne relationship in detail, seeming to take its homoerotic elements largely for granted. Rather, Creech found textual evidence in *Pierre* itself to make the most forceful case for Melville's homosexuality: Isabel, who is ambiguously identified in the novel as possibly Pierre's half-sister (but possibly not), becomes identified with Pierre's longings for his deceased father: indeed, Isabel's "transvested incarnation of the father is all-determining" (155).

As with Elizabeth Renker's discussion of Melville's possible domestic violence as an analogue to his writing, Creech's "epistemology of the wink" was both endlessly suggestive and frustratingly difficult to demonstrate conclusively. There is unquestionably a strand of allusion to same-sex desire that runs throughout Melville's career — in his novels, his poetry, and even his correspondence. Whether noting this strand of allusion constitutes a demonstration of Melville's sexual identity as homosexual or heterosexual is less clear, and as with religiously oriented readings of Melville that confidently locate him in a particular variety of faith or doubt, it seems possible that the critic's desire can be as important as Melville's in determining where Melville is placed on a sexual continuum. In some ways, moreover, Creech was less ambitious than Martin in his claims: Martin had seen a renewal of the value placed on male friendships, including homosexual couples, as a force that could transform Euro-American civilization, whereas Creech's emphasis on demonstrating Melville's homosexuality by means of a series of carefully decoded coy allusions from *Pierre* tended to bracket out the large-scale geopolitical concerns in which Martin was invested. Nonetheless, Creech's work represented a substantial advance in considerations of Melville's sexuality as the result of his careful close reading and his conceptualization of his reading strategy through the metaphor of the wink.

Perhaps the most broadly influential consideration of the homoerotic element in Melville's work was Eve Kosofsky Sedgwick's 1990 study *The Epistemology of the Closet*, now an acknowledged classic in the field of queer theory. Sedgwick devoted a chapter of this seminal work to an extended reading of *Billy Budd* in light of questions of sexuality, and she responded directly to Ann Douglas's earlier discussions of gender in Melville in *The Feminization of American Culture*. Sedgwick read

Billy Budd as representative of the "deadlock between what I have been calling more generally *universalizing* and *minoritizing* accounts of the relation of homosexual desires or persons to the wider field of all desires or persons" (91). She located this deadlock in the tension between John Claggart's status as "*a homosexual*" (her emphasis) and the evidence that "*every* impulse of *every* person in this book that could at all be called desire could be called homosexual desire, being directed by men exclusively toward men" (92). The question posed by *Billy Budd*, for Sedgwick, was whether same-sex desire could be celebrated, as the early parts of the narrative seem to suggest, or if the only way in which Melville's culture and its successors could deal with homosexuality was through the "minoritizing discourse" represented by Claggart's death and the deaths of Billy and Captain Vere that it sets in motion — a discourse, which, Sedgwick suggested, ends in the exclusion and even genocide of those who do not conform to a heterosexual majority. Sedgwick contended that *Billy Budd*, written as it was at the very time that modern concepts of homosexuality were being formulated, expose the degree to which the concepts themselves are tainted by a homophobia that threatens not only homosexuals as a group, but humanity as a whole (128).

Even as Sedgwick focused attention on the homoerotic aspects and anxieties of *Billy Budd*, other scholars extended readings of these aspects of Melville's work to his earlier novels. By 1994 it had become a commonplace to suggest that the incest plot in *Pierre* was a means of speaking indirectly about homosexuality, both Melville's own possible experiences of same-sex desire and wide cultural anxieties about homoeroticism. Caleb Crain's 1994 essay "Lovers of Human Flesh" found a similar strategy at work in Melville's representations of cannibalism in his sea novels. Crain noted that while the existence of cannibalism in nineteenth-century Marquesan society is questionable, the existence of publicly acknowledged homosexuality in the nineteenth-century Marquesas is well documented. Making use of Sedgwick's concept of "homosexual panic," Crain argued that many of the anxieties about cannibalism expressed in *Typee* can be read as displaced anxieties about homosexual desire and practice, which Melville would have had occasion to observe during his time as a guest of the Taipei people. Also in 1994, Leland Person's article "Melville's Cassock: Putting on Masculinity in *Moby-Dick*" both consolidated and expanded on the body of work that had developed on sexuality in *Moby-Dick*, arguing that the phallic jokes that earlier critics had noted in *Moby-Dick* were indicative of a major thematic emphasis on the performance of masculinity.

Although Melville's sexual jokes from *Moby-Dick* and "The Paradise of Bachelors and The Tartarus of Maids" had been thoroughly explicated by the early twenty-first century, by Person and Crain and their predecessors, Henry Hughes's audacious essay, "Fish, Sex and Cannibalism"

(2004), discovered subversive sexual undercurrents in Melville's first major work. Hughes pointed to both the descriptions of Marquesan modes of eating raw fish and to the discussions of cannibalism in *Typee*, suggesting that Melville had encoded references to oral sex and other practices regarded as sexually subversive in nineteenth-century America and England. Following Caleb Crain and Robert K. Martin, Hughes suggested that food functions as a metaphor for sexuality throughout Melville's work, and argued that Tommo's willingness to eat raw fish and refusal of cannibalism indicated the limits of his ability to take on the cultural and sexual norms of Marquesan society.[9]

Perhaps the most important consideration of Melville's sexuality from a biographical standpoint was Jana L. Argersinger and Leland Person's edited collection *Hawthorne and Melville: Writing a Relationship* (2008). Melville's impassioned letters to Hawthorne had been the source of much of the speculation about Melville's sexual orientation over the years, and this collection sought to illuminate the Melville-Hawthorne relationship in light of the application of theories of gender to Melville's work as well as biographical research into the history of the two authors' interactions.

Brenda Wineapple and Laurie Robertson-Lorant provided careful biographical overviews of what is known about the Melville-Hawthorne relationship, with Robertson-Lorant providing the details on Melville's side of the relationship, and the distinguished Hawthorne biographer Wineapple providing a view of the relationship from Hawthorne's standpoint. Building on this biographical foundation, Gale Temple's essay "'Ineffable Socialities'" examined the constraints which the requirements of publication in nineteenth-century America placed on the possibilities for the sort of alternative masculine identities that Melville imagined in *Moby-Dick*.

Robert Milder's contribution "The Ugly Socrates: Melville, Hawthorne, and the Varieties of Homoerotic Experience," which was also included in Milder's single-author study *Exiled Royalties* (2006), provided what is to date the most careful exploration of the relationship among homosexuality, homosociality, and homoeroticism in Melville's work. Milder argued that while Melville's personal sexuality cannot be known based on the rather scanty biographical evidence, his representations of homosocial networks and his allusions to homoerotic desire can be fruitfully examined. Milder concluded that Melville was not himself primarily interested in questions of homosexual identity, but that Melville's art was shaped decisively by homoerotic feelings that were defined in no small part by his relationship to Hawthorne.

Christopher Castiglia's essay examined the nexus of sexuality and politics using methods reminiscent of Robert K. Martin's work from the 1980s. Castiglia, himself one of the most influential of nineteenth-century Americanists studying sexuality in literature in the late twentieth and early twenty-first centuries, suggested that the Melville-Hawthorne relationship offers readers the opportunity to "avoid judging intimate relationships by the criteria of nationalism and start judging nationalism by the criteria of intimacy" (323). Castiglia thus continued Martin's quest to discover ways in which the alternative sexualities suggested by Melville's fiction and poetry and his personal relationship to Hawthorne could in turn suggest alternative approaches to politics, and particularly international affairs. Castiglia's reading was given breadth by the fact that he devoted a significant portion of his essay to the role of Vine (often understood as a stand-in for Hawthorne) in *Clarel* as an embodiment of these possibilities. Like many of the pieces in the collection, Castiglia's work indicated the degree to which biography, textual analysis, and literary and cultural theory intermingle in readings of Melville concerned with gender and sexuality.

Reading the Body in Melville's Fiction and Poetry

Melville's relationship with women and his own sexuality have been recurrent themes in Melville criticism, but in recent years a third dominant subject of discussion related to sexuality has emerged in Melville studies: the question of Melville's representations of the human body. These studies have frequently overlapped with the issues raised in work more directly concerned with sexuality, but they have also broadened the scope of these studies considerably, and it is frequently the case that studies focused on sexuality in Melville and studies associated with the body in Melville prove mutually enriching.

Sharon Cameron's *The Corporeal Self* (1981) was the first study to center its critical attention on the role of the body in Melville's work. Cameron dealt with Melville's treatment of the body in both its literal and metaphorical aspects, tracking the presence of bodily description in *Moby-Dick*, and in a series of scintillating readings, exploring the ways in which the body as a concept was thematically central to the novel. Cameron justified her emphasis on the body in part by pointing to the tattooed body of Queequeg and the bodily affection between Ishmael and Queequeg in the early chapters of *Moby-Dick*, but Queequeg ultimately was peripheral to her argument. Central to Cameron's argument is the relationship between Captain Ahab and Pip, the young black sailor and tambourine player who lost his mind as a result of his abandonment at sea and became the most incisive commentator in *Moby-Dick* on his fellow characters' motivations. Cameron noted that Pip compensates for both Ahab's physical and psychological deficiencies, and that Ahab's desire for Pip's company reflects both Ahab's own bodily incompleteness and his desire for spiritual fulfillment. Ultimately, Cameron regarded the desire to find an equivalence between one's own body and the "body of the world" and the tragic clash between this urge and its inevitable frustration as the central distinctive features of *Moby-Dick*. This aspect of Cameron's work also shed new light on a very old area of Melville studies by offering an explanation for why *King Lear* in particular was so important for the characterization of Ahab. Cameron argued that Ahab and Lear were joined most essentially by the craving to establish a correspondence between one's own body and the surrounding world.

A decade after Cameron's pioneering work on the body in *Moby-Dick*, Peter J. Bellis re-opened the investigation of questions of identity and the relation of the body to the world that had figurely so largely in Cameron's work in *No Mysteries out of Ourselves* (1990). Bellis's work reflected the influence of French philosopher and historian Michel Foucault on literary studies throughout the 1980s and 1990s. Bellis explored the ways in which the physical body and its relation to personal identity could be compared to the identities shaped by families (with family serving as a trope for larger social networks as well) and with the texts that constructed and author's fictive identity. He began by examining the effects of tattooing and amputation on bodily identity, and then turned to the sorts of wrenching emotional dislocations that occur when family identities are destabilized, before concluding with an analysis of creation of self in *Moby-Dick* and *Pierre*. Like Charles Haberstroh and Edwin Haviland Miller, Bellis regarded the loss of a father and of paternal affection as crucial to understanding the vexed state of identity through Melville's work.

Clark Davis's *After the Whale: Melville in the Wake of* Moby-Dick (1995) came to a consideration of the body in Melville through one of Melville's most important sources. Like Edward Rosenberry and other earlier critics who examined Melville's humor, Davis found the influence of Rabelais to be particularly decisive in shaping *Moby-Dick*, and he used this Rabelaisian line of influence to open Melville up to a reading based on the theories of Russian theorist Mikhail Bakhtin. Davis used Bakhtin's theories of heteroglossia and the carnivalesque to gain a critical purchase on Melville's work. In his discussion of the carnivalesque, he highlighted the congruence between Rabelais and Melville's respective uses of the human body for both serious and comic effect. From the Rabelaisian bodily comedy of the earlier chapters, Davis traced Melville's presentations of damaged bodies through the short fiction and *The Confidence-Man*. Davis also made an important intervention into discussions of the body in Melville's work by dealing at length with *Battle-Pieces* and *Clarel*. One of the most insightful and original portions of Davis's study was his reading of *Clarel*, in which he argued perceptively that "Clarel's 'pilgrimage' becomes a double search for the 'body' of theology, on the one hand, and for his own bodily reality on the other" (129). This formulation showed that Cameron's reading of the body in Melville's work as significant both in itself and as a metaphor could be extended throughout every portion of Melville's career. It was the ability to embrace both a rigorous theological and philosophical reading of Melville and a theoretically informed consideration of the role of the body throughout Melville's later work that make Davis's study a particularly important point of departure in Melville studies.

Samuel Otter's *Melville's Anatomies* (1999) was a stunningly complex work that wove sexuality and the body into its discussion of Melville's thought in the broader context of nineteenth-century American literary culture. Using the body as the defining trope for his study, Otter tracked Melville's use of the body throughout his fiction, from *Typee* to *Pierre* (omitting the short fiction and *The Confidence-Man* as well as all of the poetry from his study on the grounds that Melville turned away from the body as a determinative metaphor after *Pierre*). In *Typee*, the body came to the fore through representations of cannibalism and tattooing, and Otter demonstrated carefully the ways in which Melville had both incorporated tropes derived from predecessors and contemporaries and revised those tropes to fit his own purposes. In *White-Jacket*, Otter found the body once again proved a determinative metaphor, this time because of the emphasis on flogging and the analogies between the corporal punishment of sailors in US military vessels and that inflicted as part of the regime of chattel slavery in the antebellum South. Meanwhile, both the "white jacket" the narrator wears (and is nicknamed for) and the ship in which he voyages become metaphorical bodies that also impose lasting consequences upon the literal bodies that are laboring and being punished on board the ship. Otter's ingenious linking of the bodily punishments of sailors with the violence of antebellum slavery made his discussion of *White-Jacket* particularly resonant in relation to the broader shape of American literary culture, and it allowed Otter to put Melville in conversation with such a figure as the great African-American abolitionist leader Frederick Douglass. Having laid this foundation, Otter turned to what is surely the richest source of bodily imagery in Melville's entire literary corpus: *Moby-Dick*.

Few novels in world literature provide as much bodily imagery as *Moby-Dick*, and Otter carefully anatomized the full range of this imagery, putting the lengthy cetological discussions of the head of the whale that so often prove an obstacle to undergraduates' appreciation of the novel into conversation with the nineteenth-century pseudo-sciences such as phrenology and the craniometry of Samuel George Morton and other leading ethnologists. This opened the way for a discussion of bodily understandings of race and the relationship between Melville's critique of racism in *Moby-Dick* and the critiques mounted by William Apess, Frederick Douglass, James Russell Lowell, and William Wells Brown. For Otter, a concern with the body turned insistently toward broader social, cultural, and political concerns related to race and slavery throughout Melville's work. Finally, with *Pierre*, the last of the works that Otter considered in *Melville's Anatomies*, Otter found that the landscape itself became a body, felicitously locating *Pierre*'s meaning in "the body of the landscape and . . . the hidden landscape of the body" (173). Throughout his book, Otter showed an astonishing (and quite Melvillean) ability to connect the concrete and the bodily with the largest and most important social, cultural, and political strands in nineteenth-century America.

Otter contributed as well to one of the most important new directions in Melville scholarship in the early twenty-first century: the turn toward disability studies. In a 2006 special issue of *Leviathan*, David T. Mitchell and Otter edited a group of essays dealing with the subject of disability, and as with many emerging intuitions in Melville studies, or for that matter, literary studies in general, the connection seemed quite intuitive once it was made, even if it had not been among the topics most Melville scholars had addressed in detail previously. Captain Ahab, after all is one of the most famous characters to suffer from a missing limb, and Billy Budd suffers from one of the best-known speech impediments in all of literature. Mitchell had in fact been among the very earliest critics to consider these aspects of Melville's work in detail, in a 1999 essay entitled "'Too Much of a Cripple': Ahab, Dire Bodies, and the Language of Prosthesis in *Moby-Dick*" (also included in *Narrative Prosthesis*, 2000, co-written with Sharon L. Snyder). In the 1999 essay Mitchell had argued that Melville's depiction of a link between Ahab's physical dismemberment and use of a prosthesis in the form a his whale-bone leg, and his psychological instability was an example of a common motif in Victorian literature, particularly Victorian women's writing. Mitchell suggested that this characteristic Victorian trope of disability and prosthesis was crucial in shaping the trajectory of Melville's narrative:

> Ahab is not so much doomed to a "natural" fate bequeathed by the gods, but rather an artificially prescribed destiny that props up the captain's figure for a time and then "gives out" under the pressures of historically constructed expectations about disability. . . . This sense of being simultaneously immobilized and towed by another vessel proffers a vision of the disabled body firmly yoked to the tragic logic of nineteenth-century discourses on physical difference. (22)

Mitchell thus demonstrated the centrality of nineteenth-century discourses of disability to some of Melville's most important work. Much like many of Melville's gender-oriented critics of the 1990s and 2000s, he also showed that Melville was deeply indebted to the literature of his time, and especially to literature written by his female contemporaries.

The essays in the 2006 disability issue of *Leviathan* expanded these initial connections by considering a wider range of disabilities, beginning with those that shape Ishmael's narration in *Moby-Dick*. In James Emmett

Ryan's "Ishmael's Recovery," Ryan read Ishmael's hypos as a species of disability, arguing that the arc of the narrative in *Moby-Dick* is shaped by Ishmael's gradual recovery from a variety of physical and mental diseases as well as by the numerous injuries and illnesses affecting Ahab and even, toward the end of the novel, Queequeg. Thus, the crucial contrast at the heart of *Moby-Dick* between Ishmael and Ahab was most fundamentally between Ishmael's ability to recover from both his bodily and spiritual ailments and Ahab's inability to do the same. The effect of Ryan's argument was ultimately to weave together Melville's spiritual and philosophical concerns with his demonstrable obsession with the health of the body, and with the corresponding obsessions with the medical relationship between the mind and the body that permeated nineteenth-century American culture.

In addition to Ryan's work on *Moby-Dick*, the special issue of *Leviathan* featured several articles on *The Confidence-Man*, one by David T. Mitchell and Sharon L. Snyder that broadened the investigations of disability in Melville they had begun in the late 1990s. In "Masquerades of Impairment," Mitchell and Snyder argued that *The Confidence-Man* demonstrated how disability could be used as "a disruption of the rationales of national personhood and morality" (35). Their essay also comprised the first chapter of another full-length study of disability in literature by Snyder and Mitchell, *Cultural Locations of Disability* (2006), further demonstrating Melville's importance to this burgeoning field of literary study. Meanwhile, in "From Melville to Eddie Murphy: The Disability Con in American Literature and Film," Ellen Samuels explored the ways in which *The Confidence-Man* connected with twentieth-century cultural artifacts.

When the diverse body of work on gender, sexuality, and the body in Melville's work is considered, it becomes evident that these matters are anything but peripheral to Melville's artistic production. Melville's own sexuality and the presence of same-sex desire and affection in his work seem likely to generate considerable further exploration, and Melville's treatment of female sexuality and his representations of women have finally begun to receive the attention they deserve. Although the tendency to identify Melville specifically as a "gay" or "straight" author seems perhaps to have run its course, explorations of the idiosyncratic contours of the sexualities expressed in Melville's writing continue to be productive of much rich and absorbing scholarship (this probability is very much in keeping with the concern with the fluidity of sexual identity evinced by queer theorists). A particularly stimulating body of scholarship in the area of gender is the work that shows how Melville interacted with his female contemporaries, both appropriating and resisting characteristic elements of some of the most popular and influential work of his time. As of 2010, Melville seems more than ever to be an author who resonates with readers across the boundaries of gender, sexual orientation, and disability, speaking powerfully to his readers on the grounds of shared bodily experience. What this has meant, and continues to mean for scholars, is that the Melville behind the beard has emerged as a much more complex, human writer than the disembodied voice of wisdom imagined at times by some of his earlier critics.

Notes

[1] It is noteworthy that fictional treatments of Melville's life in recent years, including Sena Jeter Naslund's *Ahab's Wife* (1999), Frederick Busch's *The Night Inspector* (1999), and Jay Parini's *The Passages of H.M.* (2011), have been informed by this body of work.

[2] Kring and Carey's findings were published in several venues, first as an article in *Proceedings of the Massachusetts Historical Society* entitled "Two Discoveries Concerning Herman Melville" (1975), and then as a pamphlet co-written with Donald Yannella and Hershel Parker entitled "The Endless Winding Way in Melville: New Charts by Kring and Carey" (1981).

[3] Avallone's career has been marked by several important essays on Melville, most notably "What American Renaissance?" (1997), which included a discussion of Melville in its broader critique of the idea of the American Renaissance, which Avallone argued helped to maintain gendered hierarchies in the literary canon.

[4] A reference that lurks in the background of most work on *Pierre* and sexuality is Henry Murray's 1949 Hendricks House introduction to *Pierre*, which emphasized the importance of the Pierre-Isabel relationship and the corresponding incest plot.

[5] Parker has made this observation at several points in his two-volume biography of Melville, which is discussed in chapter 1.

[6] Robert Shulman followed up on Fiedler's consideration of phallic jokes and innuendos in *Moby-Dick* with his 1961 essay "The Serious Functions of Melville's Phallic Jokes," in which he argued that these jokes concealed satire of "conventional religious, economic, and social values" and powerful self-assertion as an author. Shulman and Fiedler had been preceded in their considerations of Melville's sexual humor by E. H. Eby's "Herman Melville's Tartarus of Maids" (1940), which had first pointed out the use of female genital imagery in the topographical descriptions in Melville's diptych "The Paradise of Bachelors and the Tartarus of Maids." Carol Fabricant's 1977 article "*Tristram Shandy* and *Moby-Dick*: A Cock and Bull Story and a Tale of the Tub" discussed Laurence Sterne's influence on Melville's sexual humor.

[7] Robyn Wiegman's "Melville's Geography of Gender" (1989) struck a cautionary note with regard to considerations of the homoerotic element in Melville's work and argued that critics like Martin and Boone underestimated Melville's skepticism toward the varieties of "male bonding" described in his novels (735). From a very different vantage point in terms of sexual politics Camille Paglia's *Sexual Personae: Art and Decadence from Nefertiti to Emily Dickinson* (1990), found *Moby-Dick* to be representative of a more conventional sort of masculinity than what they had found in Melville, arguing that femininity appeared in

Moby-Dick as a ghastly apparition to be resisted (as in the case of the great squid, which Paglia identified with female sexuality), and that the novel as a whole was an expression of an embattled but defiantly self-assertive masculinity. While Wiegman's and Paglia's views in general were very different, both found Martin and Boone to be excessively sanguine in their depiction of a Melville who developed alternative masculinities.

[8] For more on the role of mourning in Melville's writing, see Peter Balaam's *Misery's Mathematics* (2009). Balaam expanded the analysis of the relation between Melville's works and those of Catherine Maria Sedgwick that he had begun to develop in his article in *Melville and Women* discussed above.

[9] For more on the role of sexuality in Melville's representations of the Pacific, see William Heath's "Melville and Marquesan Eroticism" (1988) and T. Walter Herbert's *Marquesan Encounters* (1980), which are discussed in chapter 6, and John Bryant's *Melville Unfolding* (2008), which is discussed in chapters 1 and 6, as well as Bryant's *Melville and Repose* (1993), which is discussed in chapter 2. Herbert, Bryant, and Heath all served as sources for Hughes's speculations, and the implications of Melville's Marquesan writings for our understanding of the role of sexuality throughout his career formed an important subplot in both Herbert and Bryant's books and Heath's essay.

5: Aspects of America: Democracy, Nationalism, and War

ONE QUESTION THAT HAS BEEN INESCAPABLE for nearly all Melville scholars is that of Melville's relation to his country. Is Melville the ultimate American author, the writer of the "great American novel" in *Moby-Dick* and the American Shakespeare that he himself prophesied in "Hawthorne and his Mosses"? Or is Melville a fundamentally oppositional figure, standing outside his culture and alternately pouring scorn on its materialism and philistinism and being wounded by its indifference? Or is Melville a symptom of a sicknesses at the heart of American culture — a sign and symbol of American exceptionalism, imperialism, and arrogance? Melville the American classic, Melville the counter-cultural prophet, and Melville the American chauvinist jostle uncomfortably with each other in these readings, raising questions that will run throughout this chapter and recur in the next.

Inquiry into Melville's "Americanness" has been marked more than most areas of Melville study by the willingness, even eagerness, of scholars who do not identify themselves primarily, or in some cases even secondarily as Melvilleans to write extensively on Melville's work — or at the least, carefully selected portions of Melville's work. What this has meant in practical terms is that Americanist discussions of Melville's work have shown the pressure of the wider-ranging arguments within the disciplines of American literature and American history and the interdisciplinary enterprise of American studies into which they were incorporated. Most concretely, it has meant that rather than the full-length studies considered in the earlier chapters of this volume, scholars dealing with Melville from the vantage of American studies have tended to produce chapters devoted to Melville in the midst of longer studies, and as a result, their views of Melville tend to be shaped by larger ideological considerations regarding the shape American literature. This also means that there is perhaps a little less room for the idiosyncratic in these scholars' work, and more of a tendency for individual scholars to arrange themselves into reasonably discrete "schools" of thought on Melville. In this chapter, I examine three angles from which Melville has been viewed as an American author and citizen: as an exemplar and critic of American literary nationalism, as an allegorist of American law and the democratic process, and as narrator and uneasy critic of war and violence in nineteenth-century America.

American Nationalism: Identity and Critique

Many of the early scholars of the Melville Revival were most interested in presenting Melville as a giant of world literature. Perhaps paradoxically, it was an Englishman who inaugurated the tradition of writing about Melville as a characteristic American. D. H. Lawrence's *Studies in Classic American Literature* (1923) took the lead in proclaiming Melville as a central writer in an American canon. Like most of *Studies in Classic American Literature*, Lawrence's chapters on Melville are highly idiosyncratic. What makes Lawrence's criticism in general, and his chapters on Melville in particular, entertaining and engaging, is his propensity to mock and argue with the authors he discusses almost as if he were talking to them in person. (One of the most memorable examples of this from Lawrence's discussion of Melville is "And that's Melville. Oh dear, when the solemn ass brays, brays, brays!" [158].) Lawrence devoted two chapters to Melville, one to *Typee* and *Omoo*, and one to *Moby-Dick*. In the first chapter, Lawrence portrayed Melville as characteristically "American," according to Lawrence's definition, in his attraction to "primitive" South Pacific paradises and his inability ultimately to embrace them. The second chapter is more distinctive, however. There, Lawrence, using his typically colloquial tone, celebrates the strangeness of the novel, highlighting its internal tensions between American respectability and American audacity: "It is the same thing as in all Americans. They keep their old-fashioned ideal frock-coats on, and an old-fashioned silk hat, and they do the most impossible things" (158). Melville was for Lawrence an uptight New Englander who had somehow nonetheless tapped into the most obscure parts of the human soul and unconscious and the most terrifying realities of nature. This tension between staid materialism and mad depths of cosmic insight was not the only element of *Moby-Dick* that Lawrence regarded as characteristically American, however. He also saw the multi-racial, multi-ethnic cast of characters as representative of American experience, and the conclusion as the death of an American identity predicated upon whiteness. Moby Dick himself was, in Lawrence's view, a symbol of "the last phallic being of the white man" (173). Lawrence thus pointed toward later readings of *Moby-Dick* as the great American multicultural novel and toward psychologically oriented readings of *Moby-Dick* as a novel of racial and imperial anxieties. Charles Olson's *Call Me Ishmael* (1947), which is discussed in chapter 2, both followed and expanded Lawrence's model, emphasizing the frontier and the sheer size of America as shaping factors in Melville's art, and adopting much of Lawrence's colloquial and whimsical tone.

On the heels of Lawrence's reading of Melville from the British side of the Atlantic came the first extended effort by an American to put Melville at the center of the American literary canon, Van Wyck Brooks's *The*

Times of Melville and Whitman (1924), in which Brooks made the seemingly rash move of putting Melville alongside Whitman as a representative figure at the heart of the American literary canon. Brooks did this in part by emphasizing the massive popular appeal of *Typee* in the late 1840s, a strategy for establishing Melville's significance that would reemerge only with the cultural studies-oriented approaches to Melville of the 1990s, and in part by describing the alienated genius of *Moby-Dick*, a strategy for establishing Melville's significance that would be common for decades. Less than a decade later, in 1930, the seminal American literary historian Vernon Louis Parrington would inaugurate a crucial strand in Americanist Melville criticism with his observation regarding Melville that "Such a man would not so much turn critic as embody criticism. His life — even more than Emerson's — laid upon America, was a yardstick to measure the shortcomings of a professed civilization" (266). Parrington's words would prove prophetic of a general tendency in Americanist criticism to view Melville as the ultimate cultural outsider in nineteenth-century America — with the paradoxical result that Melville has been surprisingly resilient, more so perhaps even than figures like Emerson, Hawthorne, and Poe, in the face of challenges to the American literary canon.

F. O. Matthiessen's 1941 study *American Renaissance* (discussed in chapter 2), was primarily concerned with aesthetic questions, but it was an exercise in literary nationalism insofar as Matthiessen located the distinctiveness of American literature in its "devotion to the possibilities of democracy" (xiv). Even though Matthiessen did not develop the political implications of his reading of American literature from the 1850s, he was among the most important figures in the discussions of literary nationalism in American literature generally and Melville's work specifically, both because he had done so much to define the contours of a distinctively American canon and because the canon he created (male, white, northern, Romantic) provided later critics with much to react against. Moreover, the tension between Matthiessen the literary critic who established the conventional narrative of the American canon, and Matthiessen the individual, a gay socialist clergyman, would prove irresistible for cultural critics and historians.[1]

Yvor Winters's essay "Herman Melville and the Problems of Moral Navigation" (1938), collected in his large polemical critique of New Critical methods, *In Defense of Reason* (1947), came at the question of Melville's Americanness from another angle. In keeping with much of the criticism of the Melville Revival, Winters began his discussion of Melville with an analysis of the tragic and Calvinistic elements within the novel's implied philosophy and theology, but after making some fairly standard observations along these lines, he turned to the question of literary nationalism. *Moby-Dick* was notable for Winters in that Melville had managed to escape what Winters called "Maule's curse" — a persistent irrationalism characteristic of much

American literature. Winters argued that Melville, by creating Ahab, had diagnosed much of what was wrong with nineteenth-century American literature, and, by doing so, had escaped it.

The distinctiveness of American literature, a key theme for Lawrence, Matthiessen, and Winters, was picked up by Richard Chase during the formative years of American literary studies as an academic discipline. Chase's *The American Novel and Its Tradition* (1957) stood at the head of a long line of studies in the 1950s and 1960s that sought to define American literature as a distinctive tradition: different from European literatures, yes, but also cohesive in its own right. Each of these studies tended to propose a specific key for understanding what made American literature both different and cohesive. The model that Chase proposed for defining the "Americanness" of American literature was that of the romance, a model that would prove enduring both as an influence on other scholars of Chase's generation and as a mystification in need of unmasking for scholars of later generations. Chase built his model on the foundation of the earlier work he had done on Melville: in 1949, he had argued in *Herman Melville: A Critical Study* that Melville was a vital model for post–World War II American culture because he offered a vision of liberalism tempered by tragedy in his work. Melville thus became a sort of premonition of Reinhold Niebuhr and Neo-Orthodox theology with important political implications. In *The American Novel and Its Tradition*, Chase suggested that major American writers distinguished themselves by their ability to overcome facile optimism and by their embrace of the romance rather than the novel as their characteristic literary genre. This choice came with a cost, because it meant that the social texture of American literature was gravely reduced in comparison to English and European models. In making this observation, Chase was indebted to Lionel Trilling's *The Liberal Imagination* (1950), which had initially identified the American literary tradition with the romance rather than the more realistic novel.

Harry Levin's *The Power of Blackness* (1958) focused on the role of canonical American literature as an alternative to materialism and facile optimism in American culture. American literature recognized tragedy and its centrality to human existence, and for Levin as for Chase, Melville enjoyed a commanding position at the pinnacle of a dissident American romance tradition. Richard Sewall, in his *The Vision of Tragedy* (1959), also found *Moby-Dick* to be the supreme American expression of a wider strand of tragedy in world literature. Marius Bewley's *The Eccentric Design: Form in the Classic American Novel* (1959) situated Melville's work in the wider frame of American literature, again by portraying him as a cultural outsider among cultural outsiders, transcending his context in much the same way as his fellow canonical American writers, only more so. Bewley had begun to make his case for Melville earlier, in *The Complex Fate* (1952), and he extended it here, arguing that Melville's perception of the tragic intermixture of moral good and moral evil in human endeavors was the quality that most distinguished him among American writers. It is worth noting, of course, that the understanding of American literature put forward in such studies depended on excluding the sentimental and domestic strand within American writing from serious literary consideration.[2]

R. W. B. Lewis's *The American Adam* (1955) found common ground between the archetypal literary criticism in vogue in the late 1950s and early 1960s and Americanist cultural scholarship, and Lewis continued the tradition of finding Melville's work to be a culmination of the central strands in antebellum American literature and an inescapable influence on the American writers who followed him. In a chapter entitled "Melville: The Apotheosis of Adam," Lewis argues that Melville defined the figure of the "American Adam" as

> the young innocent, liberated from family and social history or bereft of them; advancing hopefully into a complex world he knows not of; radically affecting the world and radically affected by it; perhaps even destroyed — in various versions of the recurring anecdote hanged, beaten, shot, betrayed, abandoned — but leaving his mark upon the world, and a sign in which conquest may later become possible for the survivors. *In hoc signo vince*: the analogy is inescapable, and it was Herman Melville who first made it manifest. (127–28)

Lewis's reference to the dream of the Roman emperor Constantine in which he was promised conquest through the sign of the cross becomes particularly interesting in light of later developments in Melville criticism: although Lewis was not centrally interested in discussing questions of imperialism, the quotation demonstrates the way in which such issues might arise unbidden. For Lewis, however, the prime significance of the American Adam in Melville flowed from the way in which Melville realized the conception of the male outsider as hero. This apotheosis of the outsider, Lewis suggested, was the quintessence of the American literary tradition. Joining Lewis in the emphasis on Melville as a mythmaker and a reconciler of opposites was Leo Marx, whose *The Machine in the Garden* (1964) grouped Melville with Hawthorne as a fierce critic of the "soft pastoralism" of much nineteenth-century American writing, including that of more optimistic Transcendentalists like Emerson and Thoreau (282). What united Americanist critics from Chase to Marx, from the late 1940s to the early 1960s, was their view of Melville as the prototype of the American without illusions, the man who was able to look steadily at his culture and identify its shortcomings.

Joel Porte put particular emphasis on the oppositional quality of the American Romance tradition in general and Melville's writing in particular in his 1969 study *The Romance in America*. Porte focused on those of Melville's works that were typically regarded as falling outside the American canon and as being Melville's angriest and most critical of the American literary mainstream. What connected Melville with Hawthorne and Poe was his "self-conscious concern with the premises of art" (153), which Porte explored in a reading of Melville's little-discussed tale "The Piazza." From there, Porte turned to *The Confidence-Man* and *Pierre*, arguing that both represented a kind of retreat from a revolt against the very idea of romance as it appeared in other nineteenth-century American writers. If Melville had frequently been portrayed as a dissenter from the mainstream pieties of sentimentalism, Porte went further and portrayed him as a figure disillusioned even with his own counter-tradition of the romance. By the time of *Billy Budd*, Porte suggested, Melville had become utterly possessed by his doubts about the possibility of reaching the truth through fiction. As with many of his predecessors, Porte saw Melville as occupying the most extreme outposts of the American literary tradition, taking doubts and uncertainties that appeared in passing in other writers' works relentlessly to their logical conclusions. Melville thus became an outsider among outsiders, a critic even of those who, like Melville, positioned themselves as critics of mainstream American literary culture. It is worth noting, however, that Melville the anti-romance romancer described by Porte was a Melville stripped of the achievements of his early career, including *Moby-Dick*, and of his poetry — a difficulty highlighting one of the challenges Melville's Americanist critics faced: for Melville's position in relation to his national and cultural milieu shifted frequently over the course of his career. Still, the central role that *The Confidence-Man* played in Porte's reading also highlighted the broader direction of Melville studies in the 1960s, mirroring as it did H. Bruce Franklin's and Edgar Dryden's vigorous defenses of the place of *The Confidence-Man* in the Melville canon.

No figure among Melville's American contemporaries was as important to discussions of Melville's status as an American writer as Nathaniel Hawthorne. Richard Brodhead's study *Hawthorne, Melville, and the Novel* (1976) was one of the most broadly influential studies to examine the significance of the Melville-Hawthorne relationship for the development of American literature. Brodhead regarded Melville as an intellectual and spiritual explorer — a "diver" — to use the metaphor that Melville himself applied to Emerson, and he thus stressed Melville's connections with the visionary goals of Emerson and Thoreau, arguing that Melville sought consistently to relate "organic reality" to consciousness (152). For Brodhead, then, Melville's status as an American writer derived from his affinities with other writers who connected the physical and spiritual or intellectual worlds in compelling ways.

Even as Brodhead was setting Melville and Hawthorne together in the context of New England Transcendentalism and the accompanying spiritual ferment, other writers were looking further west in order to understand Melville's American art. In keeping with the growing emphasis on the eminence of *The Confidence-Man* among Melville's works in the 1960s and 1970s, Warwick Wadlington placed Melville's *The Confidence-Man* within the wider context of confidence games in nineteenth-century America in his ambitious study *The Confidence Game in American Literature* (1975), which narrated the development of the confidence man as a figure in American popular culture and folklore, using Melville as its point of departure.

The impulse to incorporate Melville into broadly explanatory frameworks for understanding American culture reached a kind of zenith with Sacvan Bercovitch's *The American Jeremiad* (1978), which reshaped American Studies as a whole and Melville studies in particular through its emphasis on the power of the sermon to create opinion in nineteenth-century America. As discussed in chapter 2, R. P. Blackmur had in the 1930s identified the sermon as Melville's most characteristic genre; Bercovitch found that a specific subgenre of the sermon, the jeremiad, had been determinative for the development of American culture in the nineteenth century and earlier, and he read Melville as a vital commentator on this influence. The jeremiad, a sermonic form named for the biblical prophet Jeremiah and built around a call for a chosen people to return to a vanished virtue, was central to American culture according to Bercovitch because of the way in which it encompassed both severe critiques of social norms and affirmations of a larger national mission. Melville was especially important for Bercovitch because he cleverly revealed the ways in which critique and consensus coexisted in American culture. *Pierre* was essential to understanding this side of Melville, because in the chapter "The Journey and the Pamphlet," Melville had shown how Plotinus Plinlimmon, a radical reformer, could at the same time put forward a cynical reconciliation of God's time and human time. For Bercovitch, this curious mixture of idealism and cynicism was also at the heart of the Ishmael-Ahab contrast in *Moby-Dick*. Melville was essential for understanding the contradictions of American culture, Bercovitch suggested, precisely because he had understood them so well, while still being shaped by them. Bercovitch's work was a watershed moment in both American literary criticism and Americanist Melville criticism because it suggested that the gap between mainstream American society and the prophetic role of its most revered writers was smaller than might initially appear.

This insight would be developed further in a very influential collection edited by Bercovitch and Myra Jehlen a few years later: *Ideology and Classic American Literature* (1986), in which, in an essay entitled "Art, Religion, and the Problem of Cultural Authority in *Pierre*" the distinguished scholar of Puritanism and the American Revolution Emory Elliott argued that major American writers "argued with" but ultimately "preserved . . . an American ideological consensus" (337). Between his work in writing *The American Jeremiad* and editing *Ideology and Classic American Literature*, Bercovitch became a leading inspiration for the scholars who were sometimes loosely grouped together as the "New Americanist" movement during the 1980s and 1990s — first by their detractors, and then by the scholars in question themselves. His suspicion of the view that nineteenth-century American writers could be seen as exclusively critics of the follies of the wider culture became a part of the received wisdom for a generation of Americanist critics.[3]

The idea of the romance as a peculiarly American form, which had been widely influential from the 1950s through the 1970s, was both resonant and contested in the 1980s. In an exceptionally illuminating study, Michael Davitt Bell took up the question of the romance as a tool for understanding American literary culture in his 1980 study *The Development of American Romance: The Sacrifice of Relation*. Bell argued that the story of the American Romance as a genre extending from Charles Brockden Brown and Washington Irving through Poe, Hawthorne, and Melville was not simply an escape from social reality, but an expression of active alienation from the world as it was, and thus suffused with revolutionary potential, at the same time that many of its practitioners were uncomfortable with its potential revolutionary political implications. As was the case with so many studies of antebellum American literature, Melville appeared at the end of the study, and Bell explicitly argued Melville represented a "culmination" of the American Romance tradition, suggesting that tensions between the revolutionary and the conservative elements within the romance were raised to a particularly high pitch in Melville's work (195). Bell tracked the early revolutionary promptings in Melville's novels of the South Pacific and *White-Jacket* through what he regarded as Melville's self-conscious confrontations of the tension between these promptings and Melville's ironic perceptions of the illusions associated with Messianic revolutionary assertion in *Moby-Dick* and *Pierre*. These last two works, Bell suggested, represented the point in Melville's career when he posed most directly the central question of the American Romance: the question of whether there could be a "relation" (to use the term from Bell's subtitle) between revolutionary or (to use a psychological-sociological term Bell favored) deviant promptings, and one's actual life in the world. Bell found that these questions were answered, or at least evaded meaningfully, through the self-conscious irony of the utterances of characters like Ishmael in *Moby-Dick* and Plotinus Plinlimmon in *Pierre*. By the time of the *The Confidence-Man*, Melville's vision of truth, and the American Romance tradition as a whole, had dissolved completely into irony, demonstrating the ultimate failure of the tradition to manage successfully its own contradictions.

John Carlos Rowe was a leading voice in the rethinking of American literary history that followed in the wake of Bercovitch's broadly influential work. Rowe applied the methodologies of deconstruction and the

New Historicism in his studies. In *Through the Custom-House* (1982) Rowe focused on *Pierre*, *The Confidence-Man*, and "Bartleby the Scrivener." In a chapter entitled "Ecliptic Voyaging: Orbits of the Sign in Melville's 'Bartleby the Scrivener,'" Rowe argued that within a wider body of nineteenth-century American literature that objected to America's "increasing neglect of our spiritual nature," Melville's work indicated the gaps and self-delusion that inhabited this critique (111). A decade and a half later, in *At Emerson's Tomb* (1997), Rowe took up Elliott's consideration of *Pierre* from *Ideology and Classic American Literature* and argued that Melville was uniquely critical of "the ideological consequences of literary production" in nineteenth-century America and thus "anticipated the cultural criticism of our own present moment" (95). As the examples of Bercovitch, Bell, and Rowe make clear, even as scholars rethought their basic assumptions about the meaning of American literature in general, Melville still continued to enjoy nearly as special a place among the New Americanist critics of the 1980s and 1990s as he did among earlier generations. Poe, Hawthorne, and Emerson were all being revaluated quite critically, but Melville was still treated as an exception, a writer who always maintained a critical distance from the foibles of his times.

John P. McWilliams's *Hawthorne, Melville, and the American Character* (1984) tracked the evolution of Melville's ideas about America. McWilliams started with an analysis of the views of America put forward in Melville's early novels, emphasizing Melville's optimism about the American democratic prospect. In this way, McWilliams departed from what had become accepted wisdom for many critics — the view that Melville was always primarily a critic of his culture and a cultural outsider throughout his career. When he turned to *Moby-Dick*, McWilliams concentrated on Melville's consistent application of landscape imagery from America to the sea and noted the frequent metaphors that made a western prairie of the Pacific and the implicit analogies between Queequeg and James Fenimore Cooper's Indian heroes. Ultimately, McWilliams argued, *Moby-Dick* marked a turning point in Melville's relationship with his culture: his choice to kill off the imposing figure of Bulkington indicated his disillusionment with the possibility of a truly American hero appearing. McWilliams saw Melville's magazine fiction, *The Confidence-Man* and *Pierre*, and later *Battle-Pieces* and *Clarel* as reflections of the increasingly bitter disillusionment that followed *Moby-Dick*, and thus he concluded with the idea of Melville as literary outsider that he had initially seemed to be undermining. Reflecting on the tension between early nationalistic optimism and later disillusionment, McWilliams concludes, "The substance of Melville's heroic national vision can never now be attained, but the vision itself is not likely to be abandoned. It is the ineradicable, ever-receding future that our cultural heritage inflicts upon us" (225). In a way, McWilliams's narrative of Melville's career was a mirror image of Bell's, but with reverse politicial implications: for Bell, an early revolutionary impulse was eroded by irony, whereas for McWilliams, an early nationalist and cultural chauvinism became replaced by a more critical attitude.

Despite the generally accepted view of Melville as an outsider to the American literary marketplace, his position in relation to this marketplace has always been important to Melville criticism. Indeed, when William Charvat was pioneering the field of scholarly studies of the American literary marketplace in the nineteenth century, Melville was among the authors he considered at the greatest length. And in *American Romanticism and the Marketplace* (1985), Michael Gilmore compared Melville with such other leading American Romantics as Emerson, Thoreau, and Hawthorne. Gilmore argued that Melville's two most enduring works, *Moby-Dick* and "Bartleby, the Scrivener," were both conceived in reaction to a culture in which money was presumed to buy everything. Ahab's pursuit of *Moby-Dick* in this reading is not so much a grand metaphysical quest as an attempt at "attacking the commodity form" — making the world a place where human values supersede commercial ones (116). In "Bartleby," by the same token, Gilmore focused especially on the significance of its subtitle, "A Tale of Wall Street," arguing that the story that the lawyer-narrator tells in the short story is a narrative of the shift in America to an increasingly "impersonal market system" (135). For Gilmore, Melville was particularly astute as a narrator and critic of the increasing commodification of American culture in the nineteenth century.

Myra Jehlen's *American Incarnation: The Individual, the Nation, and the Continent* (1986), also placed Melville firmly in the context of nineteenth-century American material history. Jehlen argued that *Pierre* embodies both the seductions and perils of American individualism, with its incest plot functioning as a metaphor for self-contained individualism, and the collapse first of Pierre's literary ambitions and then his sanity demonstrating the inevitable deconstruction of a culture built on individualism. For Jehlen, "Pierre is the stone on which the church of his civilization had been built, and the stone that, self-hurled at the altar, has toppled it forever" (185). Thus Jehlen suggested that Pierre, more than Ishmael or Ahab, represented in one person the perennial crisis of American individualistic identity.

The question of individualism as a central American trait would be addressed powerfully by Donald Pease one year later. Of all the critics loosely grouped together under the name "New Americanists," none had a wider-ranging influence. Pease was both an editor of several important New Americanist collections and the author of what many supporters and opponents of the New Americanists saw as the paradigmatic New Americanist essay on Melville. In "Moby-Dick and the Cold War" in *The American Renaissance Reconsidered* (1985), which Pease co-edited with Walter Benn Michaels, and "Melville and Cultural

Persuasion," the capstone chapter in Pease's influential study *Visionary Compacts: American Renaissance Writings in Cultural Context* (1987), Pease analyzed the role that *Moby-Dick* had played in the imagination of twentieth-century American culture. For Pease, the story of nineteenth-century American literature could only be understood by those who comprehended the role of twentieth-century politics, and particularly the Cold War between the United States and the Soviet Union, in shaping the very definition of nineteenth-century American literature as it was studied and taught in the twentieth century. Nineteenth-century American literature was, in Pease's view, used to give legitimacy to a twentieth-century cultural consensus that identified America with liberty and the Soviet Union with totalitarianism, and thus helped justify the Cold War and the policies associated with it. Pease saw the work of critics like Richard Chase and Charles Feidelson as reinforcing a Cold War consensus that separated culture from politics and led intellectuals toward quietism. Twentieth-century individualism, expressed as a preference for symbolism and aesthetic complexity over allegory and political virtue by critics like Chase and Feidelson, cut literary intellectuals off from the crucial moral, social, and economic issues of their time.

This did not mean that Pease regarded nineteenth-century American literature only through the lens of the Cold War himself. Rather, he suggested that in its own context, nineteenth-century American literature was concerned with developing a sense of shared endeavor and community that could make American liberty something more than individualistic license, and with undermining facile tendencies towards consensus that arose out of the mythology of the American Revolution as the defining event for the new nation — thus inverting the goals that Pease attributed to critics of American literature in the Cold War era. Melville was particularly important to Pease's reading of the relation between nineteenth and twentieth-century American cultures, because, Pease argued, "*Moby-Dick*, the nineteenth-century social text, resists the procedures involved in forming a modern canon, just as its subject matter resisted or more precisely disarticulated the ruling mythos in the nineteenth century" (235). Captain Ahab, for Pease, stood in for the consensus-building power of invocations of the American Revolution in nineteenth-century America, whereas Ishmael represented "subversive narrative energies" (243). Moreover, Captain Ahab's method of stifling dissent by co-opting his dissenters (specifically Starbuck, in the quarter-deck passage that Pease analyzes) could be seen as a premonition of the modes of persuasion used during the Cold War, where an absolute opposition between Soviet totalitarianism and American democracy could be used to stifle all debate. Indeed, Pease suggested that even the subversive Ishmael is ultimately absorbed by Ahab's rhetoric, finally constituting "a single self-conflicted will" (274). Having made this connection, Pease then turned to F. O. Matthiessen's *American Renaissance* (1941), to show how Matthiessen, himself a socialist and dissenter from the Cold War consensus, wrote dissent out of the story of American literature — with *American Renaissance*, Matthiessen's most influential work, operating as the consensual device that excludes Matthiessen's own personal and political dissent. In an ingenious if convoluted argument, Pease identified *Moby-Dick* in its status as a classic of American literature as an embodiment of an oppressive consensus, and *Moby-Dick* in its status as a nineteenth-century artifact written by Melville as a critique of that same consensus. This double suggestion, of Melville as both a relic of a previous generation of criticism that must be overcome and as a fierce dissenter from the earlier generation's consensus who must be rehabilitated in order to be read properly, would prove persuasive to many Americanist critics in the 1980s and 1990s, as would Pease's suggestion that Melville's work exposed the means by which dissent was often co-opted. As clever and influential as Pease's argument was, it is hard not to find it a bit confined by its own Cold War context, and by Pease's tendency to engage with a relatively limited range of prior Melville criticism. Nonetheless, Pease unquestionably opened a wider range of possibilities for political readings of Melville than had previously existed.

Following Pease, both chronologically and thematically, William V. Spanos's *The Errant Art of "Moby-Dick"* (1995) captured much of what was curious about the New Americanist controversy as it impinged on Melville studies. Ostensibly about Melville and *Moby-Dick*, the study was heavily framed by a mix of Martin Heidegger's theory of reading as *destruction* and an understanding of American history in which the period from roughly the landing of the Separatists at Plymouth in the early seventeenth century to the escalation in Vietnam in the mid-1960s was a long, fairly uniform prologue to the Vietnam War, and the decades since were a dismal afterword to the war. Crowning these philosophical and historical standpoints was the literary historical view, supported heavily with quotations from Donald Pease, that the "American Renaissance" was an invention of American Cold War discourse. This perhaps explains why a book with "*Moby-Dick*" in the title could devote less time than one might expect to Melville.

Spanos reassured readers that in fact Melville had "proleptically delegitimated" the discourses responsible for the Vietnam War, but this reassurance was not supported by a particularly detailed discussion of *Moby-Dick*, Melville's own political context, or specific details of Melville criticism as it had developed over the years. Most Melvilleans, it seemed, were "Old Americanists," and thus part of the problem. One of the most curious omissions in this regard was the fact that H. Bruce Franklin, who had enlisted Melville on behalf of the anti-war movement in the 1960s and 1970s, was absent from the study altogether. Spanos's ingenious readings of some elements of *Moby-Dick* and his eminently defensible conclusion that Melville was a critic of rather than a cheerleader for American expansionism, were compromised by a lack of engagement with prior Melville scholarship and a tendency to engage in political speculations that, whatever their own merits, seemed to have a slender basis in Melville's novel. Spanos's 2007 study *Herman Melville and the American Calling* expanded the scope of his earlier work to include Melville's later fiction (albeit none of his poetry). The argument remained consistent, in that Spanos again saw Melville as a misunderstood and prescient critic of mainstream American culture, and particularly American exceptionalism, in the nineteenth century and beyond, and he regarded previous Melville criticism as being largely unaware of this crucial insight. Although Spanos's own readings of Melville were often highly defensible, it is hard to see that they marked an absolute break from prior Melville criticism, as these two studies at times seem to imply.

From the 1980s on, a variety of critiques of the New Americanist approaches to nineteenth-century American literature appeared, most notably Frederick Crews's "Whose American Renaissance?" (1988). Crews's criticisms of the New Americanists drew a variety of responses; among the most measured and judicious was Michael P. Kramer's "Imagining Authorship in America: 'Whose American Renaissance' Revisited" (2001). In one of the more expansive treatments of the New Americanist controversy, G. R. Thompson and Eric Carl Link contributed a careful and exhaustive critique of New Americanist strategies for engaging Melville in *Neutral Ground: New Traditionalism and the American Romance Controversy* (1999). Thompson and Link were especially concerned to demonstrate that the idea of the American romance was not an invention either of Cold War literary critics or even of Nathaniel Hawthorne, but was rather the product of nineteenth-century America's engagement with Europe. Thompson and Link criticized the New Americanists for a lack of historical perspective while acknowledging that their scholarship had contributed substantially to an expanded and enriched literary canon. They advocated what they called a "New Traditionalism," which would make the most of the expanded canon while preserving a respect for the accomplishments of earlier Americanist scholars. With regard to Melville, they argued that Pease's view of *Moby-Dick* as having been reinvented as a Cold War text by earlier Americanist critics was overstated and ignored the significance of the romance designation for Melville himself. Ultimately, Thompson and Link argued for an understanding of Melville that attended carefully to the critical milieu of his own time.

Lawrence Buell revisited the recurring questions of both Melville's literary greatness and his representative Americanness in his 2008 essay "The Unkillable Dream of the Great American Novel." Buell traced the origin of the idea of the Great American Novel to John William DeForest's introduction of the term less than two decades after Melville's publication of *Moby-Dick*, and followed it through its permutations over the years. Buell argued that *Moby-Dick*'s prinicipal claim to the title of Great American Novel status was derived somewhat paradoxically from Ishmael's cosmopolitan references to the crew of the *Pequod* as an "Anacharsis Clootz deputation" and from the novel's sense of American identity as an unfinished work in progress. For Buell, Melville's references to Anacharsis Clootz and his deputation before the Parliament of Man in the days after the French Revolution suggested prominent nineteenth-century historian "Eric Foner's glass-half-empty, ironic but hopeful scenario of freedom in US history as a history of not-yet-realization" (149). Buell's argument here demonstrated how thoroughly and decisively readings of Melville and American literary nationalism had shifted their focus to America's relationship with the broader world.

It was appropriate, then, that Hester Blum reintroduced the strand in Melville scholarship that emphasized his affiliation with the sea, that most universal of sources of human experience, in her 2008 study *The View from the Masthead* (2008). Blum examined the ways in which Melville's work was enmeshed in already existing paradigms for maritime literature and how it influenced new developments in the field. Perhaps Blum's most significant contribution to Melville scholarship was her insistence that rather than moving quickly from anonymous sailor's narratives or those by little-known authors in the background to Melville in the foreground, readers and scholars should follow Melville back into a deeper engagement with the American literature of the sea. It is not difficult to suppose that Melville would have approved this call for deeper engagement with the literal lives and livelihoods of sailors.

Melville and Democracy: Politics, Law, and the Democratic Process

The question of what it meant to be an American was not the sole question Melville critics have asked regarding Melville's association with his country, however. A more pressing question in recent years has concerned what sort of American Melville was. How did he fit into the cultural and political spectrum of his time? Is there any way to think of him other than as either a conformist or a critic? What were Melville's views on matters of politics and law, the stuff of both democracy generally and of his own family life? The studies discussed below attempted to answer just such questions. Perry Miller's *The Raven and the Whale* (1956) presented a Melville who was not so much a man of the sea as an author shaped by urban literary environments and conventions. Miller examined Poe and Melville in light of the competing cultural and political factions in New

York City: "Young America," associated with the northern wing of the Democratic Party and literary intellectuals like Evert Duyckinck, and the Knickerbocker Set, associated with the Whig Party and literati like Henry Wadsworth Longfellow and Lewis Gaylord Clark. The Knickerbocker Set carried on the literary traditions of Washington Irving, a benefactor of Melville's whom Melville somewhat ungratefully criticized in "Hawthorne and His Mosses," while the Young America movement had close connections to Melville's family, and was led by the Evert and George Duyckinck, two of Melville's most important supporters during the time he was writing *Moby-Dick*. Miller's study was the first to consider seriously how Melville fit into the divergent political and social views of his time.

It would be easy to forget, in the midst of all the analysis of the specific character of American literature, that nineteenth-century Americans were deeply divided, most profoundly by slavery, but also by a host of other issues. Charles H. Foster took a political angle into his consideration of *Moby-Dick*, arguing that the novel could be read as an attack on the Fugitive Slave Act in his article "Something in the Emblems: A Reinterpretation of *Moby-Dick*" (1961). On a more ambitious scale, Alan Heimert put forward one the most explicitly political readings of *Moby-Dick* in his essay "*Moby-Dick* and American Political Symbolism" (1963, which analyzed the competing sea metaphors used by Democrats and Whigs during the 1840s and 1850s and used these metaphors as a background for understanding Melville's political stance in *Moby-Dick*, drawing on the rhetoric of the "Young America" wing of the Democratic party and the oratory of Daniel Webster and the poetry of Henry Wadsworth Longfellow from the Whig party. Heimert brilliantly sums up the ways in which the form of *Moby-Dick* was shaped by the political and oratorical cultures of the 1850s:

> In the *Pequod* Melville created a ship strikingly similar to those which rode the oratorical seas of 1850. It sails under a red flag, and its crew — in all its "democratic dignity" — comprises a "deputation from all the isles of the earth." But the *Pequod* is clearly reminiscent of Longfellow's *Union*; it is put together of "all contrasting things" from the three sections of the United States: "oak and maple, and pine wood, iron and pitch and hemp." And the *Pequod* is manned (as we are reminded at each crucial moment along its career) by *thirty* isolatoes — all, Melville remarked "federated along one keel." (501)

Heimert demonstrated that Melville's achievement in *Moby-Dick* was in part the product of his ability to draw on metaphors from widely divergent political viewpoints, but he also argued that Melville took sides in the most important disputes of his day. In particular, Heimert read *Moby-Dick* and the earlier *Mardi* as implicit (and at times explicit) critiques of the tendency toward imperialism in the rhetoric of the national Democratic party, and especially of its Southern wing. Controversially, Heimert suggested that Captain Ahab had a clear counterpart on the American political scene in 1850: the pro-slavery South Carolina Democratic Senator John C. Calhoun. In this, Heimert differed with Charles Foster's earlier identification of Ahab with Daniel Webster, and re-oriented Foster's view of *Moby-Dick* as an attack on the Fugitive Slave Law to a broader attack on imperialism and racism in nineteenth-century America and an expression of revulsion on the part of the Northern "Young America" wing of the Democratic Party against the extremism and "monomania" of Southern Democrats. Heimert also found Melville's stance to be ambivalent — that Melville hated slavery but was uncomfortable with abolitionists, whom he also parodied as monomaniacs. The central monomaniac, however, was always Calhoun as Ahab, with Daniel Webster and his federalism taking the place of Moby Dick, understood as a metaphor for a Hobbesian political "leviathan." Heimert even managed to find a political corollary for one of *Moby-Dick*'s shortest-lived characters, identifying Bulkington, who is lost at the outset of the *Pequod*'s journey, with Western Democratic Senator Thomas Hart Benton. Heimert's Melville was thus anything but an apolitical figure musing upon the tragedy of the human condition: he was a man fully engaged in the politics of his time and nation.

Marvin Fisher's *Going Under* (1977) provided an analysis of Melville's short fiction that acknowledged the political pressures of Melville's time. Social and political issues were especially relevant to Melville's magazine fiction because of the degree to which magazines embraced the specific political line of one or another of the major political parties, and Fisher showed how Melville's work fit into wider impulses within the field of American magazine publishing. Fisher saw Melville as an "underground messiah of American letters" who chronicled the political, social, and religious crises of one of the most divisive decades in American history in a fundamentally subversive manner (213).

Henry Nash Smith examined Melville's relationship to democracy in his study *Democracy and the Novel* (1978), but curiously he did so largely by focusing on the dictatorial personality of Ahab. Making use of psychological approaches to the novel, Smith argued that Ahab resists reductive political readings of his character, as Melville refuses to supply sufficient sociological justification for the captain's madness. Ultimately, for Smith, *Moby-Dick*'s status as a tragedy outweighed its relation to democratic culture: Ahab is an individual inexplicable by reference to sociological analysis, and thus the chapter devoted to *Moby-Dick* proved to be a sort of anomaly in a study otherwise concerned with democracy. What Smith recognized that seems significant is Melville's resistance to being taken on other terms than his own, a resistance that parallels Ahab's own intransigence.

The question of justice and the role of political power came to the fore in Barbara Johnson's "Melville's Fist: The Execution of Billy Budd"

(1979). Johnson, who made her name by applying the methods of deconstructive and psychoanalytic literary theory to the work of nineteenth-century American authors, traced the contradictions and oppositions at the heart of Melville's portrait of military justice on the high seas in *Billy Budd*. She argued that it was possible to start with the question of the justice of Billy's execution, and to move from there to an inquiry about the nature of knowledge itself and its relationship to language. Johnson's essay forecast both the growing interest in *Billy Budd* on the part of legal studies scholars through her discussion of the language of military justice, and the emphasis on the part of these scholars on matters of language and epistemology.

Like Johnson, Larzer Ziff addressed questions of authority and history in his 1981 study *Literary Democracy*. Ziff's wide-ranging study of nineteenth-century American writers from George Lippard to Harriet Beecher Stowe was framed by chapters on Melville, with a chapter on *Typee* that made Melville's preference for history over myth in that novel the grounds for the development of the democratic novel at the beginning, and chapters on *Moby-Dick* and *The Confidence-Man* at the end. The concluding chapters examined the tension in these two works between the energies unleashed by democracy on the one hand, and the potentially negative effects of democracy on the possibilities of literary art, which after all had its roots in myth, on the other.

Michael Paul Rogin's *Subversive Genealogy* (1983) expanded the concern with American politics that had appeared in the work of Sacvan Bercovitch and John Carlos Rowe, drawing particularly on Melville's family history. Although Rogin used a psychoanalytical framework reminiscent of Edwin Haviland Miller's to understand Melville's relations with his father and brothers, Rogin was less concerned with the psychology of Melville's familial relationships than with the roles these family members, including Melville's brothers Gansevoort and Allan, and his father-in-law Lemuel Shaw, played in the public sphere. As a political scientist and historian, Rogin was well situated to comment on Gansevoort Melville's engagement with Democratic Party politics and Shaw's influence on American jurisprudence and business practices. Rogin argued that Herman Melville defined himself in part by resistance to the more standard political allegiances of his family members, thus subverting both familial hierarchies and American capitalist and expansionist ideologies.

Discussions of democracy have enduring links to discussions of the social mechanisms and disciplines necessary to run a self-governing society, and in the late 1980s, two aspects of social discipline came to be of special interest to Melville scholars. Robert Shulman's ambitious study *Social Criticism and Nineteenth-Century American Fictions* (1987) considered Melville alongside such other major American authors as Hawthorne and Poe in their concern with the American penal system. In

1989, meanwhile, *Cardozo Studies in Law and Literature* published a special issue examining *Billy Budd* in the light of contemporary legal studies. Legal theory and crime and punishment would flourish as topics for Melville criticism throughout the 1990s and beyond.

Law had been a concern of Melville scholarship before 1989; as discussed above, Barbara Johnson had dealt with matters of law and justice in her 1979 essay "Melville's Fist," and even earlier, C. B. Ives had argued on the basis of British case law that Billy Budd was not hanged out of absolute legal necessity in his article "*Billy Budd* and the Articles of War" (1962). Charles Reich had introduced *Billy Budd* to the field of law and literature with his essay "The Tragedy of Justice in *Billy Budd*" (1967), and five years later, Jack W. Ledbetter had followed suit with the essay "The Trial of Billy Budd, Foretopman" (1972). Christopher Sten, who was to make a name for himself as a Melville scholar in the areas of aesthetics and the visual arts, had weighed in in 1975 in "Vere's Use of 'Forms': Means and Ends in *Billy Budd*," considering the ethical question that he believed Vere had to face: "Does the end — civilization — justify the inevitable sacrifice of the natural man?" (38). Robert Cover's "Of Creon and Captain Vere" from *Justice Accused* (1975), meanwhile, had used Captain Vere, along with the character of Creon from *Antigone*, as examples of judicial inflexibility. In the early 1980s, Richard H. Weisberg had brought Billy Budd into the context of modern jurisprudence with his essay "How Judges Speak: Some Lessons for Adjudication in Billy Budd, Sailor, with an Application to Justice Rehnquist" (1982) and his book-length study *The Failure of the Word* (1984), in which he had gone beyond Cover to argue that Captain Vere was an absolute villain who had manipulated the law for his own purposes, including the tawdry motive of professional envy, rather than following the law. By 1984, William Domnarski had been able to write a precis of prior legal criticism on *Billy Budd*, suggesting that the novella was firmly established as a standard law and literature text. Meanwhile, Robert Ferguson's 1984 study *Law and Letters in American Culture* had stressed the relation between Vere's reasoning in *Billy Budd* and both the movement in literature from Romanticism to Realism and in law from moralism to professionalism, with particular reference to the opinions of Oliver Wendell Holmes, Jr. Ferguson also expanded the number of Melville texts under consideration by law and literature scholars by bringing Melville's early novel *White-Jacket* into the mix as an example of the earlier moralism and Romanticism of American legal and literary cultures. Several years later, Brook Thomas's 1987 study *Cross-Examinations of Law and Literature* had been more expansive still, considering *Benito Cereno*, "Bartleby, the Scrivener," and *The Confidence-Man*. Like Michael Paul Rogin, Thomas found Melville's relation to his father-in-law, Lemuel Shaw, to be particularly important to understanding his view of the law.

Despite the volume of previously published legal criticism on *Billy Budd*, however, the special issue of *Cardozo Studies in Law and Literature* devoted to the novella represented an important departure, in that it both consolidated earlier scholarship and indicated Melville's arrival as part of a select group of seminal literary authors for study among legal scholars. Several articles were of particular interest. Judith Schenck Koffler's "The Feminine in *Billy Budd*" suggested that the importance of *Billy Budd* for legal scholarship lay not so much in traditional readings of the justice or injustice of Billy Budd's execution as in the novella's representation of "the feminine in man." Koffler contended that *Billy Budd* could be read profitably in a legal context for its invocations of homo-eroticism and androgyny, an approach that, as chapter 4 of this study notes, was becoming increasingly influential elsewhere in literary and cultural studies at the time. Melville, Koffler believed, was trying to "preserve from the strangulating gaze of modern society the life-giving possibility of erotic love, the love of men for men" (2). Richard H. Weisberg continued to expand his scathing critique of Captain Vere in his essay "Accepting the Insider Narrator's Challenge: Billy Budd and the 'Legalistic' Reader." Richard A. Posner's "Comment on Richard Weisberg's Interpretation of 'Billy Budd'" suggested that in vilifying Vere so thoroughly Weisberg had misread the novella; Vere, for Posner, was a legal thinker trying to reach wise decisions on utilitarian grounds, possibly mistaken, but not indefensible. Posner, himself as of this writing a judge on the US Court of Appeals for the Seventh Circuit, had also dealt with *Billy Budd* in *Law and Literature: A Misunderstood Relation* (1988). Steven Mailloux also responded to Weisberg in his essay "Judging the Judge," in which he argued that Captain Vere executes Billy Budd because he cannot deal with "the threat of political and intellectual chaos," and that his readings of the law are ultimately meant to be persuasive (86). Taken as a whole, the special *Cardoza* issue announced that *Billy Budd* could now be regarded as an inescapable part of the law and literature canon in America, and it framed the terms for future debate on *Billy Budd* in much the same way that the concept of a "testament of acceptance" had for religiously oriented criticism of the novella sixty years earlier.

Moving away from specifically legal topics, but still closely concerned with matters of politics and democratic procedure, Nancy Fredericks picked up the question of Melville's relation to democracy in her study *Melville's Art of Democracy* (1995). Fredericks wrote that democracy, far from being peripheral to Melville's work, formed a kind of conceptual core for Melville's fiction. Fredericks investigated Melville's use of the Kantian philosophical categories to diagnose potential threats to democracy, and she also put forward a series of readings that argued for Melville's sympathy with those subject to class, race, and gender-based exploitation. Fredericks's driving aim was to contend that Melville deserved to be seen as a nineteenth-century prophet of radical democracy in many of his antebellum works, and that aesthetic analysis of Melville's work could confirm this generally political argument.

Synthesizing the concern with broad political principles that appears in Fredericks's work with the more technical legal consideration explored by the legal studies critics, David Suchoff's "Melville: Ironic Democracy" in *Critical Theory and the Novel* (1994) also made Melville's approach to the democratic process central to a re-reading of Melville's significance. Drawing on Theodor Adorno and Max Horkheimer's theories of the "culture industry," Suchoff argued that Melville's work constituted an important critique of the cultural illusions and mystifications of nineteenth-century America. Several years later, Wai-Chee Dimock made Melville a small but important component of her entry into legal studies, *Residues of Justice* (1997), in which she argued that Melville's "The Paradise of Bachelors and the Tartarus of Maids" used gender to highlight class-based oppression. H. Bruce Franklin's essay "Billy Budd and Capital Punishment" (1997) also dealt with the nexus of legal and social matters, arguing that the novella represented an important critique of the justice and morality of capital punishment.

Jeffrey Westover's essay "The Impressments of Billy Budd" (1998) brought concepts from international law to bear on Melville's lasts novella. Westover read *Billy Budd* in view of the British practice of the impressments of American sailors in the course of its wars with France, and found that Melville had probed carefully the ways in which liberties in which Englishmen gloried were undergirded by coercive practices like impressment. As Westover's essay suggested, questions of law in Melville become interesting not only relation to legal theory, but also in relation to the concrete social practices of crime and punishment. Carol Colatrella's *Literature and Moral Reform: Melville and the Discipline of Reading* (2002), looked at Melville's career as a writer of fiction in light of the understanding of rehabilitation and punishment current in nineteenth-century American society. Influenced by Michel Foucault's *Discipline and Punish* (1977), Colatrella tracked images of Melville's protagonists as prisoners from throughout his career, using "Bartleby, the Scrivener" and *Billy Budd* as bookends. Colatrella's Melville was a staunch critic of his society and culture, rejecting religiously oriented and ultimately superficial reformist movements in favor of a more thorough-going social and economic critique.[4] For Colatrella, "Melville's fictions subvert optimistic religious rhetoric in describing how social structures unjustly imprison individuals" (19). The tradition of viewing Melville as an outsider with exceptional insight into his culture thus continued into the twenty-first century. *Billy Budd* would continue to provide grounds for reflection for those wrestling with the legal and moral questions of their own day, as Daniel Solove's 2005 article "Melville's *Billy Budd* and Security in Times of Crisis" would indicate. Solove read the novella as a remarkable premonition of the ethical choices facing American policy-makers in the wake of 9/11, and he found that Melville's last work resonated powerfully with the specific concerns of the early years of the twenty-first century.

The question of Melville's relation to democracy also implied that the social context in which he lived and worked would be of great importance to understanding his art. In the rush to identify Melville as an American, scholars often lost sight of the fact that he was a particular sort of urban American: a man whose life revolved in no small part around New York City. Wyn Kelley followed a path that had been neglected since Perry Miller's work in the 1950s in considering Melville as a writer shaped by urban coteries and urban metaphors in *Melville's City* (1996). Kelley analyzed both Melville's use of urban metaphors and the role that New York and a variety of other cities around the world played in his work. After examining the pressure that New York City's vicissitudes had exerted on Melville's life and family, Kelley turned to the fiction and poetry, beginning with Melville's appropriation of the urbane (and presumptively urban) persona of the flaneur in his novels of the South Pacific. From there, she traced Melville's representations of decaying urban spaces in *Redburn, White-Jacket*, and *Pierre*, and his representations of travelers dealing with a variety of urban spaces in his work as a whole. Particularly insightful was Kelley's division of Melville's work between an early concern with "Sojourners in the City of Man" (chapter 5) and a later interest, reaching its climax in *Clarel*, with "Pilgrims in the City of God" (chapter 6). The great strength of Kelley's study was its Melvillean capacity to take seriously both material realities and spiritual significances in Melville's work, and at the same time to examine Melville as both a representative and a fierce critic of American urban life.

John Evelev also provided an alternative to the view of Melville as a lonely literary outsider in American culture in *Tolerable Entertainment* (2006). Evelev found Melville to be a compelling exemplar of the development of professionalism, literary and otherwise, in nineteenth-century American culture. Evelev followed the steps of Melville's career from his initial success with *Typee* through his more famous failures that followed and his modestly commercially successful magazine fiction, always with an eye to understanding what Melville's work and its fate could teach us about the development of the professions in antebellum America. What was particularly noteworthy about Evelev's work on Melville and professionalism, like that of Hester Blum on the subject of Melville and the sea, was that it demonstrated that Melville was increasingly being used by scholars of American cultural studies as a conduit into discussions of topics that were of great importance to him, such as the life of the sailor or the life of the literary professional. It seems appropriate that an author so deeply invested in the particularities of his time and place, as well as of the books that he loved, should draw later scholars back to those particularities.

Clare Spark's *Hunting Captain Ahab* (2001) was the product of an almost unimaginable amount of archival research, and it was also among the most polemical studies of Melville and the Melville Revival ever written. Spark's project resembled the New Americanist critique of earlier Americanist scholarship in that she saw many earlier Melvilleans as agents of American Cold War ideologies. Unlike the New Americanists, Spark saw Melville himself as being, at least in the years surrounding the writing of *Moby-Dick*, a truly radical critic of conservative American Christianity and capitalism, on behalf of a radically egalitarian vision. Spark also saw Ahab himself as being a truly radical figure — not the imperialist and hubristic John C. Calhoun of Alan Heimert's reading — but a sympathetic expression of Melville's resistance to the nineteenth-century American mainstream. Ishmael, in Spark's reading, was a pitiful expression of an impulse toward conformity. The other major distinction between Spark's work and virtually anyone else's was her intensive research into the papers of many of the most eminent scholars of the Melville Revival, from Raymond Weaver to Henry Murray, Charles Olson, and Richard Chase.

Robert Milder, who has done so much to illuminate Melville's work from the perspectives of both religion and philosophy and gender and sexuality, wrote several important pieces of criticism analyzing Melville's work in relation to democracy. In three pieces that were collected in *Exiled Royalties* (2006), Milder discussed the role of democracy throughout Melville's body of work. In "Melville's Metaphysics of Democracy: Hawthorne and His Mosses" and "Ishmael's Grand Erections," Milder elegantly elucidated the lines of tension in Melville's work between his attitudes as a "political egalitarian" and as "cultural aristocrat" (63). In "Uncivil Wars," Milder analyzed the divisions in Melville's country during the Civil War in relation to the divisions in his family in the 1860s.

Alfred S. Konefsky's "The Accidental Legal Historian" (2004) made the most ambitious claim yet for Melville's significance to legal studies. Konefsky asserted that Melville, one of America's most revered authors, was also one of America's most unjustly ignored legal historians. In fact, Melville's fiction constituted an alternative history of American jurisprudence in the nineteenth-century, and the inequities of American legal practice in the nineteenth century could best be understood by reference to the juridical inanities that Melville described in his magazine fiction and *Billy Budd* in particular. Melville understood the contradictions at the heart of the nineteenth-century conception of freedom in American much better than many professional legal historians.

This viewpoint coincided with the views of a number of Melvilleans in the first decade of the twenty-first century, who more than their predecessors in earlier decades, extended the consideration of Melville and law beyond the confines of *Billy Budd*. John Matteson raised the issue of Melville's treatment of the law and legal issues in two major articles: "'Deadly

Voids and Unbidden Infidelities'" (2006) and "'A New Race Has Sprung Up'" (2008). In the first article, drawing on his reading of that most public of antebellum American lawyers, Daniel Webster, Matteson argued that Melville was an "outlaw writer" who offered in *Moby-Dick* a critique of "outmoded, confining legal forms and institutions" (117, 119). In the second article, Matteson found that the concept of "prudence" advocated at such length by the attorney who narrates "Bartleby, the Scrivener" was in fact a crucial legal and cultural concept in nineteenth-century America. In a line of argument reminiscent of the work of Robert Ferguson from the 1980s, Matteson argued that Melville's probing of the moral rightness of prudence was closely connected to his reflections on the cautious jurisprudence of his father-in-law, Massachusetts chief justice Lemuel Shaw. In Matteson's reading, the narrator of "Bartleby," like Lemuel Shaw, strives to reconcile Christian charity with practical considerations, while in both the story and its historical context, a younger generation is prepared to subordinate all moral considerations to economic ones. "Bartleby," then, became the story of the creation of a new prudential cultural and legal consensus to replace an earlier theological consensus.

Deak Nabers also brought legal studies approaches with cultural studies implications to Melville into the twenty-first century. Nabers devoted the first chapter of his study *Victory of Law* (2006) to a consideration of how *Battle-Pieces* and *Billy Budd* addressed the legal issues surrounding the war and its aftermath. Nabers argued that Melville built *Battle-Pieces* around the legal questions that followed from the Thirteenth and Fourteenth Amendments to the United States Constitution, and that recognizing this fact leads us to realize that there is a greater continuity between Melville's fiction and poetry than is often acknowledged. Nabers suggests that "Melville's newfound legalism does not represent a retreat from his previous interest in unstable characters and insoluble questions. It is, instead, an extension of it" (22). The ambiguities and formal anomalies that shaped *Battle-Pieces* were, for Nabers, an aesthetic corollary to the ambiguities surrounding the status of law in Reconstruction America. Most importantly, perhaps, Nabers pointed out that questions of law and democracy could not avoid taking into account the significance of war, and particularly the Civil War, for any Americanist reading of Melville's work. It is to this matter that we now turn.

"All wars are boyish, and are fought by boys": War, Violence, and Pacifism in Melville's Art

War disrupted Melville's career, the life of the nation, and the story of twentieth-century American literary criticism in different but complementary ways. Melville's career as a writer coincided in its beginning with the Mexican-American War. Melville's abandonment of fiction and embrace of poetry as his prime métier corresponded to the cataclysmic events of the American Civil War, and the story of Melville criticism in the twentieth and twenty-first centuries was punctuated by the First and Second World Wars, the Cold War and its concomitant hot wars in Korea and Vietnam, the two Gulf Wars, and the American war in Afghanistan. Many of the critics discussed above touched on the relevance of war to Melville's work to one degree or another: for the critics whose work is discussed in the remainder of this chapter, war and violence became crucial for any meaningful understanding of Melville's work.

No work by Melville was more explicitly concerned with war than his first published collection of poetry, *Battle-Pieces, and Aspects of the War* (1866). Oddly, however, the statement of one of America's most revered writers on one of its central conflicts was largely ignored for a long time. For example, Edmund Wilson's *Patriotic Gore* (1962), which was the first major twentieth study of the literature of the Civil War, had little to say about Melville, seemingly taking for granted one of the most devastating early critiques of *Battle-Pieces*, distinguished American Realist William Dean Howells's review in *The Atlantic*, which branded the collection as "like no poetry you have every read, and no life you have ever known" (Higgins and Parker, 527). Howells's review would cast a long shadow, and only in the years surrounding the turn of the twenty-first century would *Battle-Pieces* truly receive the respectful attention it deserved.

By the end of the 1960s, contemporary events were pushing Melville scholarship to consider the contemporary political implications of Melville's work with increasing urgency. H. Bruce Franklin was the leading indicator of a shift in Melville studies that would make political readings more central to the enterprise. Franklin had become an increasingly outspoken critic of the Vietnam War during the late 1960s, and he argued that Melville would have shared his sense of the immorality of America's involvement in Southeast Asia. In articles like "The Tarry Hand of Herman Melville" (1976), Franklin argued that the moral intuition behind *Moby-Dick* was a sort of refutation of the rationale for the Vietnam war: pacifist rather than violent, socialist rather than capitalist. If these readings lacked the subtlety of Franklin's earlier scholarly work on Melville, they demonstrated the urgency with which Melville's work could be brought to bear on contemporary conflicts.

Perhaps because the turn to Melville's depictions of war and violence was so much influenced by the events of the 1960s rather than by memories of the 1860s, war and violence would come to the fore in Melville criticism not through *Battle-Pieces*, but through *Moby-Dick*. Richard Slotkin's *Regeneration through Violence* (1973) analyzed Melville's work with a view to understanding the violent undercurrents in American history. Like Franklin, Slotkin wrote in the immediate context of America's involvement in Vietnam, and sought to explain this involvement in terms of America's broader cultural and literary history. Slotkin built his argument that American history was inflected powerfully by the idea of redemptive violence largely with reference to frontier narratives and novels, but he found that Melville was a particularly powerful commentator on this strand in American culture, even though his work rarely dealt directly with the frontier. Slotkin argued that *Moby-Dick* was the great American epic because of Melville's fusing of the tropes of the frontier narrative with the mythology of the sea by means of the hunt, a frontier metaphor transposed into a sea novel by the device of whaling. Slotkin noted that the hunt itself was a form of sacred violence for many of the indigenous cultures of the Americas, and he used the contrast of Ahab and Queequeg to suggest the different mythologies and attitudes toward the natural world of indigenous American and Americans of European descent. Slotkin did not stop with a simple opposition between Ahab and Queequeg, however. Ahab, for Slotkin, represented a compendium of all the characteristics of the nineteenth-century American nation: Ahab is

> the true American hero, worthy to be captain of a ship "whose wood could only be American" and whose name could only be Indian. Like the American pioneer, he has bound men of God and men of nature, Christians and pagans, captives and captors, Chingachgook and Simon Girty, Boone and Mather, Mary Rowlandson and King Philip within the framework of a single, purposeful endeavor, a quest fraught with complex ironies. (549)

Ahab's status as a "true American hero" was rendered ominous for Slotkin by the endeavor in which he and his crew were engaged: "to seek out and murder the very spirit and essence of mind, world, and wilderness" (549). Melville had, in Slotkin's view, given the grandeur and the horror of violence in America its ultimate expression in *Moby-Dick*.

Surely no event in American history epitomizes both the grandeur and the horror that Slotkin diagnosed in Ahab like the Civil War, which began ten years after the publication of Melville's greatest novel. Daniel Aaron's *The Unwritten War* (1973), made Melville a much more important part of its narrative than had Edmund Wilson's earlier *Patriotic Gore*. In a chapter entitled "Melville: The Conflict of Convictions," Aaron suggests that Melville was distinguished from other American authors, like Walt Whitman, by his profound ambivalence about the war:

> Melville read no happy auguries of the War's outcome, nationalist though he was. Whitman detected a providential Hand behind the "Secession War," as if the United States advanced according to some heavenly time table. For him, the War tested American manhood and tempered a nation; for Melville, the massive bloodletting may

have taught Americans something, but in the process mocked the democratic dream. (77)

In a set of observations reminiscent of Leo Marx's *The Machine in the Garden*, Aaron also examined how Melville's poetry stressed the dehumanizing effect of the military technology of ironclad ships in the Civil War in poems such as "A Utilitarian View of the Monitor's Fight," and in Melville's later collection *John Marr and Other Sailors* in the poem "Bridegroom Dick." After a series of readings of poems from *Battle-Pieces* and the Prose Supplement attached to *Battle-Pieces*, Aaron closed by noting that Melville's concern with the Civil War, and his ambivalence about the war, continued to exercise his imagination a decade later, with the appearance of the character of Ungar in Melville's 1876 long poem *Clarel*. The war, Aaron made clear, was an enduring part of Melville's literary legacy.

Aaron's willingness to take seriously Melville's engagement with the Civil War was to gain adherents over the following decades. As we have seen, twentieth-century wars played an important role in shaping Melville's literary reputation, from the First World War to the Cold War and the "hot wars" associated with it, particularly Vietnam. Joyce Sparer Adler was, however, the first to make Melville's general attitude toward war the keystone of her study of Melville. In *War in Melville's Imagination* (1981), Adler argued that Melville was a committed and thoroughgoing pacifist, that "Melville's passion against war was a great dynamic in his imagination and a main shaping force in his art" (3). She supported this argument with evidence from the entire range of works from Melville's career, from *Typee* to *Billy Budd*. In Melville's early novels, Adler examined the way that Melville critiqued a warlike European civilization by contrast with peaceful Marquesan "savagery," thus performing the dual feat of repudiating European cultural and religious chauvinism and renouncing the violence associated with war. When Adler turned to *Mardi* she found that Melville's most explicitly allegorical work moves through a series of critiques of violent societies to the realized utopia of a society of peace in Serenia, the portion of the Mardian archipelago devoted to the pacifist ethical principles of primitive Christianity. Not surprisingly, *White-Jacket* provided Adler with some of her most persuasive evidence for Melville's pacifism, with its powerful depiction of a depraved "man-of-war world" and invocations of pacifist alternatives like the Quakers. Like so many studies of Melville, Adler's reached a crescendo with her discussion of *Moby-Dick*, which she suggested anticipated the twentieth-century terror of a world that could actually be destroyed by the technological progress in the methods of making war. Ahab and the whale thus became particularly evocative for readers in a nuclear age, and Adler's reading of *Moby-Dick* at the beginning of the 1980s can be seen as a reflection of the growing fears of nuclear holocaust that characterized the penultimate decade of the twentieth century. Adler saw the theme of war and peace extending through the material on "Indian-Hating" in *The Confidence-Man* and in Melville's deeply ambivalent Civil War poems in *Battle-Pieces*. Finally, she found Melville's "philosophy of war and peace" to be contained in *Billy Budd* (160): in the case of Captain Vere, war utterly removes the human ability to make a decision based on conscience rather than martial necessity, and is thus absolutely dehumanizing.

If Adler had analyzed Melville's view of war throughout his career, the task of discussing his specific attitude toward the Civil War remained. No single event refuted the idea of a stable nineteenth-century American identity, or an unambiguous definition of American democracy more thoroughly than the Civil War, with its massive bloodshed and its revelation of intractable ideological differences at the heart of the American experiment.[5] Stanton Garner's *The Civil War World of Herman Melville* (1993) took up the challenge of explaining the relationship between Melville's career and the most vital political events of his time. Garner examined the role that each of the members of Melville's extended family of Melvilles, Gansevoorts, Shaws, and Hoadleys played in relation to the war, tracing the various Democratic and Republican political influences on Melville's artistry. Garner used close readings of numerous poems from *Battle-Pieces* to illustrate the complexity of Melville's allegiances during the Civil War. Especially notable were Garner's readings of poems that dealt with the tensions in Northern society during the war, such as "The House-Top." One of the less persuasive aspects of Garner's readings is his occasional eagerness to separate Melville from the views expressed by narrators in the poems. Although Garner's reminder that the speakers in *Battle-Pieces* are not necessarily identical in their views to Melville himself is salutary, it is also true that the sort of totally independent narrators that appear in the dramatic monologues of Robert Browning are hard to identify in Melville's lyrics: indeed, from his earliest novels to his latest poetry, Melville's narrators tend to share important characteristics with Melville himself.[6] When Garner claims that, for example, "The House-Top" is a dramatic monologue on the Browning model and that Melville did not share his speaker's strong distaste for the draft rioters (who caused extensive destruction in New York City during the war and lynched African-Americans) or his ambivalent approval of the riots' suppression, the claim is considerably less persuasive than the portions of the book that are based on extensive historical and familial research (255–57). Nevertheless, the big picture that Garner created of both Melville's personal engagement with the war and the decisive influence of the war on Melville's art remains one of the most compelling treatments of any phase of Melville's career by anyone. In addition to his exhaustive accounting for Melville and his family's activities during the war, Garner showed how the concept of fratricide became integral to Melville's work after the war, from *Battle-Pieces* to *Billy Budd*, and he provided a moving intellectual biography of Melville's development in response to the tension between Melville's own pacifism and his equally personal devotion to the cause of the Union in the Civil War.

The Civil War had played a relatively minor role in Melville criticism prior to Garner's magisterial study of Melville's entanglements with the politics of the war, and as highly respected as Garner's work had been, it did not produce an immediate flood of studies taking up Melville's representations of the war. In the early years of the twenty-first century, however, interest in Melville's poetry and in his relation to the Civil War grew side by side. Two studies along these lines from the end of the twentieth century were Rosanna Warren's "Dark Knowledge: Melville's Poems of the Civil War" (1999) and Helen Vendler's "Melville and the Lyric of History" (1999). Warren, the daughter of the influential novelist, poet, and editor of Melville's poetry Robert Penn Warren, argued that Melville had come closer to writing what Walt Whitman called "the real war" than any of his contemporaries — a position that challenged directly William Dean Howells's initial negative reviews of the poetry and the consensus to which it led (102). Warren believed that the greatness of *Battle-Pieces* ultimately proceeded from the way in which it "war[red] on illusion" through the very unorthodox prosody for which it was frequently despised (103). Vendler, meanwhile, found that Melville was vastly underrated as a Civil War poet, arguing that the war was "the external equivalent of Melville's internal crisis" and that the story of the second half of Melville's career is the story of a self-educated poet creating forms that conform to the complexity of his inner and outer experience (580). She also contended that it was the moral ambiguity of Melville's work that prevented it from achieving the acclaim of better-known contemporaries like Whitman and Dickinson. Warren and Vendler made especially important contributions to the body of criticism on *Battle-Pieces* because their work took seriously both the cultural context for the collection of poems and the technical prosody that Melville had employed. A third study of Melville's Civil War poetry from the same year was Lawrence Buell's "American Civil War Poetry and the Meaning of Literary Commodification" (1999), in which Buell, like Vendler, compared Melville's poetic reflections on the Civil War with those of his contemporaries. Melville's poetry was distinguished from his contemporaries, Buell found, by its resistance to being made into a commodity for popular consumption.

Michael Warner's essay "What Like a Bullet Can Undeceive?" (2003) continued the developing tradition of considering Melville's poetry in the light of war, conflict, and anti-war rhetoric. Taking the aftermath of September 11, 2001, as his point of departure, Warner probed the moral dilemmas of war, and particularly of the Civil War as understood by

Northerners who were both anti-slavery and appalled by the violence of modern warfare. As the September 11 starting point indicates, Warner was concerned especially with the way that these dilemmas continue to resonate in the twenty-first century. Calling into question Stanton Garner's reading of the poem as "a soft, elegiac, conciliatory poem" (qtd. in Warner, 47), Warner regarded Melville's poem "Shiloh," which was perhaps the most memorable poem in his Civil War collection *Battle-Pieces*, as a refutation of the providentially inflected patriotism of "The Battle Hymn of the Republic" and other attempts to provide religious justifications for warfare. Warner then drew "Shiloh" into a broader argument about the origins and meanings of the idea of redemptive violence, contending that Melville's poem has profound implications for our understanding of secularism, religion, and state and nonstate violence in our own times.[7] It is surely noteworthy that Americanist scholarship on Melville has converged in the twenty-first century with so many other strands of Melville scholarship in concluding that the way forward into a richer understanding of Melville's work and its implication is through his poetry, and in the first decade of the twenty-first century, this tendency became particularly pronounced as numerous younger scholars began to address Melville's work in *Battle-Pieces*.

Faith Barrett found yet another novel approach to *Battle-Pieces* and its representation of the Civil war in her essay "'They Answered Him Aloud'" (2007). Barrett argued that far from being an essentially private collection of responses to the war, *Battle-Pieces* in fact drew widely from popular culture, thus emphasizing the continuity between Melville's fiction and his poetry. Cody Marrs's essay "A Wayward Art: Battle-Pieces and Melville's Poetic Turn" (2010) criticized the conventional critical narrative that Melville's turn to poetry in the 1860s represented a renunciation of Melville's "antebellum predilections for subversion and egalitarianism" (92). Marrs argued that instead, *Battle-Pieces* represented a transformation of Melville's "entire artistic project, shuttling from the relative boundlessness of the novel to the generative boundedness of the lyric" (115). Both Barrett and Marrs showed that Melville's poetry is still capable of opening up almost unlimited aesthetic and cultural perspectives that had scarcely begun to be viewed ten years into the twenty-first century.[8]

In this chapter, I have gently pushed against the tendency to recruit Melville as an accessory to our own wars, both literal and ideological. There is no escaping the fact, however, that as Warner's perceptive reading of "Shiloh" illustrates, our readings of Melville have often been illumined by the flickering light of the crises of our times. His earliest works have been read retrospectively in the context of the Mexican-American War, a conflict that his brother Gansevoort supported, but about which Herman Melville was ambivalent when not silent. The American Civil War has shed considerable, if at times distorting, light backwards upon Melville's fiction, and most of his poetry was written by its ambiguous glow. As the New Americanist critics have accurately noted, the Second World War and the Cold War shifted the terms of Melville interpretation considerably. The New Americanists' own readings of the Vietnam War had perhaps an even more substantial, and at times distorting, effect on their readings of Melville. As of 2010, in our own new century, the wars in Iraq and Afghanistan (which, as Peter Szendy has noted, *Moby-Dick* has the effect of weirdly seeming to prophesy) have already begun to provide new contexts for reading Melville. What their meaning for our understanding of Melville will be, and what Melville's significance for our understanding of this phase in American history will be, remains to be seen.

Throughout this chapter, I have emphasized the pressure of contemporary events on literary criticism., Now, in the early years of the twenty-first century, our readings of Melville may well be in the midst of a significant reshaping as a result of the events. It is noteworthy that America's first African-American president, Barack Obama, has publicly identified *Moby-Dick* as one of his favorite novels, and as America increasingly becomes defined, not just by ethnic diversity among peoples of European descent, but also by a populace of truly global origins, Melville is becoming a representative American author in ways that D. H. Lawrence could scarcely have imagined in 1923. If the critics discussed in this chapter saw Melville as representative of the America of the nineteenth and twentieth centuries, those in the next suggest ways in which he is likely to be read in the century to come.

Notes

[1] For considerations of Matthiessen's politics and sexuality, see Jonathan Arac's "F. O. Matthiessen: Authorizing an American Renaissance" (1985) and Jay Grossman's "The Canon in the Closet: Matthiessen's Whitman, Whitman's Matthiessen" (1998).

[2] For a consideration of where Melville criticism as a whole was at this time from an Americanist perspective, see Philip Rahv's "Melville and the Critics" (1950).

[3] Bercovitch himself was more circumspect than some of those he influenced in this regard. In *The Rites of Assent* (1993), he made clear that he was not suggesting that dissent was impossible in nineteenth-century America, but merely that its status was more ambiguous than might initially appear.

[4] Sianne Ngai's *Ugly Feelings* (2005) also suggested readings of Melville as an acute social and legal critic, especially through "Bartleby the Scrivener" and *The Confidence-Man*.

[5] An anticipation of the turn towards thinking of Melville as a Civil War poet had appeared in 1990 in the form of Timothy Sweet's *Traces of War: Poetry, Photography, and the Crisis of the Union*.

[6] This is the case even when Melville uses speakers who are separated from himself by time period and gender, as is the case with the speaker in "After the Pleasure Party," who is a woman in the declining days of the Roman Empire. Although she clearly is not Melville, her sense of alienation and ambivalence about her sexuality have compelling analogues in Melville's own personal history.

[7] Randall Fuller's *From Battlefields Rising* (2011) offered still further explorations of the influence of the Civil War on Melville's political and artistic development, in the context of a wide-ranging discussion of the Civil War's effects on American literature.

[8] I have reserved the rich body of recent scholarship on Melville and Frederick Douglass for chapter 6. I have also kept many of the considerations of racial issues in *Benito Cereno* for that chapter. Both strands are clearly relevant to the Civil War, but they resonate most powerfully with Melville's understanding of race.

6: "An Anacharsis Clootz Deputation": Race, Ethnicity, Empire, and Cosmopolitanism

MELVILLE BELONGS TO THE WORLD. If this seems like a potentially controversial statement regarding a figure who so often has been examined within the context of American nationalism, it is not because of any lack of transnationalism in Melville's own works. Melville began his career with representations of travel at the crossroads of European and Euro-American imperialism and indigenous cultures in the South Pacific. His first two books not focused on the islands of the South Pacific, *Redburn* and *White-Jacket*, both dealt with the cosmopolitan world of the sea, with characters appearing from all over Europe, the Americas, Asia, and Africa; and in *Redburn* specifically, Melville celebrated America's own cosmopolitan makeup. *Moby-Dick* made Melville's global concerns explicit, with its famous description of the crew of the *Pequod* as an "Anacharsis Clootz deputation, from all the isles of the sea, and all the ends of the earth" (121). Anacharsis Clootz was an eccentric Prussian nobleman who brought what he believed to be a representative sampling of the human race before the French National Constituent Assembly in 1790, so this reference connects Melville's work to the ideal of international human fraternity. The sketches in *The Encantadas* deal with Latin America, as do substantial frame stories within *Moby-Dick*. Melville's late long poem *Clarel* features pilgrims in the Near East from throughout Europe, Asia, and the Americas, and late works like *John Marr, Sailor* and *Billy Budd* are defined by the internationalism of the sea. And throughout Melville's body of work he draws on an astonishingly cosmopolitan array of allusions and references.

If Americanists old and new have found varieties of Americanness both reflected and critiqued in Melville's work, both they and critics from around the planet have found that Melville has at least as much to say about the world at large. Indeed, Melville's works are among the most resolutely international in American literature. When critics began to make this aspect of Melville's work a central component of Melville criticism in the 1980s and 1990s, they drew readers' attention to a strand in Melville's work that seemed overwhelmingly evident once it was acknowledged. Likewise, Melville's concern with questions of race and slavery only really began to receive the attention it deserved in the 1970s, but once readers began to look closely, it became evident that questions of race and slavery were to be found everywhere in Melville's work. Readers interested in Melville's treatment of race, ethnicity, and cosmopolitanism now have a diverse array of criticism to contemplate as the result of scholars' efforts during the last three decades.

Although the 1980s marked the initiation of a broad critical consensus on the political significance of Melville's internationalism, the work that truly inaugurated this tendency appeared in the early 1950s. C. L. R. James's *Mariners, Renegades, and Castaways* (1953) took Melville's description of the *Pequod*'s crew as an "Anacharsis Clootz deputation" very seriously indeed, and James's personal circumstances meant that Melville's discussion of these matters resonated with especial poignancy. James wrote his study of Melville as a detainee at Ellis Island, and in a move unusual in literary criticism, he devoted the final chapter of his study to a discussion of his own experiences in light of his reading of Melville. In keeping with the political landscape of the 1950s, James had focused partly on the relationship between totalitarianism and democracy. Another central theme, however, was the question of nationality and the quest to move beyond national divisions (like those indicated by the practice of detention at Ellis Island) that James found in Melville's text. James found that *Moby-Dick* was cosmopolitan in its sensibility precisely because of the fact that it is a novel about work, in which workers play the central roles. James found in Captain Ahab the totalitarian impulses and the propagandistic manipulative capability of a Hitler or a Stalin (as a former Trotskyist, James loathed Stalin, while remaining himself invested in Marxist political thought), and he credited Melville for recognizing in the nineteenth century the emergence of tendencies that would create totalitarian dictatorships in the twentieth century. At the same time, James wrote, Melville had recognized the centrality of workers of all races and nationalities to the alternatives to the totalitarian systems embodied by Ahab, and both the cosmic greatness of these workers and the necessity for equality among them. James sums this viewpoint up in writing about Queequeg: "In Queequeg therefore was embodied the mystery of the universe and the attainment of truth. But in his nobility of spirit, his relation to Nature, his relation to other beings, and his philosophical attitude to the world, Queequeg was merely a member of the anonymous crew" (35). The workers on the *Pequod* then, appeared as democratic nobility personified, even as Ahab as the captain represented the most dangerous and fatally seductive possibilities for mass manipulation.

Given the broader tendency of critics to oppose Ishmael to Ahab and see Ishmael as a positive alternative to Ahab's madness, one might expect James to follow this route when he turns to an extended consideration of Ishmael's character. This is not the case, however. James identifies Ishmael as an educated, middle-to-upper-class young man who is both sympathetic to the workers and their varieties of cultures and faiths, and powerless to resist Ahab's lethal magnetism. Ishmael's famous discussion of his response to *Moby-Dick* in "The Whiteness of the Whale" James analyzes in light of Ishmael's status as an intellectual, viewing Ishmael's intellectualism as signaling a lack of commitment and arguing that the crucial question confronting Ishmael is whether to side with Captain Ahab or the crew (47). In James's view, Ishmael chooses to escape this decision, and as a result, James's treatment of Ishmael is among the most contemptuous of any by a Melville critic: Ishmael, for James, is a coward, of the sort "for whom life consists of nothing else but fine cambrics and tea on the piazza" (53).

Having established to his satisfaction that Melville, writing in 1851, had anticipated the central political and economic questions of the 1950s perfectly, James turned his attention to the question of how Melville had managed to do this. James created a narrative of increased insight into the birth of the modern world that, while dismissive of the metaphysics of *Mardi*, built Melville's other early works into a trajectory that necessarily led up to Melville's profoundest insights into totalitarianism and working class consciousness in *Moby-Dick*. After *Moby-Dick*, Melville was largely wrapping up some unfinished business, dealing prophetically with modern psychology in *Pierre*, the wastefulness of modern industrial society in "Bartleby" (Bartleby is a "human typewriter" [128]), and revolution in *Benito Cereno*. For James, *Benito Cereno* was the end of Melville's work as an important author, and it represented a failure of nerve in that it addressed the issue of slavery but did not contain a direct and unambiguous denunciation of slavery. In his best work, however, and preeminently in *Moby-Dick*, Melville was among the greatest representative authors in American literature, and indeed of all human civilization.

> For consider. What Melville did was to place within the covers of one book a presentation of a whole civilization so that any ordinary human being today can read it in a few days and grasp the essentials of the world he lived in. To do this a man must contain, in his single self, at one and the same time, the whole history of the past, the most significant experiences of the world around him, and a clear vision of the future. Of all this he creates an ordered whole. No philosopher, statesman, scientist, or soldier exceeds him in creative effort. (138)

James's statement of the enduring power of Melville's work, and its ability to speak to situations far beyond those of Melville's lifetime, is among the most powerful explanations of the continuing importance and appeal of Melville's writing. The degree to which James's engagement with Melville was deeply personal was shown by the extended autobiographical epilogue dealing with his own experiences as an inmate on Ellis Island, imprisoned for being an alien and a political dissenter. James himself, as a Trinidadian intimately connected to major moral and political issues within the United States, thus became an exemplar of the "Anacharsis Clootz deputation" that Melville created in *Moby-Dick*. This chapter has the effect of tying Melville, not only to James's world, but also, given the events of the early years of the twenty-first century, to ours.

Because James's work is so powerful, insightful, and influential, it is worth attending as well to some of the shortcomings of his reading of *Moby-Dick*. The schematic arrangement James employed, identifying Ahab with totalitarianism, the crew with egalitarian, multi-racial social democracy threatened by totalitarianism, and Ishmael with uncommitted and therefore cowardly intellectualism, can feel rather wooden today. If Ahab was, in Starbuck's words, a "tyrant to all below," he was also a "democrat to all above" — a tendency both Melville and James doubtless found attractive. Moreover, James's dismissal of Ishmael seems oddly counter-intuitive, given that much of the praise of the crew's democratic possibilities comes precisely through Ishmael's voice. Nonetheless, it is hard to escape the conviction, after reading *Mariners, Renegades, and Castaways*, that few readers have experienced the Melvillean "shock of recognition" more powerfully than C. L. R. James. James's influence has also been immense: many figures discussed in this chapter, and such eminent New Americanists as Donald Pease and William Spanos (both discussed in chapter 5) have acknowledged substantial debts to James.[1]

An alternative route into Melville's portrayal of international contexts appeared in 1961 in the form of Dorothee Metlitsky Finkelstein's *Melville's Orienda*. Finkelstein examined Melville's treatment of Asia, examining Melville's reading carefully in search of sources for his allusions to Egyptian, Assyrian, Persian, and Arab cultural and religious traditions, with particular emphasis on his treatment of the faiths of Islam and Zoroastrianism. Finkelstein demonstrated comprehensively that Melville had pursued a rigorous course of reading in developing his allusions to the Near East, and she teased out the implications of this long-term engagement for the future of Melville criticism. Of particular interest in the twenty-first century is the extensive space that she devoted to unraveling the Zoroastrian and Muslim strands that went into making up the character of Fedallah in *Moby-Dick*. Finkelstein argued that Fedallah was compounded out the snippets of the gothic romance *Vathek* and travelers' accounts describing the Ismailiya Muslim sect from Persia, particularly the subset of this sect known in Western Europe as the Assassins (225–32). Finkelstein also devoted substantial space to identifying the source material for *Clarel*. As Finkelstein acknowledged, textual scholarship had served an important function in establishing the basis for studies such as hers: Howard Horsford's edition of Melville's *Journal of a Visit to Europe and the Levant* (1955; later incorporated into the Northwestern-Newberry volume *Journals*) would lay the groundwork for a multitude of future transnationally oriented studies of Melville.

Melville was also attracting admirers from Asia as early as the 1960s, as Indian scholar A. N. Kaul's *The American Vision* (1963) would illustrate. In a chapter entitled "Herman Melville: New World Voyageur," Kaul focused especially on Melville's status as a traveler, examining his works set in the Marquesas and his exploration of the Galpagos Islands in *The Encantadas* in light of a wider impulse toward "rejection and quest" in American literature (216). Indeed, Kaul resolved the conventional conflict between Melville's Americanness and his cosmopolitanism by seeing cosmopolitanism and ethnic and racial diversity as a hallmark of American literature generally that was simply intensified in Melville:

> It is a significant fact that whereas the actual crew of the *Acushnet* [the real-life whale-ship on which Melville himself sailed] was composed of twenty-one Americans, three Portuguese, and one Englishman, the crew of the whaling boat as we have it in *Moby-Dick* is a motley crowd drawn from all the nationalities of the world. . . . In this respect, [Melville] was as hopelessly ungenteel and as hopefully American as Natty Bumppo or Whitman. (219)

For Kaul, an Indian national and academic, Melville's nineteenth-century Americanness lay precisely in a principled egalitarian internationalism, and the facts that had been seen as distinctive to the American experience by previous critics became grounds for making broader connections for Kaul, who argued that "the great American fact of space" had the effect of making American literature analogous to the early Vedic literatures of India (220). For Kaul, then, as for Melville, American literary nationalism and cosmopolitanism were not contradictory, but complementary.

In-depth treatment of Melville as a writer of anti-racist and postcolonial sensibilities was deferred, however, until the period in which these sorts of readings came more generally into vogue: the 1980s, 1990s, and the opening decade of the twenty-first century. The trend began to manifest itself with the publication of two important books at the start of the 1980s: T. Walter Herbert's *Marquesan Encounters* (1980) and Carolyn L. Karcher's *Shadow Over the Promised Land* (1979). Herbert drew his readers' attention to the multicultural implications of Melville's representations of the South Seas early in his career, while Karcher investigated the attitudes that Melville expressed toward race and slavery throughout his entire career. Both books would stand at the head of a rich tradition of inquiry into race, ethnicity, and cosmopolitanism in Melville.

At least since Charles R. Anderson's pioneering work in the 1930s, Melvilleans had been interested in Melville's engagement with the Marquesas, but Herbert was the first to place Melville in the context of a broader exploration of the American encounter with the Marquesas. In *Marquesan Encounters*, he carefully examined Marquesan culture and its representations by Melville and his fellow nineteenth-century Americans, emphasizing the ways in which literary and anthropological study can complement and parallel each other. Using a vocabulary derived from modern anthropological concepts of Claude Levi-Strauss and Bronislaw Malinowski, Herbert could discuss the cultures of the West and the Marquesas in a comparative framework. He also examined the development of the broad American encounter with the Marquesas, tracing the representations of the Marquesas found in missionary reports and ship captains' narratives as well as Melville's own early novels, with particular emphasis on the cross-cultural misunderstandings that informed much missionary and government policy in the Marquesas. Melville's place in the US encounter with the Marquesas, Herbert found, was that of a "beachcomber" — a white man who was able in many cases to understand the Marquesans better than his Euro-American contemporaries because he was in a position of powerlessness rather than power in relation to the Marquesan islanders. Moreover, Melville's response to the Marquesas was less romanticized than, for example, James Fenimore Cooper's representations of American Indians because of the "critical ambivalences" Melville was able to maintain in his discussions of Marquesan cultures (156). Melville's humility was the ultimate source of his advantage over his contemporaries in representing the Marquesas, Herbert suggested, contending that Melville, who presented himself with comic understatement as "a man eating bananas," could avoid the hubris of missionaries and military officers in dealing with other cultures (157).

Following in the wake of Herbert's refocusing of Melvilleans' attention on the Marquesas, William Heath dealt with Melville's representation of sexuality in the Marquesas in his 1988 article "Melville and Marquesan Eroticism," which put Melville's writings about the Marquesas, and particularly Melville's representations of sexuality in the Marquesas, into conversation with the anthropological findings of the second half of the twentieth century.

Even as Melville's obsession with the meaning of the Civil War was long ignored by Melvilleans and Americanists alike, his deep concern with the crime of slavery languished for decades in the background of Melville criticism. Carolyn L. Karcher changed this dramatically with *Shadow Over the Promised Land*, in which she mapped Melville's response to slavery from throughout his career, starting with a thorough biographical overview of what we know about Melville and slavery, and moving through readings of each of his major fictional works between *Redburn* and *White-Jacket* and *The Confidence-Man*. Karcher found that these works contained a powerful critique of slaveholding culture in the United States. As a point of departure she took Melville's own experiences as a sailor. Melville had been a virtual slave in the Marquesas himself, and he had experienced various forms of oppression and exploitation as a sailor on whale-ships and a naval ship. Moreover, his close contact with non-Christian cultures meant that he was inoculated against the Christian chauvinism of most of his American contemporaries. Karcher found that Melville's attitude toward slavery was the product of a dialectic between Melville's hatred of arbitrary authority and his anxieties about violent revolution. Thus, Melville could pen stunningly caustic denunciations of slavery in *Mardi*, but draw back from completely embracing abolitionism altogether, and in *Benito Cereno* he could examine the psychology of slave revolt sympathetically but still recoil from the prospect of violent resistance. Melville's post-Civil War works, however, Karcher found to be less prepossessing in their discussions of matters related to race and slavery — in these works, Karcher thought, Melville's anti-authoritarianism had been overshadowed by his fears of revolution.

Karcher made race and slavery a permanent part of Melville criticism with *Shadow over the Promised Land*, and the centrality of her work is emphasized in part by the important work that it made possible. Following Karcher, Eric Sundquist was the source of a constellation of work on Melville in relation to race and slavery that in tandem with Karcher's work redefined the field of Melville studies, especially because of the close examination to which Sundquist subjected Melville's representations of race in *Benito Cereno*. The possibility that *Benito Cereno* could prove congenial to anti-racist analysis should have been clear at least since the great mid-twentieth-century African-American novelist Ralph Ellison mined it for the epigraph to his 1950 novel *Invisible Man*, and it had served as one piece of Karcher's puzzle in her study of Melville and slavery, but before Sundquist, no one had attempted to pursue its implications regarding race in an exhaustive manner. Moreover, Sundquist used *Benito Cereno* to open up more broadly comparative perspectives for understanding New World slavery by considering the implications Melville's novella for understanding race in the Caribbean and Latin America as well as in the United States.

In "Melville, Delany, and New World Slavery," which made up a substantial portion of his 1993 study *To Wake the Nations*, Sundquist drew special attention to the fact that the great slave rebellion that created an independent Haiti hovered in the background of *Benito Cereno*, and that Melville's renaming Cereno's ship the Santo Domingo pointed to the Haitian Revolution as an important point of reference.[2] Nor was this all. Melville had specifically chosen his source material to implicate the Spanish-speaking, Portuguese-speaking, and English-speaking nations of the Western Hemisphere as accomplices in the slave trade and the crimes of New World slavery. Melville thus pointed the way to a truly "hemispheric" method of examining the literature of slavery and freedom, considering the interrelatedness of the institution of slavery throughout the Anglophone, Francophone, Hispanophone, and Lusophone Americas (136). Rejecting C. L. R. James's suggestion that *Benito Cereno* represented a falling away from the antiracism of Melville's earlier work, Sundquist suggested that instead, Melville's accomplishment in *Benito Cereno* had been to "reconfigure[] the machinery of slavery as a masquerade, exposing its appeal to natural law as the utmost artifice" (139). In this way, Melville had "suggested that there was *no future* [emphasis in original], as it were, for the experiment of American democracy so long as the paralysis of inequality continued" — a radical statement indeed for a nineteenth-century writer (139). Emily Miller Budick's *Engendering Romance* (1994) provided a similar approach, arguing that *Benito Cereno* was actually more progressive in its racial politics than more famous and influential works like *Uncle Tom's Cabin*, because it unmasked the deceptiveness of conventional racial categories.

At the same time that Sundquist and Budick were recovering the radical potential of *Benito Cereno*, Toni Morrison's *Playing in the Dark* (1992) emerged as a watershed text for critics who read American literature in relation to race. Morrison, while she did not engage in extended readings of Melville's work, drew on him to suggest that the metaphorical "power of blackness" Melville described in "Hawthorne and His Mosses" had implications for understanding "American Africanism — a fabricated brew of darkness, otherness, alarm and desire that is uniquely American" (38). Morrison's thesis proved important for Melville studies, opening up a more expansive range of possibilities for critics considering Melville in relation to race and slavery. An important application to Melville of the efforts of African-Americanist critics like Morrison and Henry Louis Gates, Jr. to situate African-American literature within the wider body of American literature appeared in 1994 in the form of Michael Berthold's "*Moby-Dick* and the American Slave Narrative," which argued that many of the frame stories within the narrative of *Moby-Dick* owed much to the conventions of the slave narratives published in antebellum America.

Melville's status as a critic of racism, slavery, and imperialism was not uncontested in the late 1980s and early 1990s, however. Given Melville's status as a generally acknowledged countercultural critic of US expansionism and cultural chauvinism in criticism from earlier in the 1980s, Wai-Chee Dimock's *Empire for Liberty: Melville and the Poetics of Individualism* (1989) made a resoundingly contrarian argument. Dimock concentrated especially on Melville's early work, arguing that an imperialist aesthetic lurked behind Melville's famous declaration to Hawthorne that "You must have plenty of sea-room to tell the Truth in" (in Dimock, 3). Melville's interest in size and expansiveness shaded for Dimock into a reflection of the expansionist ideologies current in the America of the 1840s and 1850s, and particularly within the Democratic Party, for which

Herman Melville's brother Gansevoort was an important spokesman. Dimock's title, taken from Jefferson, played with the idea that individualism and imperialism could go hand in hand, and she argued that they did so in Melville's fiction. In *Mardi*, for example, Dimock contended that the authorial persona appeared as a kind of monarch, suggesting an imperial selfhood corresponding to the imperial demands and prerogatives of national expansion. In *Redburn* and *White-Jacket*, on the other hand, the authorial persona corresponds to the demands of the bourgeois self, thus creating a fit subjectivity for imperial expansion — in a witty turn of phrase, Dimock surmises that the "manifest subjectivity" in these novels "might even be said to have a Manifest Destiny of its own" (79). In *Moby-Dick* as well, freedom is always imagined, as the freedom of individual self-sufficiency and self-reliance — the very sense of freedom endorsed in the political rhetoric of Manifest Destiny. *Pierre* and *The Confidence-Man*, for Dimock, reiterate the same theme of the imperial authorial self, each embodying in its own way "authorial unaccountability" (175). Melville thus became, for Dimock, not a lonely anti-imperialist dissenter, but the very voice of an American individualism that was imperial in both its scope and it designs. Dimock's work fit in well with the New Americanist readings of American literature in vogue in the 1980s for precisely this reason — like many New Americanists, Dimock emphasized the limits of dissent in American culture.

Dimock's argument for an imperial Melville coincided with a body of work that used similar methods and theories drawn from postcolonial criticism to reach an opposite conclusion. John Samson's *White Lies: Melville's Narratives of Facts* (1989), by shedding new light on works which had long been seen as secondary within Melville's literary corpus, demonstrated the potential of postcolonial criticism to open up the internal canon within Melville studies. Samson argued that Melville had in fact undermined imperialism and expansionism especially in his lesser known works of fiction, which were distinguished by a strong nonfictional component. The "white lies" of his title were the lies that undergirded white racial privilege in antebellum America, and the function of Melville's "narratives of facts" was to expose these lies for what they were. Melville did so through a form of dramatic irony that pointed out the folly and self-delusion of his narrators. But Samson made a sharp distinction between a self-aware narrator like Ishmael, and the narrators of the early novels, *Israel Potter*, and *Billy Budd*, whom Samson saw as exhibiting the very cultural delusions that Melville himself scorned. When considered together, Samson and Dimock, while they drew very different conclusions about the nature of Melville's own investment in debates over race and imperialism, demonstrate conclusively that race, ethnicity, the postcolonial, and the transnational, would predominate in Melville studies in the years to come.

Samson's work found parallels in considerations of Melville's attitude toward slavery and revolution. In *Conspiracy and Romance* (1989) Robert Levine discussed *Benito Cereno* as a manifestation of the impulse toward narratives of conspiracy in American literature, and a powerful and disturbing reflection on complicity, even among whites who did not see themselves as being pro-slavery, in the crimes of slavery. Levine argued that *Benito Cereno* in its original form (unlike the dramatic version crafted by Robert Lowell in the 1960s) was not only a critique of slavery, but also an "implicating narrative that addresses [Melville's] and his readers complicitous entanglement in a web of anxiety, desire, and power" (168). Levine was particularly concerned with the shaping force that the idea of revolutionary conspiracy and the anxieties associated with it had for nineteenth-century American literary culture, and he saw Melville as commenting self-consciously on the role that these anxieties played in American racial ideologies.

Melville's cosmopolitanism would prove to be a subject of considerable interest for one of the most influential critics of the later twentieth century. Edward Said's polemical study *Orientalism* was one of the defining texts of late twentieth-century literary and cultural criticism, and it led to a tremendous upsurge in interest in travel and cross-cultural encounters and representations in literature. Said brought his argument — that much nineteenth-century European travel literature and anthropology served the purposes of empire — to bear in his introduction to the 1991 Library of America edition of *Moby-Dick*, subsequently included in *Reflections on Exile and Other Essays*. As in much Americanist literary and cultural criticism of Melville, Said regarded Melville as having punctured the illusions of Orientalism, and drawing on C. L. R. James, found Melville to be a sharp critic of empire and a visionary who embraced a multiplicity of global cultures. Said parted company with James, however, in his reading of Ahab, noting that if Melville presented Ahab as a dictatorial and dangerous personality, he also presented him as a powerfully admirable figure. Said attributed this duality to the combination of Melville's attachment to American literary nationalism and the energies unleashed by empire with a mistrust of the morality of imperialism. Said was thus able to both celebrate James's reading of Melville and revise it, and he made a powerful case for reading *Moby-Dick* as an "occasion for prophesy, world-historical vision, genius and madness close allied" (369).

Said's view that the postcolonial was already present in Melville's work was taken up the next year by Lawrence Buell's "Melville and the Question of American Decolonization" (1992), which was both a response to the work of scholars like Wai-Chee Dimock who had pioneered postcolonial approaches to Melville and an attempt to show the relevance of postcolonial theory to the cultural situation of nineteenth-century Americans. Buell argued that Melville's work demonstrated a kind of "postcolonial anxiety" characteristic of nineteenth-century American literature. *Billy Budd* became especially important for Buell in this regard, as it featured contact between American sailors and British men-of-war in the years immediately following the American Revolution. Buell's essay was an important milestone, in that a well-established senior Americanist was putting transnational and postcolonial issues in a central position within his reading of Melville. Another sign of the centrality of race and the postcolonial and transnational for understanding Melville in the 1990s appeared in 1995, in the form of Jonathan Arac's contribution to *The Cambridge History of American Literature*, "Narrative Forms." Arac traced the critiques of imperialism in *Typee* and *Omoo* and the emphasis on human rights in *White-Jacket*, suggesting that Melville's engagement with political questions in *White-Jacket* indicated his unwillingness to be trammeled by the limits of conventionally literary discourse, and thus contributed to his marginalization as a writer of fiction in the nineteenth century.

Race, ethnicity, and postcolonial theory came together in a particularly compelling way in Malini Johar Schueller's 1998 study *U.S. Orientalisms*, which was an explicit response Said's omission of American literature in *Orientalism*. Correcting an oversight in much of the earlier postcolonial readings of Melville's work, Schueller devoted the bulk of her discussion to *Clarel*, arguing that Melville had absorbed earlier Orientalist writings by American authors, but that what he had produced in *Clarel* constituted a subversion of the norms implicit in the earlier texts. Schueller regarded *Clarel* as a keen critique of racism, national chauvinism, and heteronormativity all at once. As a result, the Melville who emerged from Schueller's work wore a much different aspect from the promoter of imperial selfhood that Wai-Chee Dimock had found him to be a decade earlier.

Russ Castronovo's *Fathering the Nation* (1995) presented a version of Melville that was fundamentally iconoclastic, subverting not just the political rhetoric of contemporaries but assumptions about race and cultural difference that had been present in American public life since (and before) the founding of the nation. Castronovo, like John Samson, found that Melville's putatively minor works offered unexpectedly bracing criticisms of the shared cultural assumptions of nineteenth-century Americans. In *Israel Potter*, Castronovo argued, Melville had created a revisionary history of the American Revolution, emphasizing the gaps and inconsistencies in the national narratives surrounding the Revolution, rather than tamely submitting to patriotic piety. In *The Confidence-Man*, Melville had gone further and undermined any justification for westward expansion with a parody that consistently dismantled the national narratives used in support of such territorial expansion. And in *Moby-Dick*, Melville had further undermined the patriarchal authority that obtained in nineteenth-century American political discourse by comparing George

Washington and Queequeg freely. Melville could thus be seen as an American writer who had shattered the cultural consensus of his time. In a move that was to become increasingly common, Castronovo found that considering Melville's work through the prism of race meant that his genuine radicalism would no longer be obscured. Castronovo continued to address the matter of race and slavery in relation to Melville's radicalism in a particularly provocative manner in an article that he co-authored with Christopher Castiglia, "A 'Hive of Subtlety'" (2004), which argued that in *Benito Cereno*, Melville had demonstrated the political efficacy of aesthetics by using the aesthetic responses of his readers to undermine their cultural preconceptions. The wider import of this was that Melville showed that aesthetic analyses of literature could not be dismissed as mere evasions of the real world of cultural life, thus extending Castronovo's earlier arguments for Melville's iconoclastic radicalism.

Sanford Marovitz's contributions to understanding Melville as an international author were wide-ranging and numerous, and with A. C. Christodolou, he edited the collection *Melville "Among the Nations"* (2001), a collection of essays from the 1997 international Melville conference in Greece.[3] This collection drew special attention to the growing consensus that Melville was the American writer most eminently adapted to being read by the light of postcolonial theory. Three articles in particular stood out in relation to colonialism and race: Christopher Sten's "Melville's Cosmopolitanism," Wyn Kelley's "The Style of Lima," and Yukiko Oshima's "The Red Flag of the *Pequod*/ Pequot." Sten suggested that for Melville, art and cosmopolitanism were virtually inseparable and that "cosmopolitanism had become a defining activity of the imagination for Melville, in politics and in art" (47). Kelley found that the Latin-American elements of *Moby-Dick* had often been underrated in terms of their significance. For Kelley, Melville's use of Lima, Peru, as the site for the telling of "The Town-Ho's Story" called attention to the history of colonialism in the Americas, and she argued that Melville was engaged in a running debate with the most popular of US historians of Latin America, William Hickling Prescott, throughout *Moby-Dick* and especially in "The Whiteness of the Whale." Like Kelley, Oshima addressed a strand of *Moby-Dick* that is both easily visible and often ignored, suggesting that the naming of the *Pequod* after the indigenous Pequot nation of New England pointed to an allegory of European violence against American Indians that worked its way through *Moby-Dick*.

Marovitz's collection had the effect of drawing attention to the truly global matter and audience of Melville's work. A parallel strand in criticism during the late 1990s and the early 2000s was an increasing interest in Melville's specific relation to the Near East. Hilton Obenzinger's *American Palestin* (1999) had the effect of redirecting studies of *Clarel*, which of all of Melville's work was most directly concerned with the Near

East, from religious issues to more broadly cultural concerns. For Obenzinger, who focused primarily on *Clarel* and Melville's travel journals in his discussion of Melville, Melville had resisted the compulsions of American exceptionalism and created an "infidel countertext" that questioned imperialist and expansionist assumptions and, by drawing connections between the Arabs of Palestine and the indigenous peoples of the Americas, had called into doubt covenantal narratives of American history.[4]

Continuing Obenzinger's trajectory of emphasizing the relationship between imperialism and national identity in Melville's work, Bruce Harvey connected sexuality with race, ethnicity, and travel in his readings of *Typee* and *Clarel* in *American Geographies* (2001). Harvey's discussion of *Typee* and *Clarel* both contextualized Melville's first novel and his most ambitious poem in light of other American travel writing and of geography textbooks, and, like Schueller's and Obenzinger's work, emphasized the substantial differences between Melville and his contemporaries. Harvey was concerned particularly with Melville's use of concepts associated with natural law, finding that Melville employed the idea of natural law in the service of anti-imperial critique in *Typee* and of an exploration of Melville's own complex sexuality in *Clarel*.

Like Obenzinger, Timothy Marr was centrally interested in Melville's reaction to the people of the Near East and the power relations associated with the confrontation between Eastern and Western cultures in the nineteenth-century Levant. Marr's *The Cultural Roots of American Islamicism* (2006) argued that Melville drew heavily on models for characters and concepts taken from Islam throughout his career. Marr focused particularly on Melville's use of Islamic models in *Moby-Dick* and in *Clarel* and the later poetry. His book-length study followed a series of important essays he had written on the subject of ethnicity and cosmopolitanism in Melville's work. In "Without the Pale" (2001) Marr examined the significance of the multiracial and multicultural make-up of the *Pequod*'s crew.

> Unlike many Americans of his time, Melville refused to repress his exposure to the enigma of human variety. Instead, he actively celebrated it as a fresh and original dimension of a new world literature that lay claim to a more global genealogy. Melville used the shipboard society of multicultural sailors and the phenomenon of the gam — the coincidental meeting of two ships at sea — to dramatize the continuing need for liberation. (135)

Marr found that cosmopolitanism and the embrace of diversity were not so much an intriguing feature of Melville's project as the soul of his entire body of work, a theme that Marr developed both in his studies of ethnic cosmopolitanism and of Melville's engagement with Islam and the Near East.

Running parallel to the resurgence of interest in Melville's representation of the Near East was a particularly urgent strand of work focused on the Pacific as the site of Melville's earliest work. Participating in the transnationally charged milieu of Melville scholarship near the turn of the twenty-first century, Geoffrey Sanborn's *The Sign of the Cannibal* (1998) provided a detailed and theoretically informed engagement with Melville's representations of cultural otherness, making particular use of Melville's representations of tattooing and cannibalism. *Typee*, *Moby-Dick*, and *Benito Cereno* served as Sanborn's central occasions for analysis, showing the shifting meanings of cannibalism in Melville's early South Seas romance, his mature masterpiece, and his novella of a slave revolt at sea. Sanborn emphasized the difficulties and subtleties of interpretation, suggesting that Melville's acknowledgment of the uncertainties of interpretation provided him with his most compelling subversions of racism and imperialism. Epistemological humility thus became for Sanborn a crucial element in Melville practice of cross-cultural representation.

Sanborn followed his work on Marquesan tattooing practices with an important article on the subject of Queequeg's import for understanding the view of both intercultural dialogue and sexuality implicit in *Moby-Dick*. In "Whence Come You, Queequeg?" (2005), Sanborn tracked the printed sources for Melville's descriptions of tattooing in his early novels, identifying the New Zealand Maori leader Te Pehi Kupe (or Tupai Cupa, as the name was spelled in George Lillie Craik's *The New Zealanders* [1830], the source of Melville's information about Kupe) as the model for Queequeg's facial tattoos. Sanborn made this identification through careful analysis of both Ishmael's description of Queequeg's tattoos and the specific traditions of tattooing that existed among the Maori people during the nineteenth century. Sanborn used this identification and a reading of *Moby-Dick* in juxtaposition with Craik's *The New Zealanders* in order to consider the nature of the interracial bond between Ishmael and Queequeg. He argued that Queequeg's character provides a critique of global trade in the nineteenth century and the systems of domination and subordination that undergirded it, and that it does so through probing the implications of Queequeg and Ishmael's shared humanity and their mutual respect for a universal human bond. After considering the Ishmael-Queequeg relationship in light of the Hawthorne-Melville relationship to which the title of his essay alludes ("Whence come you, Hawthorne" is from the most famous of Melville's letters to Nathaniel Hawthorne), Sanborn concluded with a beautiful image of what intercultural and interracial contact and friendship means in *Moby-Dick*. For Sanborn, the relationship of Ishmael and Queequeg "presents us with a way of being alone in which we are nonetheless together, and a way of being together in which we are no longer ourselves" (251). Sanborn's essay thus had the effect of showing the wider cultural implications of the most winsome and intimate elements within *Moby-Dick*.

Similar studies of Melville in relation to Pacific cultures emerged in the late 1990s and early 2000s. In 1997 Juniper Ellis argued in "Melville's Literary Cartographies of the South Seas" that Melville had attacked Western imperialism but had failed to provide an accurate or adequate account of the indigenous cultures of the Pacific. John Carlos Rowe, who did much to promote the scholarly investigation of the imperial impulse in American literature, found Melville to be an acute critic of imperialism and racism in *Typee*. In his study *Literary Culture and U.S. Imperialism* (2000), Rowe brought together the two major strands discussed in this chapter, arguing that Melville's critique of imperialism in *Typee* was intimately connected with a critique of slavery. In "'The Thrice Mysterious Taboo'" (1999), Alex Calder suggests that Melville had acknowledged his own inability to serve as an authoritative interpreter of Marquesan culture: "I don't believe Melville supposes that he can get to the bottom of any of these mysteries. Rather he has a way of writing that undoes settled conclusions, even as he reproduces, as carefully and exactly as he can, the very circumstances of outsider doubt" (29). Melville was thus praiseworthy precisely for his willingness to acknowledge what he did not know about the culture of the Typee people.

Intensified discussion of themes associated with race in Melville's work grew alongside the cross-cultural and postcolonial discussions by Sanborn, Rowe, Ellis, and Calder. Fred V. Bernard's "The Question of Race in *Moby-Dick*" (2002) helped forecast a growing concern with Melville's representation of race, particularly as it related to antebellum African Americans, in the first decade of the twenty-first century, and in combination with Michael Berthold's earlier work, it also ensured that considerations of race in Melville would reach into the central text of the Melville canon as well as into works like *Typee* and *Benito Cereno*. Bernard made the counterintuitive but compelling argument that both Ishmael and Ahab can be read as characters of mixed racial heritage — and thus imagined as "black" in terms of nineteenth-century American racial hierarchies. One of the most powerful aspects of this reading was that it provided a motivation for both Ahab's rage and Ishmael's melancholy based in the concrete social facts of nineteenth-century America. Bernard also demonstrated links between Melville's work and one of his more unlikely contemporaries, the fiery abolitionist William Lloyd Garrison. The possibility that Ahab and Ishmael can be seen as African American characters lends new significance to "the whiteness of the whale." As of this writing, the full implications of Bernard's daring suggestion have yet to be explored.

Even as discussion of Melville's treatment of race reached a crescendo, the transnational element in his work came in for increasingly wide-ranging attention. Most considerations of Melville's transnationalism have looked across the Pacific to Oceania and beyond to Asia, or else to the Near Eastern and Mediterranean sources for *Clarel*. Paul Giles's *Virtual Americas*

(2002) looked across the Atlantic to England in a chapter entitled "Bewildering Entanglement: Melville's Engagement with the British Tradition." Giles acknowledged a paradox in the history of Melville's critical reception: while British critics had been virtually alone in recognizing Melville as a significant American writer in the years leading up to the Melville Revival, they had relatively little to say about him during the years of Melville's ascendance among American literary critics. Giles presented what he believed could be an antidote to this neglect, discussing at length the depth and the breadth of Melville's engagement with British culture. For Giles, the perception of Melville as a fundamentally apolitical writer, which he suggested helped to explain Melville's recent neglect by British critics, was misguided. Indeed, throughout his career Melville had "play[ed] off British and American idioms against each other, thereby relativizing the assumptions of both national cultures" (85). Giles made a compelling case that Melville is as much a part of global Anglophone literary culture as he is an icon of American literature. Melville's personal history and his reception history, then, is not only the product of American culture and the emergent American empire, but also of Britain and its empire.

Like Giles's study, Anne Baker's *Heartless Immensity* (2006) extended the interest in travel and geography in Melville's fiction that had appeared in the work of Schueller, Obenzinger, and Harvey in recent years. Baker found that geography had been fundamental in shaping Melville's imagination in that the sheer size of the United States called out for new forms of expression. This line of argument hearkened back to Charles Olson's *Call Me Ishmael*, but in Baker's hands it took on significant new resonances, tempering Olson's literary nationalism with the insights of postcolonial and transnational literary and cultural theory. Baker explored the ways in which Ahab's use of maps in *Moby-Dick* paralleled the discussions of mapping in Charles's Wilkes's 1845 *Narrative of the First United States Exploring Expedition*, suggesting that Melville parodied the emergent imperialism of Wilkes's text. She also found important parallels between Margaret Fuller's subversive account of the American West in *A Summer on the Lakes* (1843) and Melville's subversions of imperial ambitions in *Typee* and his other works on the South Seas. Baker thus was able to provide a careful description of Melville's particular variety of literary nationalism, rather than simply falling into celebration or condemnation.

Melville's time in the Marquesas was also the subject of an ambitious 2006 special issue of *ESQ* edited by G. R. Thompson, "Melville in the Marquesas," that sought to map out the relationship between Melville's depictions of the Marquesas in *Typee* and his actual experiences and what we now know about nineteenth-century Marquesan history and culture. The issue featured anthropologist Robert C. Suggs's vigorous critique of the factual grounds for *Typee* and a series of responses by eminent Melville scholars, some of whom, like John Bryant, found Suggs's arguments against Melville's veracity unpersuasive, and some of whom objected to the necessity of confirming the factual basis of Melville's account on literary grounds. Samuel Otter argued for an interpretation of Melville's time in the Marquesas that both acknowledged the force of Suggs's objections to Melville's depictions of the Marquesas and preserved a sense of Melville's artistic autonomy as a novelist, and G. R. Thompson contended that fictional and factual analysis could indeed coincide through the mechanism of Melville's irony.

Paul Lyons's *American Pacificism* (2006), published in the same year as the *ESQ* issue, also argued for a reading of Melville's relation to the Pacific that kept fact and fiction in tension with each other. Pointing out that no less an important source of information on Melville's beliefs than his wife Elizabeth had confirmed in 1901 that Melville himself never fully accepted allegations that the Typee people practice cannibalism, Lyons argued that *Typee* constituted an exploitation and a critique of the idea of South Seas cannibalism (89). He criticizes the exploitative element in Melville's representations of alleged Marquesan cannibalism sharply, arguing that whatever Melville's tendency to mock Western chauvinism, "it is Tommo-Melville as much as anyone, who has (parodically or not) stuck the Marquesans with the 'sign of the cannibal'" (96). Lyons found Melville's critiques of Western stereotypes insufficient to atone for the central failing of perpetuating the allegation of Marquesan cannibalism.

On the heels of Lyons's study, eminent Melvilleans Jill Barnum, Wyn Kelley, and Christopher Sten edited an important collection bringing together a variety of perspectives on Melville's engagement with the cultures of the Marquesas and Hawaii, *"Whole Oceans Away": Melville and the Pacific* (2007). This collection had the effect of bringing some of Melville's harshest critics and most ardent defenders of his treatment of the Pacific into conversation with each other. In an especially scathing indictment of Melville's Pacific writings, Monica A. Ka'imipono Kaiwi, herself a native Hawaiian, argued that Melville was a slanderer, not a defender of indigenous cultures in the Pacific islands, and particularly Hawaii. Likewise, Amy S. Greenberg found that *Typee*'s favorable reception in the expansionist 1840s may have had less to do with its mockery of imperialism than with its reinforcement of contemporary paeans to the joys of expansionism. Charlene Avallone expanded the implications of Kaiwi and Greenberg's arguments to make the case that Melville's "apprentice work" in *Typee* should no longer be given the respectful attention that it has received in the recent past, suggesting that its "casual racism" be treated with the contempt it deserves, and that "more mature achievements" like *Moby-Dick* not be sullied by excessive associations with works that are both minor and mendacious (46). Bryan Short, meanwhile, took the view that *Typee*'s failings were already being corrected in Melville's second "apprentice work": *Omoo*. In this less widely popular novel, Short writes, Melville created "a new discursive environment" that gave voice to a nascent postcolonial critique of imperialism ("Plagiarizing," 109). Melville accomplished this, Short argues, by recasting his sources on Polynesia, particularly William Ellis, to show the futility of colonialism's promises of "progress" in the Pacific. In these and the other essays throughout the collection, the question of Melville's relationship to the Pacific world, and its moral, political, and aesthetic significances were raised with a new urgency, and readers were left with a powerful impression that the last word on Melville's representations of the Marquesas and Hawaii is far from being written.

In keeping with the vigorous reemergence of discussions of Melville in the Pacific in the mid-2000s, John Bryant reentered the discussion of Melville in the South Pacific with his study *Melville Unfolding* (2008). Bryant was a leading textual critic of Melville's work who also found that textual criticism opened up important vistas in understanding Melville's treatment of race, culture and sexuality, and *Melville Unfolding* showed how textual criticism could illuminate Melville's precarious negotiations of these highly charged issues, with special attention to Melville's process of revision revealed by the discovery of manuscript portions of *Typee* in the 1980s. Bryant's work pointed toward what looks to be a fertile field for Melville scholars over the next few decades: applying increasingly sophisticated and technologically supported textual scholarship to a fuller understanding of Melville's entanglements with both culture and sexuality.

It is easy to forget that Melville's Pacific legacy is not restricted to Polynesia. Given the trajectory of the *Pequod*'s voyage around the world in *Moby-Dick*, it is perhaps not surprising that Melville has developed an important critical following in Japan, where whaling has long been culturally significant. In a special issue of *Leviathan* edited by A. Robert Lee that appeared in 2006, Japanese critics explored the state of Melville studies in Japan, suggesting that Melville continued to resonate in Asia in the twenty-first century. Among the essays included, several highlighted the expansiveness of the possibilities for scholars dealing with Melville in the context of Asia. Tomoyuki Zettsu's "Cannibal Connections: A Buddhist Reading of 'The Encantadas'" suggested that Melville had drawn on Buddhist concepts of reincarnation and merit in imagining the inner significances of the Galapagos Islands, and that even so sensational a trope as cannibalism was used by Melville to suggest alternatives to Western notions of subjectivity. Zettsu traced similarities between the possibility that the Chola widow Hunilla's deceased husband was eaten by dogs and the Japanese Buddhist tradition of Buddhist holy men who had allowed themselves to be eaten out of a sense of compassion for animals. Both Lee in his introduction and Arimichi Mankino and Dorsey Kleitz in their respective essays discussed the relevance of Commodore Perry's "opening" of Japan for an understanding of Melville, and Yuji Kato examined

Melville's reception history in Japan from the 1930s onward. Provocatively, Ikuno Saiki suggested the previously unexplored possibility of Japanese models for the pivotal character of Fedallah and his Asian crew in *Moby-Dick*, while Yukiko Oshima provided a view from Japan of the racial conflicts between American Indians and Euro-Americans in *The Confidence-Man*. The issue made clear that Melville's work had both embraced and been embraced by Japanese culture much more than had traditionally be realized.

Expanding the frame of Melville's transnationalism to encompass the globe, Robert Tally's *Melville, Mapping, and Globalization* (2009) indicated that postcolonial and transnational readings of Melville promised to continue to be a vital field for debate and placed Melville's Pacific writings within the wider frame of his fiction as a whole. Heavily influenced by the New Americanist scholarship of William Spanos and Jonathan Arac, and making bold claims for Melville's status as a radical critic of status quo, Tally viewed Melville as a writer who both exemplified the global and put forward bracing critiques of the exploitative elements of what came to be called globalization. What makes Tally's argument both distinctive and exciting is his interest in plumbing the political and cultural significances of Melville's aesthetic forms: Tally argues that by embracing the form of the baroque, with its chaotic juxtapositions of disparate elements, Melville had "offer[ed] us a fine example of that postnational literature best suited to our time" (49). Melville had, Tally suggests, been ahead, not only of his times, but of his critics.

Meanwhile, an important new area of study had opened up in the area of Melville and race that would prove immensely productive of scholarship in the second half of the 2000s. Robert K. Wallace's *Douglass and Melville* (2005) made the surprising yet deeply productive leap of putting Melville into dialogue with one of his most influential contemporaries: the African American orator and abolitionist leader Frederick Douglass. Wallace tracked the parallels between the two revered Americans biographies and examined points of shared emphasis between Melville's fiction and Douglass's abolitionist writings.

In tandem with Ivy G. Wilson, Wallace also edited a special issue of *Leviathan*, in which further complexities were unraveled in the matter of Melville's relation to Frederick Douglass.[5] Scott Peeples placed Melville and Douglass's reactions to Abraham Lincoln's assassination in conversation with each other, suggesting that these two figures, both of whom had opposed slavery long before the Civil War, diverged afterwards, with Melville tending toward ambivalence and accommodation with the South, and Douglass emerging as an impassioned supporter of an egalitarian Reconstruction. Zoe Trodd presented a complementary view to that of Peeples: where Peeples had emphasized the explicit political divergence between Melville and Douglass after the war, Trodd considered how both writers continued the practice of subverting hallowed national narratives that they had begun in the antebellum period. Trodd also discussed extensively the pessimism in *Battle-Pieces* about any redemptive "rebirth" of the American nation in the wake of the war. Anne Baker examined a particular instance of Melville's subversion of patriotic rhetoric, the Revolutionary War novella *Israel Potter*, in combination with Douglass's questioning of the patriotic rhetoric surrounding the Fourth of July. Christopher Sten found that Melville and Douglass had been shaped in unlikely ways by their encounters with Washington, DC and the political machinery there, and he concurred with Peeples in finding a sharper divergence between Douglass's politics and Melville's after the war than before, with Douglass's optimism about the federal government waxing and Melville's waning. Roosevelt Montas, finally, took the similar position that Douglass had found transcendence in the theory of liberty, whereas Melville "presented, by the end of his career, a heart-breaking picture of a world where transcendent values are inoperative as guides to interpretation, and where the formalist adherence of laws appeared to be the only way of maintaining a stable, if arbitrary, order" in the form of *Billy Budd* (69). The issue thus confirmed the centrality of Douglass and Melville to the culturally inflected literary criticism inspired by issues of slavery and freedom that flourished in American literary studies during the first decade of the twenty-first century.

Along with Wallace's book and the *Leviathan* special issue that Wallace and Wilson edited, Samuel Otter's and Robert Levine's collection of essays on the relation between Melville's works and those of Frederick Douglass, *Frederick Douglass and Herman Melville: Essays in Relation* (2008) represented a substantial reinforcement of the idea that race, slavery, and emancipation could never again be relegated to the periphery of Melville scholarship. A series of essays explored Douglass and Melville in relation to literary and cultural geographies, manhood and sexuality, and war. Several essays were especially noteworthy. Robert K. Wallace extended earlier discussions of Melville's relation to the politics and jurisprudence of his father-in-law, Lemuel Shaw, in relation to slavery, while Sterling Stuckey previewed the argument that he would develop in his book-length study (discussed below) of the influence of African culture, and especially dance, on Melville's aesthetics. John Stauffer discussed interracial friendships in both authors as a refutation of pro-slavery ideology. Steven Mailloux examined Melville and Douglass as practitioners of "political theology," arguing that both used Pauline concepts to criticize slavery, but that Douglass used political theology with a confidence Melville was unable to muster. Elisa Tamarkin explored the relative impact of England on Melville's and Douglass's work, finding that England became associated with relative freedom and human dignity for Douglass — and particularly a "gentlemanly" escape from the compulsions of capitalism — but slavery in a gracious disguise for

Melville. Hester Blum made a compelling connection between Melville and Douglass on questions of gender and masculinity, arguing that Melville's sketches in *The Encantadas* had dealt with sexual violence in a way that paralleled the treatment of sexual violence in slave narratives. Ingeniously, Blum focused on the use of punctuation — dashes — as a way into a comparison between Douglass's treatment of bodily violence in his nonfiction and Melville's representation of sexual violence in the case of Hunilla, the woman who has suffered abandonment and rape in *The Encantadas*.

   Melville has often been seen as a writer deeply concerned with East and West: connections between the United States and Asia, the Pacific, Africa, and Europe, are foregrounded in many of his works. As Blum's essay and Sundquist's work (and before that, James's work) demonstrated, Melville was also very concerned with relationships among the Americas, and a geographical model for understanding Melville's work must be concerned with North-South relations within the Americas as well as East-West relations around the globe. Several studies have pointed a way forward here. In the Douglass-Melville collection edited by Levine and Otter, one essay in particular made this point forcefully. Rodrigo Lazo, like Blum, made *The Encantadas* a central part of his consideration of Douglass and Melville, in Lazo's case in conjunction with Douglass's narrative of travel to Haiti. Lazo argued that both Douglass and Melville were concerned with the expansionist tendencies of travel writing built around the idea of "enchantment" — suggesting that romanticizing non-US cultures could contribute to imperial designs (208–9). As with many of the writers on Douglass and Melville surveyed above, Lazo found that in their respective critiques of "enchantment" Douglass tended toward the concretely political and Melville toward the metaphysical: "For Douglass, enchantment is a cover for international profiteering and Manifest Destiny. For Melville, the end of enchantment is the delusion of empire without end" (225). Writing in the tradition of Sundquist and James, Lazo pointed the way for future investigations of Melville as a writer of the Americas. His emphasis on Melville's critique of enchantment suggested connections with the work of critics like Bryan Short, who wrote in similar terms about Melville's engagement with the Pacific.

   One of the contributors to the consideration of Douglass and Melville together also made a powerful case for considering Melville in the light of African American culture more broadly. For Sterling Stuckey, Melville's interest in African and African American culture was not simply related to questions of race and slavery, but to a far wider range of cultural interests and concerns. In *African Culture and Melville's Art* (2009), Stuckey argued that Melville had been much more influenced by African culture than had previously been acknowledged, and that this had significant implications for the artistic as well as the cultural aspects of his work. By examining the historical evidence for substantial visibility of African

American culture in the Albany in which Melville grew up, Stuckey was able to establish that African traditions of song, dance, and storytelling were available to Melville from an early age. Moreover, Stuckey, argued, unmistakable traces of African influence could be found throughout Melville's body of work. In one the finest encapsulations of the significance of Melville's treatment of the relations between culture ever written, Stuckey contends that

> a certain fluidity of cultural thought and practice occurs when Melville relates one culture to another, enabling him to imagine the flow of influences, to layer one beneath, or above, the other. His is not the universality of abstraction, devoid of cultural specificity and content, but the reverse: particular human beings from different parts of the world, at times nameless, are lifted from the mundane circumstances in which Melville finds them to the dazzling heights of his art. A curious sort of immortality results from his artistry as he works from most of the world's continents. (5)

Stuckey's determination to use the cultural specificity of Melville's work to plumb the depths of his art resulted in readings of Melville's works that were both sensitive and surprising. For example, in his reading of the chapter "Midnight, Forecastle," from *Moby-Dick*, Stuckey finds that Melville made covert references to the practice of the "ring dance," a form of traditionally African dance performed in New York City during the mid-nineteenth century. Stuckey also found important evidence of African dance traditions in *Benito Cereno*. Stuckey's work demonstrated brilliantly not only that there remained much to learn about Melville and race a decade into the twenty-first century, but also that what we learn about Melville and race can powerfully illuminate Melville's literary artistry.

Transnational discussions of Melville's work have often had something of the air of manifestoes, devoting a great deal of energy to justifying their own transnationalism. When considered alongside Stuckey's work, Dennis Berthold's *American Risorgimento* (2010) offered further evidence that transnational studies of Melville had come of age. Berthold made significantly more use of concrete evidence related to Melville's engagement with other cultures than had most previous critics, taking an extended look at Melville's journals of travel in Italy and his reading of texts related to Italy and his collecting of Italian art books and art prints. The result was a highly nuanced and textured study that contributed to our understanding of the transnational Melville discussed in this chapter, the American Melville discussed in the previous chapter, and the Melville who as a devotee of the visual arts was discussed in chapter 2. Berthold found that Melville's response to Italian art went hand in hand with his interest in Italian republican politics, and Berthold deftly created readings of Italian prints Melville collected that possessed Risorgimento political resonances and connections with Melville's own works.[6] A particularly striking example of this sort of reading appeared in Berthold's discussion of how Melville mingled allusions to Dante with the 1840s American Protestant critiques of papal authority and American and Italian republicanism in *Mardi*. Here art, culture, nationalism, literature, and religion interpenetrated beautifully in one reading. Berthold's reading of moments in later texts, like his consideration of the Dominican in *Clarel*, were also provocative, but ultimately less persuasive than his brilliant analyses of the artistic and political connections between Italy and America in the 1840s and 1850s.

Berthold's concern with putting Melville's transnationalism into the specific cultural context of nineteenth-century Italian nationalism and its relation to Melville's own American nationalism provides an indication of the future direction of culturally oriented Melville scholarship. Melville's affinity for the hybrid, the transnational, and the multicultural is, by now, quite clear. His hatred of racism and cultural and religious bigotry is well established, as is the fact that this hatred stems at least in part from a broader humanism.

The future of work in this field lies, I propose, with the careful discovery of how Melville appropriated elements from the various cultures with which he was engaged, and made them into an art that could appeal, not only to the voyeuristic Western audience described by Said in *Orientalism* and by critics influenced by Said in similar works, but also to the wider world. Melville has never been only an American writer: the author who wrote "the whole world is the patrimony of the whole world" (*Redburn*, 318) always composed with a global audience in mind, and the fact that we now acknowledge this fact means that we are one step closer to seeing Melville clearly.

There is, appropriately enough given Melville's unrelenting emphasis on duality in his works, another side to the matters discussed in this chapter. Repeatedly throughout the criticism discussed so far, a very conflicted picture of Melville emerges. On the one hand, it seems indisputable at this point that few, if any, nineteenth-century Americans doubted the strictures of racist ideologies, and chauvinist national or imperial ideologies, more consistently and determinedly than Melville. The case made by Emily Miller Budick and Eric Sundquist that Melville was an exceptionally acute critic of racism is tremendously compelling. At the same time, it is also beyond dispute that Melville, whatever his affinities with Frederick Douglass, was not Douglass, nor was he William Lloyd Garrison or Harriet Beecher Stowe. The very acute critical temperament and ironic sensibility that made him such a corrosive critic of racism and political chauvinism also seems to have kept him from being a heroically outspoken advocate for the liberation of the slaves, and perhaps for admirable political causes more generally. Furthermore, if Melville could not be taken in easily by imperial ideologies, his uncertainties were such that he also could not consider resistance movements without ambivalence. It seems (and this may in itself be a rather Melvillean reflection) that as expansive as Melville's examinations of race, slavery, cosmopolitanism, and empire may be, Melville's engagement with these questions is ultimately an uncertain and incomplete project.

Notes

[1] Ten years after James made his extended argument for a revolutionary reading of Melville, his contemporary Hannah Arendt argued for more of an American Cold War reading of an anti-utopian Melville in her philosophical treatise *On Revolution* (1963). Melville was thus as contested a figure overseas in the century after his death as he was at home. Arendt's reading of Melville was also quite consistent with the view of Melville popular in the 1950s and early 1960s that saw his work as the expression of a fundamentally tragic understanding of the world.

[2] Sundquist's work in *To Wake the Nations* built on his earlier work on *Benito Cereno* in "*Benito Cereno* and New World Slavery" (1986) and "Suspense and Tautology in *Benito Cereno*" (1981), which when read with *To Wake the Nations* offer a picture of the development of Sundquist's understanding of the novella as New World writing.

[3] Another aspect of Melville's internationalism is the emergence of a number of conferences based in Europe or Asia that have been sponsored by The Melville Society and devoted to various transnational elements within Melville's body of work. Most recently, The Melville Society held an international meeting in Poland in 2007 and in Jerusalem in 2009, and there is as of this writing a Melville conference scheduled for Rome in 2011.

[4] For more on Melville's travels in the Holy Land in relation to the accounts of other travelers, see my [Brian Yothers] *The Romance of the Holy Land in American Travel Writing, 1790–1876* (2007). This study argues that Melville's work in *Clarel* makes explicit and self-conscious the concern with religious difference that to one degree or another shaped the narratives of earlier travelers.

[5] Promising to make a substantial impact on future considerations of Melville and race is Ivy G. Wilson's *Specters of Democracy: Blackness and the Aesthetics of Politics in the Antebellum U.S.* (2011). Wilson had already examined some of the legal ramifications of Melville's work in relation to slavery in his essay "'No soul above'" (2007).

[6] A significant forerunner to Berthold's work on Italian republicanism was Larry Reynolds's *European Revolutions and the American Literary Renaissance* (1988).

Epilogue: Encountering Melville

To paraphrase Ishmael: What Melville was to his critics from 1920 to 2010 has been seen. What, at times, he is to me, and what he promises to be to new readers in the new century remains to be hinted at.

Each semester that I teach *Moby-Dick*, I have a ritual to which I am drawn before the first day on which we discuss it in class. Setting aside my teaching copies of the book, I turn to myself and pick up a copy of the Riverside edition from 1956, with an introduction by the redoubtable Melvillean and Americanist Alfred Kazin. I flip through the pages, attending particularly to the notes in the margin. The copy in question is both the first copy of *Moby-Dick* that I ever read, and the reading copy of *Moby-Dick* that my mother, Esther, who died in 1988, had used as a student at Eastern Mennonite College in the late 1960s. As I look through the copious notes that she wrote in the margins, I try to imagine what her experience of Melville must have been like, as the first person to receive a GED or attend college in her family, or as a member of an often misunderstood religious minority (Old-Order Mennonite) within an often misunderstood religious minority (Mennonites more generally), and thus doubly an "Ishmael" in relation to her wider society. The notes are detailed, thorough, and neatly written, but I am certainly aware that they represent an engagement with Melville that is mediated through Kazin's introduction (also annotated) and the critical sources that informed her professor's lectures as much as through her individual response to the text. I am also aware, and have become increasingly aware in the course of writing this study, that her Melville in the late 1960s is not my Melville in the twenty-first century. Nonetheless, when I teach *Moby-Dick*, in some sense the young Esther is my imagined audience.

I bring my mother's Riverside edition up, not (entirely) out of sentimentality, but because I believe it highlights something often overlooked in our accounts of how criticism develops: the initial, informal, serendipitous acquaintances with an author that shape our critical visions. As productive of scholarly interpretation as Melville's work has been, Melville's image is not solely in the hands of literary and cultural critics. Those seeking Melville can find him in places as diverse as a public library in western Massachusetts, museums, and historical collections around the United States, not to mention a variety of venues associated with popular culture. In this brief epilogue, I wish to sketch out some of the places that someone seeking Melville in the twenty-first century can find him, and the ramifications of these potential sites of encounter for future criticism.

Travelers in the United States can find Melville in unlikely places. Perhaps the most extensive collection of Melville related materials anywhere is found in the back of a public library in small-town Massachusetts. The Melville room at the Berkshire Athenaeum, the public library for Pittsfield, Massachusetts, is a treasure trove for researchers, including Melville's collections of art prints, paintings of Melville, Melville's badge from his career as a customs officer, and, touchingly, the writing desk used by Elizabeth Shaw Melville bearing the inscription, "To know all is to forgive all" — a moving postscript to the often difficult marriage between Herman and Elizabeth Melville. Pittsfield is of course an appropriate venue for a Melville archive given his long-term residence at Arrowhead in Pittsfield and the fact that he completed *Moby-Dick* while living there, but it is a startling sensation to walk through what seems like a typical medium-sized town library and find oneself in the middle of such a remarkable collection of Melville materials. There are also ghostly resonances for the devotee of Melville scholarship: the room was endowed by the great Melville scholar Henry A. Murray, and it seems that virtually every major study of Melville takes its cover image from one of the portraits of Melville from the Berkshire Athenaeum's holdings. Moreover, the room is ringed with what must be the closest collection in existence to an exhaustive gathering of every book written about Melville.

A few miles from the Berkshire Athenaeum, in the country, is Melville's longtime home of Arrowhead, which is preserved and open for tours. Although the collection of Melville materials is less extensive than at the Berkshire Athenaeum, the impulse to see, for example, the window through which Melville looked out on Mount Greylock, the massive chimney that provided the inspiration for "I and My Chimney," and Melville's own piazza, are irresistible. Indeed, literary tourists with scholarly inclinations interested in Melville can find much to gratify them in Massachusetts. The New Bedford Whaling Museum and the New Bedford Whaling Museum Research Library have a close association with The Melville Society (the oldest of American single-author literary societies), and serves as a home for the ambitious Melville Society Cultural Project, The Melville Society Archive, and an annual marathon reading of *Moby-Dick* as well as an annual lecture on Melville's birthday. The museum also is regularly the site of institutes for high-school teachers, and in 2005, was the site of the international conference of The Melville Society devoted to Melville and Frederick Douglass that helped lead to the explosion of publications on Melville and Douglass described in chapter 6. The Houghton Library at Harvard University, meanwhile, houses substantial collections of Melville's own annotated copies of books, and has provided the foundation for numerous studies and discoveries related to Melville's life and work.

Outside of Massachusetts, Melville's presence is less concentrated, but appropriately far-flung. Southwestern University in Georgetown, Texas, features an impressive collection of Melville materials in its Osborne Collection of Herman Melville Materials, as does Princeton University in its Herman Melville Collection, 1846–56. Melville's grave in Woodlawn Cemetery in New York City is famously out of the way, but he still looms large in the collections of the New York Public Library, another site that appears frequently in the acknowledgments of studies of Melville's work and life.

Closely associated with these concrete geographical locations for Melville scholarship is the mass of electronic material that has emerged since the internet provided virtual alternatives to the physical places beloved of Melville scholars. One of the challenges of describing this material is that the world of the internet is notoriously evanescent: the listserv Ishmail, for example, which at one point was a robust venue for online discussion of Melville, is now a shadow of its former self (still vigorous and interesting, but no longer an official venue for The Melville Society), and websites both appear and disappear, or on some occasions, simply remain uncompleted after the manner of the Cologne Cathedral as described by Ishmael in *Moby-Dick*. Several substantial electronic projects bear discussing, however. The *Melville Electronic Library* (http://www2.iath.virginia.edu/melville/), while still in its earlier stages, has the potential to expand the range of contributions to textual scholarship available to students of Melville exponentially. The efforts of John Bryant and Haskell Springer, two of the most distinguished Melvilleans working today, promise to make this electronic collection of annotated Melville texts along with an electronic version of *The Melville Log* and other major contributions to Melville scholarship a truly remarkable resource for future Melvilleans. A resource that is more limited in scope but which is at this time more established than the *Melville Electronic Library*, is the ambitious website *Melville's Marginalia Online* (http://www.boisestate.edu/melville/), which has begun to gather together electronic, annotated versions of all of Melville's books that contain markings made by Melville. Steven Olsen-Smith, the editor of the site, has made *Melville's Marginalia Online* one of the most exciting venues available for younger Melvilleans to break into Melville scholarship — and it is only right that I note here that I am one of the beneficiaries of Olsen-Smith's scholarly generosity, having been given the opportunity to write the notes and introduction for Melville's markings in *The New Testament and Psalms*. Less official, but also informed by high scholarly standards, is Melville Society webmaster Robert Sandberg's *The Melville Room* (www.melvilleroom.org), a revision of Sandberg's earlier site *Herman Melville, Poet*. *The Melville Room* is under construction as of this writing, but promises to be an impressive and accessible compendium of information about Melville and his work, including his poetry and more obscure prose. Sandberg is also as of this writing the webmaster for the website of The Melville Society (www.melvillesociety.org), which contains a great deal of information about the society's activities and about Melville-related events.

Both the sheer mass of engagement with Melville in literary and popular culture and the focus of this study on criticism precludes any attempt to analyze the endless references to Melville, and particularly to *Moby-Dick*, "Bartleby, the Scrivener," and *Billy Budd* in the contexts of twentieth and twenty-first century fiction, poetry, opera, visual art, popular music, film, and television, not to mention the ubiquity of Ahab and white whale metaphors in mainstream journalism, but I do wish to consider briefly what Melville scholarship has made of these strands. Andrew Delbanco's 2005 biography of Melville begins with a collection of quotations from twentieth and twenty-first century references to Melville in public and popular culture, ranging from the debates over the second Gulf War to *The Sopranos*.

Two important discussions of Melville's relation to the popular culture of our own day appeared as a substantial section of the collection *Ungraspable Phantom: Essays on Moby-Dick* (2006) edited by John Bryant, Mary K. Bercaw Edwards, and Timothy Marr, and in a special issue of *Leviathan* from 2009. In *Ungraspable Phantom*, Samuel Otter compared the representation of Melville's work in three major performances of material from *Moby-Dick* in which dance played a major role: Laurie Anderson's multi-media performance *Songs and Stories from Moby-Dick* (1999), Rinde Eckert's chamber opera *And God Created Whales*, and John Barrymore's two film versions of *Moby-Dick* (*The Sea Beast*, silent, 1926, and *Moby Dick*, sound, 1930). Otter believed these creative engagements with the novel to be more successful than a literal reproduction of *Moby-Dick* like the 1956 film version starring Gregory Peck, and directed by John Huston with the screenplay by Ray Bradbury. Robert K. Wallace and Elizabeth Schultz, both renowned as scholars of Melville in relation to the visual arts, also contributed pieces dealing with Eckert's work. In 2007, Wallace would extend his interest in the visual aspects of performances of Melville's work in an essay published in *Leviathan* on Israeli film-maker Guy Ben-Ner's twelve-minute adaptation of *Moby-Dick* from 2000. Wyn Kelley, always known for finding fascinating new frames in which to discuss Melville, contributed a piece on *Moby-Dick* as seen through the digital culture of video and computer games, demonstrating the range of possible critical approaches available to critics considering Melville in relation to visual cultures and performance.

In a 2009 *Leviathan* special issue on popular culture edited by M. Thomas Inge, Richard Middleton-Kaplan discussed the significance of such filmic adaptations of Melville's work as *Pola X* (1999), French director Leos Carax's adaptation of *Pierre*; *Beau Travail* (1999), Claire Denis's adaptation of *Billy Budd*; and Jonathan Parker's *Bartleby* (2000). In the same issue, Carol Colatrella discussed Melville's traces in Wes Anderson's *The Life Aquatic of Steven Zissou* (2004), and Randy Laist explored Melville's influence on the film *Heathers* (1989). Yet another essay from this issue, Craig Bernardini's "Heavy Melville" discussed the afterlife of *Moby-Dick* in a death-metal concept CD entitled *Leviathan* by the band Mastodon. Meanwhile, Melville criticism helps shape contemporary fictional adaptations of Melville's models, as can be seen in Sena Jeter Naslund's *Ahab's Wife; or, The Star-Gazer* (1999) and Frederick Busch's *The Night Inspector* (1999). The fact that Melville is still so inescapable, in film versions of "Bartleby, the Scrivener" and *Moby-Dick*, in the improbable French film version of *Pierre*, *Pola X*, in Jake Heggie's operatic version of *Moby-Dick* that opened in 2010 at the Dallas opera, and in the music of Mastodon, surely indicates that we can expect Melville to be a major constituent feature of American culture for a long time to come. Encounters with Melville seem certain to continue far beyond our own generation.

But what of the tradition of critical encounters with Melville? In a review published in 1984, the eminent Melville scholar John Bryant, who has figured largely in the preceding pages, observed, "In general, Melville criticism is like *Paradise Lost*: No one wishes it longer" (90). In the years since 1984, Melville criticism has, unlike *Paradise Lost*, lengthened considerably, in no small part due to Bryant's own prodigious scholarly efforts as both an author and an editor. Bryant's statement was of course an instance of self-effacing humor, but it raises some significant issues. A question that a project such as this one inevitably touches upon is that of the value and significance of literary criticism as a field of endeavor. Few areas of critical inquiry have had the sheer fecundity of Melville studies: as of early 2011, the Modern Language Association's International Bibliography lists a staggering 5,191 hits in response to a query for critical essays, books, and dissertation abstracts that take Herman Melville as a primary subject for their work. Given this massive outpouring of scholarship, it is worth asking: What have we learned from all of this scholarly effort? Do we understand Melville better today than he was understood in the early days of the Melville Revival of the 1920s, when very little had been published on Melville's work? Is the experience of reading, teaching, and studying Melville's work enriched by this critical endeavor?

The preceding pages make some implicit arguments in response to these questions that I would like to make more explicit here. We do indeed know more about Melville and his work than anyone could have in 1920 at the outset of the Melville Revival, in 1951 at the centenary of *Moby-Dick*, in 1968, when my mother studied *Moby-Dick* as an undergraduate, or in 1995, when, as an undergraduate myself, I first picked up my mother's copy of *Moby-Dick* and read it over the summer after my freshman year in college. It has become a commonplace to assert that humanistic research, unlike scientific research, does not progress, but merely recapitulates earlier ideas under the guise of newer fads. Though like most misconceptions, this one harbors a grain of truth, it is nonetheless, a grave misconception. Melville's critics have unearthed voluminous details of Melville's life, his reading, his correspondence, and his thought — solid, verifiable facts all — that would have otherwise been unavailable to readers. Moreover, as the foregoing pages illustrate, repeatedly throughout the (currently) ninety-year history of academic criticism of Melville, critics have suggested readings of Melville that have, to borrow Melville's phrase, appeared "so terrifically true" that it has become impossible to read Melville without some recourse to those earlier readings.

The primary emotion stirred in me by the research and writing of this book is a profound sense of gratitude to the generations of scholars and critics who have created, and who continue to create, an image of Melville that is increasingly accurate and increasingly meaningful to successive generations of readers, teachers, and students. If Melville remains ungraspable, his reflection can now be seen with greater clarity than ever, through the work of the remarkable collection of men and women who have written about him over the last ninety years.

Works Cited

Aaron, Daniel. *The Unwritten War: American Writers and the Civil War.* New York: Knopf, 1973.
Adler, Joyce. *War in Melville's Imagination.* New York: New York UP, 1981.
Alter, Robert. *Pen of Iron: American Prose and the King James Bible.* Oxford; Princeton, NJ: Princeton UP, 2010.
Anderson, Charles R. *Melville in the South Seas.* New York: Columbia UP, 1939.
Arac, Jonathan. "F. O. Matthiessen: Authorizing an American Renaissance." In *The American Renaissance Reconsidered,* edited by Donald E. Pease, 90–112. Baltimore: Johns Hopkins UP, 1985.
———. "Narrative Forms." In *The Cambridge History of American Literature.* Vol. 2, *1820–1865,* edited by Cyrus R. K. Patell, 605–777. Cambridge, UK: Cambridge UP, 1995.
Arendt, Hannah. *On Revolution.* New York: Viking, 1963.
Argersinger, Jana L., and Leland S. Person, eds. *Hawthorne and Melville: Writing a Relationship.* Athens: U of Georgia P, 2008.
Arsić, Branka. *Passive Constitutions: Or, 7 1/2 Times Bartleby.* Stanford, CA: Stanford UP, 2007.
Arsić, Branka, and K. L. Evans, eds. *Melville's Philosophies.* New York: Bloomsbury, 2018.
Arvin, Newton. *Herman Melville.* New York: Sloane, 1950.
Auden, W. H. *The Enchafèd Flood: Or, the Romantic Iconography of the Sea.* Charlottesville: U of Virginia P, 1950.
Avallone, Charlene. "'Depraved and Vicious'/Urbane and Domestic: Herman Melville, Elizabeth Sanders, and the Traditions of Figuring Hawaiians." In *"Whole Oceans Away": Melville and the Pacific,* edited by Christopher Sten, 31–48. Kent, OH: Kent State UP, 2007.
———. "What American Renaissance? The Gendered Genealogy of a Critical Discourse." *PMLA* 112, no. 5 (1997): 1102–20.
———. "Women Reading Melville/Melville Reading Women." In *Melville and Women,* edited by Elizabeth A. Schultz, and Haskell S. Springer, 41–59. Kent, OH: Kent State UP, 2006.
Baird, James. *Ishmael.* Baltimore: Johns Hopkins UP, 1956.
Baker, Anne. *Heartless Immensity: Literature, Culture, and Geography in Antebellum America.* Ann Arbor: U of Michigan P, 2006.
———. "What to Israel Potter is the Fourth of July? Melville, Douglass, and the Agency of Words." *Leviathan: A Journal of Melville Studies* 10, no. 2 (2008): 5–22.

Balaam, Peter. *Misery's Mathematics: Mourning, Compensation, and Reality in Antebellum American Literature*. New York: Routledge, 2009.

———. "'Piazza to the North': Melville Reading Sedgwick." In *Melville and Women*, edited by Elizabeth A. Schultz, and Haskell S. Springer, 60–81. Kent, OH: Kent State UP, 2006.

Barnum, Jill, Wyn Kelley, and Christopher Sten, eds. *"Whole Oceans Away": Melville and the Pacific*. Kent, OH: Kent State UP, 2007.

Barrett, Faith. "'They Answered Him Aloud': Popular Voice and Nationalist Discourse in Melville's Battle-Pieces." *Leviathan: A Journal of Melville Studies* 9, no. 3 (2007): 35–49.

Barton, John Cyril. *Literary Executions: Capital Punishment and American Culture, 1820-1925* Baltimore, MD: Johns Hopkins University Press, 2014.

Baym, Nina. "The Erotic Motif in Melville's Clarel." *Texas Studies in Literature and Language: A Journal of the Humanities* 16 (1974): 315–28.

———. "Melville's Quarrel with Fiction." *PMLA* 94, no. 5 (1979): 909–23.

———. Review of *The Afterlife of Edgar Allan Poe*, by Scott Peeples. *American Literature* 77, no. 2 (2005): 414–16.

Bell, Michael Davitt. *The Development of American Romance: The Sacrifice of Relation*. Chicago: U of Chicago P, 1980.

Bell, Millicent. "Pierre Bayle and Moby Dick." *PMLA* 66, no. 5 (1951): 626–48.

Bellis, Peter J. *No Mysteries Out of Ourselves: Identity & Textual Form in the Novels of Herman Melville*. Philadelphia: U of Pennsylvania P, 1990.

Bercaw, Mary K. *Melville's Sources*. Evanston, IL: Northwestern UP, 1987.

Bercaw Edwards, Mary K. *Cannibal Old Me: Spoken Sources in Melville's Early Works*. Kent, OH: Kent State University Press, 2009.

Bercovitch, Sacvan. *The American Jeremiad*. Madison: U of Wisconsin P, 1978.

———. *The Rites of Assent: Transformations in the Symbolic Construction of America*. New York: Routledge, 1993.

Bercovitch, Sacvan, and Myra P. Jehlen. *Ideology and Classic American Literature*. Cambridge; New York: Cambridge UP, 1986.

Bernard, Fred V. "The Question of Race in Moby-Dick." *Massachusetts Review: A Quarterly of Literature, the Arts and Public Affairs* 43, no. 3 (2002): 383–404.

Bernardini, Craig. "Heavy Melville: Mastodon's Leviathan and the Popular Image of *Moby-Dick*." *Leviathan: A Journal of Melville Studies* 11, no. 3 (2009): 27–44.

Berthoff, Warner. *The Example of Melville*. Princeton, NJ: Princeton UP, 1962.

Berthold, Dennis. *American Risorgimento: Herman Melville and the Cultural Politics of Italy*. Columbus: Ohio State UP, 2009.

Berthold, Michael C. "*Moby-Dick* and American Slave Narrative." *Massachusetts Review: A Quarterly of Literature, the Arts and Public Affairs* 36, no. 1 (1994): 135–48.

Bewley, Marius. *The Complex Fate: Hawthorne, Henry James and Some Other American Writers.* London: Chatto and Windus, 1952.
———. *The Eccentric Design: Form in the Classic American Novel.* New York: Columbia UP, 1959.
Bezanson, Walter E. "Herman Melville's *Clarel.*" PhD diss., Yale University, 1943.
———. Introduction to *Clarel, A Poem and Pilgrimage in the Holy Land,* by Herman Melville, ix–cxviii. Edited by Walter E. Bezanson. New York: Hendricks House, 1960.
———. "*Moby-Dick*: A Work of Art." 1950. Reprinted in *Moby-Dick: A Norton Critical Edition,* edited by Hershel Parker and Harrison Hayford, 641–56. 2nd ed. New York: Norton, 2001.
Bickley, Robert Bruce. *The Method of Melville's Short Fiction.* Durham, NC: Duke UP, 1975.
Blackmur, R. P. "The Craft of Herman Melville: A Putative Statement." *Virginia Quarterly Review* 14 (1938): 266–82.
Blum, Hester. "Douglass's and Melville's 'Alphabets of the Blind.'" In *Frederick Douglass and Herman Melville: Essays in Relation,* edited by Robert S. Levine and Samuel Otter, 257–78. Chapel Hill: U of North Carolina P, 2008.
———. *The View from the Masthead: Maritime Imagination and Antebellum American Sea Narratives.* Chapel Hill: U of North Carolina P, 2008.
Boone, Joseph Allen. *Tradition, Counter Tradition: Love and the Form of Fiction.* Chicago: U of Chicago P, 1987.
Bowen, Merlin. *The Long Encounter: Self and Experience in the Writings of Herman Melville.* Chicago: U of Chicago P, 1960.
Braswell, William. *Melville's Religious Thought: An Essay in Interpretation.* Durham, NC: Duke UP, 1943.
Bredahl, A. Carl. *Melville's Angles of Vision.* U of Florida P, 1972.
Brodhead, Richard H. *Hawthorne, Melville, and the Novel.* Chicago: U of Chicago P, 1976.
Brodtkorb, Paul. *Ishmael's White World: A Phenomenological Reading of Moby Dick.* New Haven, CT: Yale UP, 1965.
Brodwin, Stanley. "Herman Melville's *Clarel*: An Existential Gospel." *PMLA* 86, no. 3 (1971): 375–87.
Brooks, Van Wyck. *The Times of Melville and Whitman.* New York: E. P. Dutton, 1947.
Browne, Ray B. *Melville's Drive to Humanism.* Lafayette, IN: Purdue UP, 1971.
Brumm, Ursula, and John Hooglund. *American Thought and Religious Typology.* New Brunswick, NJ: Rutgers UP, 1970.
Bryant, John. *A Companion to Melville Studies.* New York: Greenwood, 1986.
———. *The Fluid Text: A Theory of Revision and Editing for Book and Screen.* Ann Arbor: U of Michigan P, 2002.
———, ed. *Herman Melville's "Typee": A Fluid Text Edition.* Charlottesville: U of Virginia P, 2009. http://rotunda.upress.virginia.edu/melville/.

———. "How Billy Grew Black and Beautiful: Versions of Melville in the Digital Age" *Leviathan: A Journal of Melville Studies* 16, no. 1 (2014): 60-86.

———. Introduction to *Typee*, by Herman Melville, ix–xxx. New York: Penguin, 1996.

———. *Melville and Repose: The Rhetoric of Humor in the American Renaissance.* New York: Oxford UP, 1993.

———. *Melville Unfolding: Sexuality, Politics, and the Versions of Typee: A Fluid-Text Analysis, with an Edition of the Typee Manuscript.* Ann Arbor: U of Michigan P, 2008.

———. "Taipi, Tipii, Typee: Place, Memory, and Text A Response to Robert C. Suggs." *ESQ: A Journal of the American Renaissance* 51, no. 1 (2005): 137.

———. "The Ways of Creativity: Pursuing Melville's Imagination." Review of *Pursuing Melville, 1940–1980*, by Merton M. Sealts, and *Melville's Confidence Man: From Knave to Knight*, by Tom Quirk. *Modern Language Studies* 14, no. 4 (1984): 84–90.

Bryant, John, Mary K. Bercaw Edwards, and Timothy Marr, eds. *Ungraspable Phantom: Essays on Moby-Dick*. Kent, OH: Kent State UP, 2006.

Bryant, John, and Robert Milder, eds. *Melville's Evermoving Dawn*. Kent, OH: Kent State UP, 1997.

Bryant, John, and Haskell Springer, eds. *Moby-Dick: A Longman Critical Edition*. New York: Longman, 2006.

Budick, E. Miller. *Engendering Romance: Women Writers and the Hawthorne Tradition, 1850–1990*. New Haven, CT: Yale UP, 1994.

Buell, Lawrence. "American Civil War Poetry and the Meaning of Literary Commodification: Whitman, Melville, and Others." In *Reciprocal Influences: Literary Production, Distribution, and Consumption in America*, edited by Susan S. Williams, 123–38. Columbus: Ohio State UP, 1999.

———. "Melville and the Question of American Decolonization." *American Literature: A Journal of Literary History, Criticism, and Bibliography* 64, no. 2 (1992): 215–37.

———. "Melville the Poet." In *The Cambridge Companion to Herman Melville*, edited by Andrew Delbanco, 135–56. Cambridge, UK: Cambridge UP, 1998.

———. "*Moby-Dick* as Sacred Text." In *New Essays on "Moby-Dick,"* edited by Richard H. Brodhead, 53–72. London: Cambridge UP, 1986.

———. *New England Literary Culture from Revolution through Renaissance*. New York: Cambridge UP, 1986.

———. "The Unkillable Dream of the Great American Novel: *Moby-Dick* as Test Case." *American Literary History* 20, nos. 1–2 (2008): 132–55.

Busch, Frederick. *The Night Inspector: A Novel*. New York: Harmony Books, 1999.

Bush, Harold K., and Brian Yothers. *Above the American Renaissance: David S. Reynolds and the Spiritual Imagination in American Literary Studies*. Amherst, MA: University of Massachusetts Press, 2018.

Calder, Alex. "'The Thrice Mysterious Taboo': Melville's *Typee* and the Perception of Culture." *Representations* 67 (1999): 27–43.
Cameron, Sharon. *The Corporeal Self: Allegories of the Body in Melville and Hawthorne*. Baltimore: Johns Hopkins UP, 1981.
Camus, Albert. "Herman Melville." 1950. Reprinted in *Lyrical and Critical Essays*, translated by Ellen Conroy Kennedy 205-8. New York: Knopf, 1968.
Cardozo Studies in Law and Literature. Special issue on *Billy Budd*. 1, no. 1 (1989).
Castiglia, Christopher. "Alienated Affections: Hawthorne and Melville's Trans-Intimate Relationship." *Hawthorne and Melville: Writing a Relationship*, edited by Leland S. Person, 321–44. Athens: U of Georgia P, 2008.
Castiglia, Christopher, and Russ Castronovo. "Preface: A "Hive of Subtlety": Aesthetics and the End(s) of Cultural Studies." *American Literature* 76, no. 3 (2004): 423–35.
Castronovo, Russ. *Fathering the Nation: American Genealogies of Slavery and Freedom*. Berkeley: U of California P, 1995.
Chai, Leon. *The Romantic Foundations of the American Renaissance*. Ithaca, NY: Cornell UP, 1987.
Charvat, William. "Melville's Income." *American Literature: A Journal of Literary History, Criticism, and Bibliography* 15, no. 3 (1943): 251–61.
Chase, Richard Volney. *The American Novel and its Tradition*. Garden City, NY: Doubleday, 1957.
———. *Herman Melville: A Critical Study*. New York: Hafner, 1971.
Cohen, Hennig, ed. *The Battle-Pieces of Herman Melville*. London: Thomas Yoselloff, 1963.
———. *Selected Poems of Herman Melville*. Carbondale: Southern Illinois UP, 1964.
Colacurcio, Michael. "Charity and its Discontents: Pity and Politics in Melville's Fiction." *There before Us: Religion and American Literature, from Emerson to Wendell Berry*, edited by Andrew Delbanco, 49–79. Grand Rapids, MI: Eerdmans, 2007.
Colatrella, Carol. "The Life Aquatic of Melville, Cousteau, and Zissou: Narrative at Sea." *Leviathan: A Journal of Melville Studies* 11, no. 3 (2009): 79–90.
———. *Literature and Moral Reform: Melville and the Discipline of Reading*. Gainesville, FL: UP of Florida, 2002.
Coleman, Dawn. "Mahomet's Gospel and Other Revelations: Discovering Melville's Hand in *The Works of William E. Channing*." *Leviathan: A Journal of Melville Studies* 17, no. 2 (2015): 74-88.
———. "Melville and the Unitarian Conscience." In *Visionary of the Word: Melville and Religion*, ed. Jonathan A. Cook and Brian Yothers, 129-57. Evanston, IL: Northwestern University Press, 2017.
———. *Preaching and the Rise of the American Novel*. Columbus, OH: The Ohio State University Press, 2013.

---. "Whales in Cincinnati." *Leviathan: A Journal of Melville Studies* 19, no. 1 (2017): 122-39.
Cook, Jonathan A. "*Clarel* and the Victorian Crisis of Faith." In *Visionary of the Word: Melville and Religion*, ed. Jonathan A. Cook and Brian Yothers, 21-70. Evanston, IL: Northwestern University Press, 2017.
---. *Inscrutable Malice: Theodicy, Eschatology, and the Biblical Sources of Moby-Dick*. DeKalb, IL: Northern Illinois University Press, 2012.
---. *Satirical Apocalypse: An Anatomy of Melville's "The Confidence-Man."* Westport, CT: Greenwood, 1996.
Cook, Jonathan A., and Brian Yothers, eds. *Visionary of the Word: Melville and Religion*. Evanston, IL: Northwestern University Press, 2017.
Cover, Robert M. *Justice Accused: Antislavery and the Judicial Process*. New Haven, CT: Yale UP, 1975.
Cowan, Bainard. *Exiled Waters: Moby-Dick and the Crisis of Allegory*. Baton Rouge: Louisiana State UP, 1982.
Cowen, Walker, ed. *Melville's Marginalia*. New York: Garland, 1987.
Crain, Caleb. "Lovers of Human Flesh: Homosexuality and Cannibalism in Melville's Novels." *American Literature: A Journal of Literary History, Criticism, and Bibliography* 66, no. 1 (1994): 25–53.
Creech, James. *Closet Writing / Gay Reading: The Case of Melville's Pierre*. Chicago: U of Chicago P, 1993.
Crews, Frederick. "Whose American Renaissance?" *New York Review of Books* 27 (October 1988): 68–81.
Davidson, Cathy N., and Jessamyn Hatcher, eds. *No More Separate Spheres! A Next Wave American Studies Reader*. Durham, NC: Durham UP, 2002.
Davis, Clark. *After the Whale*. Tuscaloosa: U of Alabama P, 1995.
Davis, Merrell R. *Melville's "Mardi": A Chartless Voyage*. New Haven, CT: Yale UP, 1952.
Dayan, Colin. "Bartleby's Screen." *Leviathan: A Journal of Melville Studies* 17, no. 2 (2015): 1-17.
Del Tredici, Robert. *Floodgates of the Wonder-World: A Moby-Dick Pictorial*. Kent, OH: Kent State University Press, 2001.
Delbanco, Andrew. *Melville: His World and Work*. New York: Knopf, 2005.
Deleuze, Gilles. "Bartleby, or the Formula." 1989. Reprinted in *Essays Critical and Clinical*, translated by Daniel W. Smith and Michael A. Greco, 68–90. London: Verso, 1998.
Derrida, Jacques. *The Gift of Death*. Translated by David Wills. Chicago: U of Chicago P, 1995.
Dettlaff, Shirley M. "Ionian Form and Esau's Waste: Melville's View of Art in Clarel." *American Literature* 54, no. 2 (1982): 212–28.
---. "Melville's Aesthetics." In *A Companion to Melville Studies*, edited by John Bryant, 625–65. New York: Greenwood, 1986.
Dillingham, William B. *An Artist in the Rigging: The Early Work of Herman Melville*. Athens: U of Georgia P, 1972.
---. *Melville & His Circle: The Last Years*. Athens: U of Georgia P, 1996.
---. *Melville's Later Novels*. Athens: U of Georgia P, 1986.

———. *Melville's Short Fiction, 1853–1856*. Athens: U of Georgia P, 1977.
Dimock, Wai-Chee. *Empire for Liberty: Melville and the Poetics of Individualism*. Princeton, NJ: Princeton UP, 1988.
———. *Residues of Justice: Literature, Law, Philosophy*. Berkeley: U of California P, 1996.
Domnarski, William. "Law-Literature Criticism: Charting a Desirable Course with *Billy Budd*." *Journal of Legal Education* 34 (1984): 702–13.
Douglas, Ann. *The Feminization of American Culture*. New York: Knopf, 1977.
Dryden, Edgar A. *Melville's Thematics of Form: The Great Art of Telling the Truth*. Baltimore: Johns Hopkins UP, 1968.
———. *Monumental Melville: The Formation of a Literary Career*. Stanford, CA: Stanford UP, 2004.
Duban, James. *Melville's Major Fiction: Politics, Theology, and Imagination*. DeKalb, IL: Northern Illinois UP, 1983.
———. "The Translation of Pierre Bayle's an Historical and Critical Dictionary Owned by Melville." *Papers of the Bibliographical Society of America* 71 (1977): 347–51.
Eby, E. H. "Herman Melville's 'Tartarus of Maids.'" *Modern Language Quarterly* 1 (1940): 95–100.
Edwards, Mary K. Bercaw. "Questioning Typee." *Leviathan: A Journal of Melville Studies* 11, no. 2 (2009): 24–42.
Einboden, Jeffrey. "'Billy's Rendering of the Matter': Global Translations of *Billy Budd, Sailor*." In *Billy Budd, Sailor: Critical Insights*, ed. Brian Yothers, 58-72. Ipswich, MA: Salem Press, 2017.
———. *Nineteenth-Century US Literature in Middle Eastern Languages*. Edinburgh, UK: Edinburgh University Press, 2013.
Elliott, Emory. "Art, Religion, and the Problem of Authority in Pierre." In *Ideology and Classic American Literature*, edited by Sacvan Bercovitch and Myra Jehlen, 337–51. New York: Cambridge UP, 1988.
Ellis, Juniper. "Melville's Literary Cartographies of the South Seas." *Massachusetts Review: A Quarterly of Literature, the Arts and Public Affairs* 38, no. 1 (1997): 9–29.
Evans, K. L. *One Foot in the Finite: Melville's Realism Reclaimed*. Evanston, IL: Northwestern University Press, 2017.
Evans, Kim Leilani. *Whale!* Minneapolis, MN: U of Minnesota P, 2003.
Evans, Robert C., ed. *Moby-Dick: Critical Insights*. Ipswich, MA: Salem Press, 2014.
Evelev, John. *Tolerable Entertainment: Herman Melville and Professionalism in Antebellum New York*. Amherst, MA: U of Massachusetts P, 2006.
Fabricant, Carole. "*Tristram Shandy* and *Moby-Dick*: A Cock and Bull Story and a Tale of a Tub." *Journal of Narrative Technique* 7, no. 1 (1977): 57–69.
Faflik, David. *Melville and the Question of Meaning*. New York: Routledge, 2018.
Farmer, Meredith. "Herman Melville and Joseph Henry at the Albany Academy; or, Melville's Education in Mathematics and Science." *Leviathan: A Journal of Melville Studies* 18, no. 2 (2016): 4-28.

Feidelson, Charles. *Symbolism and American Literature*. Chicago: U of Chicago P, 1953.
Ferguson, Robert A. *Law and Letters in American Culture*. Cambridge, MA: Harvard UP, 1984.
Fiedler, Leslie A. *Love and Death in the American Novel*. New York: Criterion Books, 1960.
Finkelstein, Dorothee Metlitsky. *Melville's Orienda*. New Haven: Yale UP, 1961.
Fisher, Marvin. *Going Under: Melville's Short Fiction and the American 1850s*. Baton Rouge: Louisiana State UP, 1977.
Flory, Wendy Stallard. "Melville and Isabel: The Author and the Woman Within in the 'Inside Narrative' of *Pierre*." In *Melville and Women*, edited by Elizabeth A. Schultz, and Haskell S. Springer, 121–40. Kent, OH: Kent State UP, 2006.
Fogle, Richard Harter. *Melville's Shorter Tales*. Norman: U of Oklahoma P, 1960.
Foley, Brian. "Herman Melville and the Example of Sir Thomas Browne." *Modern Philology* 81, no. 3 (1984): 265–77.
Foster, Charles H. "Something in the Emblems: A Reinterpretation of *Moby-Dick*." *New England Quarterly* 34, no. 1 (1961): 3–35.
Foster, Elizabeth Sophia. Introduction to *The Confidence-Man — His Masquerade*, by Herman Melville, xiii–xcv. Edited by Elizabeth Sophia Foster. New York: Hendricks House, 1954.
Foucault, Michel. *Discipline and Punish: The Birth of the Prison*. New York: Pantheon Books, 1977.
Franchot, Jenny. "Melville's Traveling God." In *The Cambridge Companion to Herman Melville*, edited by Robert S. Levine, 157–85. New York: Cambridge UP, 1998.
———. *Roads to Rome: The Antebellum Protestant Encounter with Catholicism*. Berkeley: U of California P, 1994.
Frankel, Matthew Cordova. "Tattoo Art: The Composition of Text, Voice, and Race in Melville's Moby-Dick." *ESQ: A Journal of the American Renaissance* 53, no. 2 (2007): 114–47.
Franklin, H. Bruce. "*Billy Budd* and Capital Punishment: A Tale of Three Centuries." *American Literature: A Journal of Literary History, Criticism, and Bibliography* 69, no. 2 (1997): 337–59.
———. "The Tarry Hand of Herman Melville." In *Weapons of Criticism: Marxism in America and the Literary Tradition*, edited by Norman Rudich, 287–309. Palo Alto, CA: Ramparts, 1976.
———. *The Wake of the Gods: Melville's Mythology*. Palo Alto, CA: Stanford UP, 1963.
Franks, Jason. *A Political Companion to Herman Melville*. Lexington, KY: University of Kentucky Press, 2013.
Frederick, John T. *The Darkened Sky; Nineteenth-Century American Novelists and Religion*. South Bend, IN: U of Notre Dame P, 1969.
Fredericks, Nancy. *Melville's Art of Democracy*. Athens: U of Georgia P, 1995.

Freeburg, Christopher. *Melville and the Idea of Blackness*. New York: Cambridge University Press, 2012.
Freeman, F. Barron. *Melville's Billy Budd*. Cambridge, MA: Harvard UP, 1948.
Freeman, John. *Herman Melville*. New York: Macmillan, 1926.
Friedman, Maurice S. *Problematic Rebel: Melville, Dostoievsky, Kafka, Camus*. Rev ed. Chicago: U of Chicago P, 1970.
Fuller, Randall. *From Battlefields Rising: How the Civil War Transformed American Literature*. New York: Oxford UP, 2011.
Garner, Stanton. *The Civil War World of Herman Melville*. Lawrence: UP of Kansas, 1993.
Garner, Stanton, Lynn Horth, Hershel Parker, Robert Ryan, and Donald Yannella. "Biographers on Biography: A Panel Discussion." In *Melville's Evermoving Dawn*, edited by John Bryant and Robert Milder, 225–59. Kent, OH: Kent State UP, 1997.
Giles, Paul. *Virtual Americas: Transnational Fictions and the Transatlantic Imaginary*. Durham, NC: Duke UP, 2002.
Gilman, William H. *Melville's Early Life and Redburn*. New York: New York UP, 1951.
Gilmore, Michael T. *American Romanticism and the Marketplace*. Chicago: U of Chicago P, 1985.
Gleim, William S. *The Meaning of Moby-Dick*. New York: Russell & Russell, 1938.
Goldman, Stan. *Melville's Protest Theism: The Hidden and Silent God in Clarel*. DeKalb: Northern Illinois UP, 1993.
Grandin, Greg. *The Empire of Necessity: Slavery, Freedom, and Deception in the New World*. New York: MacMillan, 2014.
Greenberg, Amy S. "Fayaway and Her Sisters: Gender, Popular Literature, and Manifest Destiny in the Pacific, 1848–1860." In *"Whole Oceans Away": Melville and the Pacific*, edited by Christopher Sten, 17–30. Kent, OH: Kent State UP, 2007.
Greiman, Jennifer. *Democracy's Spectacle: Sovereignty and Public Life in Antebellum American Writing*. New York: Fordham University Press, 2010.
Greven, David. *Gender Protest and Same-Sex Desire in Antebellum American Literature: Margaret Fuller, Edgar Allan Poe, Nathaniel Hawthorne, and Herman Melville*. New York: Palgrave, 2014.
———. "In the Name of the Father: *Billy Budd* and the Critics from the Melville Revival to Cold War America." In *Billy Budd, Sailor: Critical Insights*, ed. Brian Yothers, 197-215. Ipswich, MA: Salem Press, 2017.
Grey, Robin. *The Complicity of Imagination: The American Renaissance, Contests of Authority, and Seventeenth-Century English Culture*. Cambridge, MA; New York: Cambridge UP, 1997.
———. *Melville & Milton: An Edition and Analysis of Melville's Annotations on Milton*. Pittsburgh, PA: Duquesne UP, 2004.
Grossman, Jay. "The Canon in the Closet: Matthiessen's Whitman, Whitman's Matthiessen." *American Literature: A Journal of Literary History, Criticism, and Bibliography* 70, no. 4 (1998): 799–832.

Gunn, Giles B. *The Interpretation of Otherness: Literature, Religion, and the American Imagination*. New York: Oxford UP, 1978.
Haberstroh, Charles. *Melville and Male Identity*. Rutherford, NJ: Fairleigh Dickinson UP, 1980.
Hancher, Michael. "Billy Budd: Famous Last Words." *Cardozo Studies in Law and Literature* 1, no. 1 (1989): 109–21.
Hardack, Richard. "Stocks and Bonds: Pantheism and the Chain of Being in the American Renaissance." *Studies in the American Renaissance* (1994): 21–42.
Hardwick, Elizabeth. *Herman Melville*. New York: Viking, 2000.
Harvey, Bruce A. *American Geographics: U.S. National Narratives and the Representation of the Non-European World, 1830–1865*. Palo Alto, CA: Stanford UP, 2001.
Hayes, Kevin J. *Melville's Folk Roots*. Kent, OH: Kent State UP, 1999.
Hayford, Harrison. "'Loomings': Yarns and Figures in the Fabric." In *Artful Thunder: Versions of the Romantic Tradition in American Life*, edited by Howard P. Vincent, 119–38. Kent, OH: Kent State UP, 1975.
———. *Melville's Prisoners*. Evanston, IL: Northwestern UP, 2003.
———. "Unnecessary Duplicates: A Key to the Writing of Moby-Dick." In *New Perspectives on "Moby-Dick,"* edited by Faith Pullin, 128–49. Edinburgh, UK: U of Edinburgh P, 1978.
Heath, William. "Melville and Marquesan Eroticism." *Massachusetts Review: A Quarterly of Literature, the Arts and Public Affairs* 29, no. 1 (1988): 43–65.
Heflin, Wilson L. *Herman Melville's Whaling Years*. Edited by Mary K. Bercaw Edwards, and Thomas Farel Heffernan. Nashville, TN: Vanderbilt UP, 2004.
Heidmann, Mark. "The Markings in Herman Melville's Bibles." *Studies in the American Renaissance* (1990): 341–98.
Heimert, Alan. "Moby-Dick and American Political Symbolism." *American Quarterly* 15, no. 4 (1963): 498–534.
Herbert, T. Walter. *Marquesan Encounters: Melville and the Meaning of Civilization*. Cambridge, MA: Harvard UP, 1980.
———. *Moby-Dick and Calvinism: A World Dismantled*. New Brunswick, NJ: Rutgers UP, 1977.
Herman, Daniel. *Zen and the White Whale*. Bethlehem, PA: Lehigh University Press, 2014.
Higgins, Brian, and Hershel Parker. *Herman Melville: The Contemporary Reviews*. Cambridge, UK: Cambridge UP, 1995.
Hoare, Philip. *Leviathan, or The Whale*. New York: HarperCollins, 2009.
Hoffman, Daniel. *Form and Fable in American Fiction*. New York: Oxford UP, 1961.
Howard, Jennifer. "Call Me Digital." *Chronicle of Higher Education*, February 17, 2006, A14.
Howard, Leon. *Herman Melville, a Biography*. Berkeley: U of California P, 1951.

Hsu, Hsuan. "War, Ekphrasis, and Elliptical Form in Melville's Battle-Pieces." *Nineteenth Century Studies* 16 (2002): 51–72.
Hughes, Henry. "Fish, Sex and Cannibalism: Appetites for Conversion in Melville's Typee." *Leviathan: A Journal of Melville Studies* 6, no. 2 (2004): 3–16.
———, ed. "Melville in the Marquesas." Special issue, *Leviathan: A Journal of Melville Studies* 11, no. 2 (2009).
Inge, M. Thomas, ed. "Melville in the Popular Imagination." Special issue, *Leviathan: A Journal of Melville Studies* 11, no. 3 (2009).
Irwin, John T. *American Hieroglyphics: The Symbol of the Egyptian Hieroglyphics in the American Renaissance.* New Haven, CT: Yale UP, 1980.
Ives, C. B. "*Billy Budd* and the Articles of War." *American Literature: A Journal of Literary History, Criticism, and Bibliography* 34, no. 1 (1962): 31–39.
Jackson, Virginia. "Who Reads Poetry?" *PMLA: Publications of the Modern Language Association of America* 123, no. 1 (2008): 181–87.
Jamali, Leyli. "Herman Melville in Iran: Translation, Interpretations, and Receptions." *Leviathan: A Journal of Melville Studies* 20, no. 1 (2018): 22-35.
James, C. L. R. *Mariners, Renegades, and Castaways: The Story of Herman Melville and the World We Live In.* 1953. Reprint, London, New York: Allison & Busby, 1985.
Jehlen, Myra. *American Incarnation: The Individual, the Nation, and the Continent.* Cambridge, MA: Harvard UP, 1986.
Johnson, Barbara. "Melville's Fist: The Execution of *Billy Budd.*" *Studies in Romanticism* 18, no. 4 (1979): 567–99.
Jonik, Michael. *Melville and the Politics of the Inhuman.* New York: Cambridge UP, 2018.
Kaiwi, Monica A. Ka'imipono. "*Typee*: Melville's 'Contribution' to the Wellbeing of Native Hawaiians." In *"Whole Oceans Away": Melville and the Pacific*, edited by Christopher Sten, 3–16. Kent, OH: Kent State UP, 2007.
Karcher, Carolyn L. *Shadow Over the Promised Land: Slavery, Race, and Violence in Melville's America.* Baton Rouge: Louisiana State UP, 1979.
Kato, Yuji. "Herman Melville and Modern Japan: A Speculative Re-Interpretation of the Critical History." *Leviathan: A Journal of Melville Studies* 8, no. 3 (2006): 11–18.
Kaul, A. N. *The American Vision; Actual and Ideal Society in Nineteenth-Century Fiction.* New Haven, CT: Yale UP, 1963.
Kazin, Alfred. *God & the American Writer.* New York: Alfred A. Knopf, 1997.
———. "On Melville as Scripture." *Partisan Review* 17 (1950): 67–75.
Kelley, Wyn. "Hawthorne and Melville in the Shoals: 'Agatha,' the Trials of Authorship, and the Dream of Collaboration." In *Hawthorne and Melville: Writing a Relationship*, edited by Leland S. Person, 173–95. Athens: U of Georgia P, 2008.
———. *Herman Melville: An Introduction.* Malden, MA: Blackwell, 2008.

———. "Lauding the Inhuman Sea." *Leviathan: A Journal of Melville Studies* 17, no. 1 (2015): 133-35.

———. "'Lying in Various Attitudes': Staging Melville's Pip in Digital Media." In *Ungraspable Phantom: Essays on Moby-Dick*, edited by John Bryant, Mary K. Bercaw Edwards, and Timothy Marr, 337–53. Kent, OH: Kent State UP, 2006.

———. "Melville by Design." In *Teaching with Digital Humanities: Tools and Methods for Nineteenth-Century American Literature*, ed. Jennifer Travis and Jessica DeSpain. Springfield, IL: University of Illinois Press, 2018.

———. *Melville's City: Literary and Urban Form in Nineteenth-Century New York*. New York: Cambridge UP, 1996.

———. "Out of the Breadbox: Eleanor Melville Metcalf and the Melville Legacy." *Leviathan: A Journal of Melville Studies* 13, no. 1 (2011): 21–33.

———. "The Style of Lima: Colonialism, Urban Form, and 'The Town-Ho's Story.'" In *Melville "Among the Nations,"* edited by Sanford E. Marovitz, and A. C. Christodoulou, 61–70. Kent, OH: Kent State UP, 2001.

———. "'Tender Kinswoman': Gail Hamilton and Gendered Justice in *Billy Budd*." In *Melville and Women*, edited by Elizabeth A. Schultz, and Haskell S. Springer, 98–117. Kent, OH: Kent State UP, 2006.

———. "'This Matter of Writing': Melville and the Manuscript Page." In *Billy Budd, Sailor: Critical Insights*, ed. Brian Yothers. Ipswich, MA: Salem Press, 2017.

———, ed. *A Companion to Herman Melville*. Malden, MA: Blackwell, 2006.

Kelley, Wyn, and Henry Jenkins. *Reading in a Participatory Culture: Remixing Moby-Dick in the English* Classroom. New York: Teacher's College Press, 2015.

Kenny, Vincent S. *Herman Melville's "Clarel": A Spiritual Autobiography*. Hamden, CT: Archon, 1973.

Kevorkian, Martin. "Faith Among the Weeds: Melville's Religious Wildings Beyond These Deserts." In *Visionary of the Word: Melville and Religion*, ed. Jonathan A. Cook and Brian Yothers, 97-125. Evanston, IL: Northwestern University Press, 2017.

———. *Writing Beyond Prophecy: Emerson, Hawthorne, and Melville After the American Renaissance*. Baton Rouge, LA: Louisiana State University Press, 2013.

Kish, Matthew. *Moby-Dick in Pictures: One Drawing for Every Page*. Portland, OR: Tin House Books, 2011.

Kleitz, Dorsey. "Herman Melville, Matthew Perry, and the Narrative of the Expedition of an American Squadron to the China Seas and Japan." *Leviathan: A Journal of Melville Studies* 8, no. 3 (2006): 25–32.

Knapp, Joseph G. *Tortured Synthesis: The Meaning of Melville's "Clarel."* New York: Philosophical Library, 1971.

Knip, Matthew. "Homosocial Desire and Erotic Communitas in Melville's Imaginary: The Evidence of Van Buskirk." *ESQ: A Journal of Nineteenth-Century American Literature and Culture* 62, no. 2 (2016): 355-414.

Koffler, Judith Schenck, and Robin West. "The Feminine Presence in *Billy Budd*." *Cardozo Studies in Law and Literature* 1, no. 1 (1989): 1–20.
Konefsky, Alfred S. "The Accidental Legal Historian: Herman Melville and the History of American Law." *Buffalo Law Review* 52, no. 4 (2004): 1179.
Kramer, Michael P. "Imagining Authorship in America: 'Whose American Renaissance?' Revisited." *American Literary History* 13, no. 1 (2001): 108–25.
Kring, Walter Donald. *Herman Melville's Religious Journey*. Raleigh, NC: Pentland Press, 1997.
Kring, Walter Donald, and Jonathan S. Carey. "Two Discoveries Concerning Herman Melville." *Proceedings of the Massachusetts Historical Society* 87 (1975): 136–41.
Kring, Walter Donald, Jonathan S. Carey, Donald Yannella, and Hershal Parker, eds. *The Endless, Winding Way in Melville: New Charts by Kring and Carey*. Glassboro, NJ: Melville Society, 1981.
Kulkarni, Hemant Balvantrao. *Moby-Dick: A Hindu Avatar, A Study of Hindu Myth and Thought in Moby-Dick*. Logan: Utah State UP, 1970.
Laist, Randy. "Profiles in Ontological Rebellion: The Presence of *Moby-Dick* in *Heathers*." *Leviathan: A Journal of Melville Studies* 11, no. 3 (2009): 72–78.
LaRue, L. H. "Paradox and Interpretation." *Cardozo Studies in Law and Literature* 1, no. 1 (1989): 97–108.
Lawrence, D. H. *Studies in Classic American Literature*. New York: Viking Press, 1964.
Lazo, Rodrigo. "The Ends of Enchantment: Douglass, Melville, and U.S. Expansion in the Americas." In *Frederick Douglass and Herman Melville: Essays in Relation*, edited by Robert S. Levine and Samuel Otter, 207–29. Chapel Hill: U of North Carolina P, 2008.
Lebowitz, Alan. *Progress into Silence: A Study of Melville's Heroes*. Bloomington: Indiana UP, 1970.
Ledbetter, Jack W. "The Trial of Billy Budd, Foretopman." *American Bar Association Journal* 58 (1972): 614–18.
Lee, A. R., ed. "Melville and Japan." Special issue, *Leviathan: A Journal of Melville Studies* 8, no. 3 (2006): 7–60.
Leverenz, David. *Manhood and the American Renaissance*. Ithaca, NY: Cornell UP, 1989.
Levin, Harry. *The Power of Blackness: Hawthorne, Poe, Melville*. New York: Knopf, 1958.
Levine, Robert S. *Conspiracy and Romance: Studies in Brockden Brown, Cooper, Hawthorne, and Melville*. Cambridge, UK; New York: Cambridge UP, 1989.
Levine, Robert S, and Samuel Otter, eds. *Frederick Douglass and Herman Melville: Essays in Relation*. Chapel Hill: U of North Carolina P, 2008.
Levine, Robert S., and Cindy Weinstein. *Pierre; or, The Ambiguities: A Norton Critical Edition*. New York: W. W. Norton, 2017.

Lewis, R. W. B. *The American Adam: Innocence, Tragedy, and Tradition in the Nineteenth Century.* Chicago: U of Chicago P, 1955.

Leyda, Jay. *The Melville Log: A Documentary Life of Herman Melville, 1819–1891.* New York: Harcourt, Brace, 1951.

Lopez Pena, Laura. *Beyond the Walls: Being with Each Other in Herman Melville's Clarel.* València: Publicacions de la Universitat de València, 2015.

Lowell, Robert. "Benito Cereno" In *The Old Glory.* New York: Farrar, Straus, and Giroux, 1965.

Lyons, Paul. *American Pacificism: Oceania in the U.S. Imagination.* New York: Routledge, 2006.

Mailloux, Steven. "Judging the Judge: *Billy Budd* and 'Proof to all Sophistries.'" *Cardozo Studies in Law and Literature* 1 no. 1 (1989): 83–88.

———. "Political Theology in Douglass and Melville." In *Frederick Douglass and Herman Melville: Essays in Relation*, edited by Robert S. Levine and Samuel Otter, 159–80. Chapel Hill: U of North Carolina P, 2008.

Maloney, Ian S. *Melville's Monumental Imagination.* New York: Routledge, 2006.

Mankino, Arimichi. "Commodore Perry as White Phantom: Moby-Dick in the Context of the Modern Age." *Leviathan: A Journal of Melville Studies* 8, no. 3 (2006): 19–23.

Marovitz, Sanford E. "The Melville Revival." In *A Companion to Herman Melville*, edited by Wyn Kelley, 515–31. New York: Blackwell, 2005.

———, ed. *Melville as Poet: The Art of "Pulsed Life."* Kent, OH: Kent State University Press, 2013.

Marovitz, Sanford E., and A. K. Christodoulou, eds. *Melville "Among the Nations": Proceedings of an International Conference, Volos, Greece, July 2–6, 1997.* Kent, OH: Kent State UP, 2001.

Marr, Timothy. *The Cultural Roots of American Islamicism.* Cambridge, UK; New York: Cambridge UP, 2006.

———. "Without the Pale: Melville and Ethnic Cosmopolitanism." In *A Historical Guide to Herman Melville*, edited by Giles Gunn, 133–66. New York: Oxford UP, 2005.

Marrs, Cody. "A Wayward Art: Battle-Pieces and Melville's Poetic Turn." *American Literature: A Journal of Literary History, Criticism, and Bibliography* 82, no. 1 (2010): 91–119.

Martin, Robert K. *Hero, Captain, and Stranger: Male Friendship, Social Critique, and Literary Form in the Sea Novels of Herman Melville.* Chapel Hill: U of North Carolina P, 1986.

Marx, Leo. *The Machine in the Garden: Technology and the Pastoral Ideal in America.* New York: Oxford UP, 1964.

———. "Melville's Parable of the Walls." *Sewanee Review* 61 (1953): 602–27.

Mason, Ronald. *The Spirit Above the Dust: A Study of Herman Melville.* London: J. Lehmann, 1951.

Matteson, John T. "'Deadly Voids and Unbidden Infidelities': Death, Memory, and the Law in Moby-Dick." In *Ungraspable Phantom: Essays on Moby-Dick*, edited by John Bryant, Mary K. Bercaw Edwards, and Timothy Marr, 117–31. Kent, OH: Kent State UP, 2006.

———. "'A New Race has Sprung Up': Prudence, Social Consensus and the Law in 'Bartleby the Scrivener.'" *Leviathan: A Journal of Melville Studies* 10, no. 1 (2008): 25–49.
Matthiessen, F. O. *American Renaissance: Art and Expression in the Age of Emerson and Whitman*. London; New York: Oxford UP, 1941.
McCall, Corey, and Tom Nurmi, eds. *Melville among the Philosophers*. Lanham, MD: Lexington Books, 2017.
McCall, Dan. *The Silence of Bartleby*. Ithaca, NY: Cornell UP, 1989.
McGettigan, Katie. *Herman Melville, Modernity, and the Material Text*. Manchester, NH: University of New Hampshire Press, 2017.
McGinnis, Eileen. "'Change Irreverent': Evolution and Faith in 'The Encantadas' and *Clarel*." In *Visionary of the Word: Melville and Religion*, ed. Jonathan A. Cook and Brian Yothers, 71-96. Evanston, IL: Northwestern University Press, 2017.
McLoughlin, Michael. *Dead Letters to the New World: Melville, Emerson, and American Transcendentalism*. New York: Routledge, 2003.
McWilliams, John P. *Hawthorne, Melville, and the American Character: A Looking-Glass Business*. New York: Cambridge UP, 1984.
Melville, Herman. *The Confidence-Man — His Masquerade*. Edited by Elizabeth Sophia Foster. New York: Hendricks House, 1954.
———. *John Marr and Other Sailors, with Some Sea Pieces*. Edited by Douglas Robillard. Facsimile edition. Kent, OH: Kent State UP, 2006.
———. *Journal of a Visit to Europe and the Levant*. Edited by Howard Horsford. Princeton, NJ: Princeton UP, 1955.
———. *Moby-Dick*. Edited by Edward W. Said. New York: Library of America, 1991.
———. *The Poems of Herman Melville*. Edited by Douglas Robillard. Kent, OH: Kent State UP, 2000.
The Melville Electronic Library. http://www2.iath.virginia.edu/melville/.
Melville's Marginalia Online. Edited by Steven Olsen-Smith, Peter Norberg, and Dennis Marnon. http://www.boisestate.edu/melville/.
Metcalf, Eleanor Melville. *Herman Melville, Cycle and Epicycle*. Cambridge, MA: Harvard UP, 1953.
Michaels, Walter Benn, and Donald E. Pease, eds. *The American Renaissance Reconsidered*. Baltimore: Johns Hopkins UP, 1985.
Middleton-Kaplan, Richard. "Play it again, Herman: Melville at the Movies." *Leviathan: A Journal of Melville Studies* 11, no. 3 (2009): 55–71.
Milder, Robert. *Exiled Royalties: Melville and the Life We Imagine*. New York: Oxford UP, 2006.
———. "'The Ugly Socrates': Melville, Hawthorne, and the Varieties of Homoerotic Experience." In *Hawthorne and Melville: Writing a Relationship*, edited by Leland S. Person, 71–111. Athens: U of Georgia P, 2008.
Miller, Edwin Haviland. *Melville*. New York: George Braziller, 1975.
Miller, Perry. *The Raven and the Whale: The War of Words and Wits in the Era of Poe and Melville*. New York: Harcourt, Brace, 1956.

Mitchell, David. "'Too Much of a Cripple': Ahab, Dire Bodies, and the Language of Prosthesis in *Moby-Dick.*" *Leviathan: A Journal of Melville Studies* 1, no. 1 (1999): 5–22.

Mitchell, David, and Samuel Otter, eds. "Melville and Disability." Special issue, *Leviathan: A Journal of Melville Studies* 8, no. 1 (2006).

Mitchell, David, and Sharon L. Snyder. "Masquerades of Impairment: Charity as a Confidence Game." *Leviathan: A Journal of Melville Studies* 8, no. 1 (2006): 35–60.

———. *Narrative Prosthesis: Disability and the Dependencies of Discourse.* Ann Arbor: U of Michigan P, 2000.

Montas, Roosevelt. "Meaning and Transcendence: Melville, Douglass, and the Anxiety of Interpretation." *Leviathan: A Journal of Melville Studies* 10, no. 2 (2008): 69–83.

Moore, Richard S. *That Cunning Alphabet: Melville's Aesthetics of Nature.* Amsterdam: Rodopi, 1982.

Morrison, Toni. *Playing in the Dark: Whiteness and the Literary Imagination.* Cambridge, MA: Harvard UP, 1992.

Mumford, Lewis. *Herman Melville: A Study of His Life and Vision.* Rev. ed. New York: Harcourt, Brace, 1962.

Murray, Henry A. Introduction to *Pierre, or the Ambiguities*, by Herman Melville, xiii–ciii. New York: Hendricks House, 1949.

———. "In Nomine Diaboli." *New England Quarterly* 24, no. 4 (1951): 435–52.

Mushabac, Jane. *Melville's Humor: A Critical Study.* Hamden, CT: Archon Books, 1981.

Nabers, Deak. *Victory of Law: The Fourteenth Amendment, the Civil War, and American Literature, 1852–1867.* Baltimore: Johns Hopkins UP, 2006.

Naslund, Sena Jeter. *Ahab's Wife; or, The Star-Gazer: A Novel.* New York: William Morrow, 1999.

New, Elisa. "Bible Leaves! Bible Leaves! Hellenism and Hebraism in Melville's *Moby-Dick.*" *Poetics Today* 19, no. 2 (1998): 281–303.

Ngai, Sianne. *Ugly Feelings.* Cambridge, MA: Harvard UP, 2005.

Nichol, John W. "Melville's 'Soiled' Fish of the Sea." *American Literature* 21, no. 3 (1949): 338–39.

Obenzinger, Hilton. *American Palestine: Melville, Twain, and the Holy Land Mania.* Princeton, NJ: Princeton UP, 1999.

———. "Wicked Books: Melville and Religion." In *A Companion to Herman Melville*, edited by Wyn Kelley, 181–96. New York: Blackwell, 2005.

Olsen-Smith, Steven. "Melville's Marginalia in Thomas Beale's *The Natural History of the Sperm Whale.*" Notes and Introduction. *Melville's Marginalia Online.* www.boisestate.edu/melville.

Olsen-Smith, Steven, Peter Norberg, and Dennis Marnon, eds. *Melville's Marginalia Online.* www.boisestate.edu/melville.

Olsen-Smith, Steven, and Merton M. Sealts. "A Cumulative Supplement to *Melville's Reading* (1988)." *Leviathan: A Journal of Melville Studies* 6, no. 1 (2004): 55–77.

Olson, Charles. *Call Me Ishmael.* New York: Reynal & Hitchcock, 1947.
———. "Lear and Moby-Dick." *Twice a year* 1 (1938): 165–89.
Osborne, Gillian. "Herman Melville: Queen of the Flowers." *Leviathan: A Journal of Melville Studies* 18, no. 3 (2016): 129-48.
Oshima, Yukiko. "Native America in *The Confidence Man*: Quite an Original Satire and Scene." *Leviathan: A Journal of Melville Studies* 8, no. 3 (2006): 51–60.
———. "The Red Flag of the Pequod/Pequot: Native American Presence in *Moby-Dick.*" In *Melville "Among the Nations,"* edited by Sanford E. Marovitz, and A. C. Christodoulou, 254–66. Kent, OH: Kent State UP, 2001.
Otter, Samuel. "How *Clarel* Works." In *A Companion to Herman Melville*, edited by Wyn Kelley, 467–81. New York: Blackwell, 2005.
———. "Leviathanic Revelations: Laurie Anderson's, Rinde Eckert's, and John Barrymore's *Moby-Dicks.*" In *Ungraspable Phantom: Essays on Moby-Dick*, edited by John Bryant, Mary K. Bercaw Edwards, and Timothy Marr, 291–304. Kent, OH: Kent State UP, 2006.
———. "Melville, Poetry, Prints." In *Melville's Philosophies*, ed. Branka Arsić and K. L. Evans, 219-60. New York: Bloomsbury, 2018.
———. *Melville's Anatomies.* Berkeley: U of California P, 1999.
———. "*Typee*: 'An Almost Incredible Book.'" *ESQ: A Journal of the American Renaissance* 51, nos. 1–3 (2005): 169–85.
Otter, Samuel, and Geoffrey Sanborn, eds. *Melville and Aesthetics.* New York: Palgrave, 2011.
Paglia, Camille. *Sexual Personae: Art and Decadence from Nefertiti to Emily Dickinson.* New Haven, CT: Yale UP, 1990.
Pardes, Ilana. *Melville's Bibles.* Berkeley: U of California P, 2008.
Parini, Jay. *The Passages of H.M.* New York: Doubleday, 2010.
Parker, Hershel. *Flawed Texts and Verbal Icons: Literary Authority in American Fiction.* Evanston, IL: Northwestern UP, 1984.
———. *Herman Melville: A Biography.* Vol. 1. Baltimore: Johns Hopkins UP, 1997.
———. *Herman Melville: A Biography.* Vol. 2. Baltimore: Johns Hopkins UP, 2002.
———. *Melville Biography: An Inside Narrative.* Evanston, IL: Northwestern University Press, 2013.
———. *Melville: The Making of the Poet.* Evanston, IL: Northwestern UP, 2008.
———. *Moby-Dick; or, The Whale: A Norton Critical Edition.* Third Edition. New York: W. W. Norton, 2017.
———. *Reading "Billy Budd."* Evanston, IL: Northwestern UP, 1990.
———. *The Recognition of Herman Melville: Selected Criticism since 1846.* Ann Arbor: U of Michigan P, 1967.
Parker, Hershel, and Harrison Hayford, eds. *Moby-Dick: A Norton Critical Edition.* 2nd ed. New York: Norton, 2001.

Parrington, Vernon Louis. *Main Currents in American Thought: An Interpretation of American Literature from the Beginnings to 1920.* New York: Harcourt, Brace, 1930.
Pease, Donald E. "Moby-Dick and the Cold War." In *The American Renaissance Reconsidered*, edited by Walter Benn Michaels and Donald E. Pease, 113–55. Baltimore: Johns Hopkins UP, 1985.
———. *Visionary Compacts: American Renaissance Writings in Cultural Context.* Madison: U of Wisconsin P, 1987.
Peeples, Scott. *The Afterlife of Edgar Allan Poe.* Rochester, NY: Camden House, 2004.
———. "Where Were Douglass and Melville on April 15, 1865." *Leviathan: A Journal of Melville Studies* 10, no. 2 (2008): 37–49.
Pellar, Brian. *Moby-Dick and Melville's Anti-Slavery Allegory.* New York: Springer, 2017.
Percival, Milton Oswin. *A Reading of Moby-Dick.* New York: Octagon Books, 1967.
Peretz, Eyal. *Literature, Disaster, and the Enigma of Power: A Reading of "Moby-Dick."* Stanford, CA: Stanford UP, 2003.
Person, Leland. "Melville's Cassock: Putting on Masculinity in *Moby-Dick*." *ESQ: A Journal of the American Renaissance* 40 (1994): 1–26.
Pommer, Henry. *Milton and Melville.* Pittsburgh, PA: U of Pittsburgh P, 1950.
Porte, Joel. *The Romance in America; Studies in Cooper, Poe, Hawthorne, Melville, and James.* Middletown, CT: Wesleyan UP, 1969.
Posner, Richard A. "Comment on Richard Weisberg's Interpretation of *Billy Budd*." *Cardozo Studies in Law and Literature* 1, no. 1 (1989): 71–81.
———. *Law and Literature.* Cambridge, MA: Harvard UP, 2009.
Post-Lauria, Sheila. *Correspondent Colorings: Melville in the Marketplace.* Amherst: U of Massachusetts P, 1996.
Potter, William. *Melville's "Clarel" and the Intersympathy of Creeds.* Kent, OH: Kent State UP, 2004.
Rahv, Philip. "Melville and His Critics." *Partisan Review* 17 (1950): 732–35.
Reed, Christian. "The Bachelor and the Orphan." *Leviathan: A Journal of Melville Studies* 17, no. 1 (2015): 1-25.
Reich, Charles A. "The Tragedy of Justice in *Billy Budd*." *Yale Review* 56 (1967): 368–89.
Renker, Elizabeth. "Herman Melville, Wife Beating, and the Written Page." *American Literature: A Journal of Literary History, Criticism, and Bibliography* 66, no. 1 (1994): 123–50.
———. "Melville the Poet: Response to William Spengemann." *American Literary History* 12, no. 1 (2000): 348–54.
———. "Melville the Realist Poet." In *A Companion to Herman Melville*, edited by Wyn Kelley, 482–96. New York: Blackwell, 2005.
———. *Strike through the Mask: Herman Melville and the Scene of Writing.* Baltimore: Johns Hopkins UP, 1996.

Renker, Elizabeth, and Douglas Robillard, eds. "Melville the Poet." Special issue, *Leviathan: A Journal of Melville Studies* 9, no. 3 (2007).
Reynolds, David S. *Beneath the American Renaissance: The Subversive Imagination in the Age of Emerson and Melville*. New York: Knopf, 1988.
Reynolds, Larry J. *European Revolutions and the American Literary Renaissance*. New Haven, CT: Yale UP, 1988.
Robertson-Lorant, Laurie. "Melville and the Women in His Life." In *Melville and Women*, edited by Elizabeth A. Schultz, and Haskell S. Springer, 15–37. Kent, OH: Kent State UP, 2006.
———. "Mr. Omoo and the Hawthornes: The Biographical Background." In *Hawthorne and Melville: Writing a Relationship*, edited by Leland S. Person, 27–49. Athens: U of Georgia P, 2008.
Robertson-Lorant, Laurie. *Melville: A Biography*. New York: Clarkson Potter, 1996.
Robillard, Douglas. *Melville and the Visual Arts: Ionian Form, Venetian Tint*. Kent, OH: Kent State UP, 1997.
Rogin, Michael Paul. *Subversive Genealogy: The Politics and Art of Herman Melville*. New York: Knopf, 1983.
Rosenberg, Warren. "'Deeper than Sappho': Melville, Poetry and the Erotic." *Modern Language Studies* 14, no. 1 (1984): 70–78.
Rosenberry, Edward H. *Melville*. London; Boston: Routledge & Kegan Paul, 1979.
———. *Melville and the Comic Spirit*. Cambridge, MA: Harvard UP, 1955.
Rowe, John Carlos. *At Emerson's Tomb: The Politics of Classic American Literature*. New York: Columbia UP, 1997.
———. *Literary Culture and U.S. Imperialism: From the Revolution to World War II*. Oxford; New York: Oxford UP, 2000.
———. *Through the Custom-House: Nineteenth-Century American Fiction and Modern Theory*. Baltimore: Johns Hopkins UP, 1982.
Ryan, James Emmett. "Ishmael's Recovery: Injury, Illness, and Convalescence in *Moby-Dick*." *Leviathan: A Journal of Melville Studies* 8, no. 1 (2006): 17–34.
Rysten, Felix S. A. *False Prophets in the Fiction of Camus, Dostoevsky, Melville, and Others*. Coral Gables, FL: U of Miami P, 1972.
Said, Edward W. "Introduction to *Moby-Dick*." 1991. Reprinted in *Reflections on Exile and Other Essays*, 356–71. Cambridge, MA: Harvard UP, 2003.
———. *Orientalism*. New York: Vintage Books, 1979.
Saiki, Ikuno. "A Shadow of the Far East: Fedallah; Or, a Japanese Sea Drifter." *Leviathan: A Journal of Melville Studies* 8, no. 3 (2006): 33–42.
Samson, John. *White Lies: Melville's Narratives of Facts*. Ithaca, NY: Cornell UP, 1989.
Samuels, Ellen. "From Melville to Eddie Murphy: The Disability Con in American Literature and Film." *Leviathan: A Journal of Melville Studies* 8, no. 1 (2006): 61–82.

Sanborn, Geoffrey. *The Sign of the Cannibal: Melville and the Making of a Postcolonial Reader*. Durham, NC: Duke UP, 1998.

———. *The Value of Herman Melville*. New York: Cambridge University Press, 2018.

———. "Whence Come You, Queequeg?" *American Literature: A Journal of Literary History, Criticism, and Bibliography* 77, no. 2 (2005): 227–57.

Sandberg, Robert, ed. *The Melville Room*. Online site (under construction). http://www.melvilleroom.org.

———. *The Melville Society*. Online site. http://www.melvillesociety.org.

Schell, Jennifer. *"A Bold and Hardy Race of Men": The Lives and Literature of American Whalemen*. Amherst, MA: University of Massachusetts Press, 2013.

———. "'We Account the Whale Immortal': Fantasies of Ecological Abundance and Discourses of Extinction in Herman Melville's *Moby-Dick*." In *Moby-Dick: Critical Insights*, ed. Robert C. Evans, 209-28. Ipswich, MA: Salem Press, 2014.

Schiffman, Joseph. "Melville's Final Stage, Irony: A Re-Examination of *Billy Budd* Criticism." *American Literature* 22, no. 2 (1950): 128–36.

Schueller, Malini Johar. *U.S. Orientalisms: Race, Nation, and Gender in Literature, 1790–1890*. Ann Arbor: U of Michigan P, 1998.

Schultz, Elizabeth A. "Feminizing *Moby-Dick*: Contemporary Women Perform the Whale." In *Ungraspable Phantom: Essays on Moby-Dick*, edited by John Bryant, Mary K. Bercaw Edwards, and Timothy Marr, 305–20. Kent, OH: Kent State UP, 2006.

———. "The New Art of *Moby-Dick*." *Leviathan: A Journal of Melville Studies* 21, no. 1 (2019): 1-76.

———. *Unpainted to the Last:* Moby-Dick *and Twentieth-Century American Art*. Lawrence: UP of Kansas, 1995.

Schultz, Elizabeth A., and Haskell S. Springer, eds. *Melville and Women*. Kent, OH: Kent State UP, 2006.

Sealts, Merton M. *Melville as Lecturer*. Cambridge, MA: Harvard UP, 1957.

———. *Melville's Reading*. Rev. and enl. ed. Columbia: U of South Carolina P, 1988.

———. *Melville's Reading: A Check-List of Books Owned and Borrowed*. Madison: U of Wisconsin P, 1966.

———. *Pursuing Melville, 1940–1980: Chapters and Essays*. Madison: U of Wisconsin P, 1982.

Sedgwick, Eve Kosofsky. *Epistemology of the Closet*. Berkeley: U of California P, 1990.

Sedgwick, William Ellery, and Sarah Cabot Sedgwick. *Herman Melville: The Tragedy of Mind*. Cambridge, MA: Harvard UP, 1944.

Seelye, John D. *Melville: The Ironic Diagram*. Evanston, IL: Northwestern UP, 1970.

Sewall, Richard Benson. *The Vision of Tragedy*. New Haven, CT: Yale UP, 1959.

Shattuck, Roger. *Forbidden Knowledge: From Prometheus to Pornography*. New York: St. Martin's, 1997.
Sherrill, Rowland A. *The Prophetic Melville: Experience, Transcendence, and Tragedy*. Athens: U of Georgia P, 1979.
Short, Bryan C. *Cast by Means of Figures: Herman Melville's Rhetorical Development*. Amherst: U of Massachusetts P, 1992.
———. "Plagiarizing Polynesia: Decolonization in Melville's *Omoo* Borrowings." In *"Whole Oceans Away": Melville and the Pacific*, edited by Christopher Sten, 98–110. Kent, OH: Kent State UP, 2007.
Shulman, Robert. "The Serious Functions of Melville's Phallic Jokes." *American Literature: A Journal of Literary History, Criticism, and Bibliography* 33, no. 2 (1961): 179–94.
———. *Social Criticism & Nineteenth-Century American Fictions*. Columbia: U of Missouri P, 1987.
Shurr, William. *The Mystery of Iniquity: Melville as Poet, 1857–1891*. Lexington: UP of Kentucky, 1972.
Simonsen, Rasmus. "Melville's Chimney: Queer Syntax and the Rhetoric of Architecture." *Leviathan: A Journal of Melville Studies* 17, no. 1 (2015): 26-40.
Slotkin, Richard. *Regeneration through Violence: The Mythology of the American Frontier, 1600–1860*. Middletown, CT: Wesleyan UP, 1973.
Smith, Henry Nash. *Democracy and the Novel: Popular Resistance to Classic American Writers*. New York: Oxford UP, 1978.
Snyder, Sharon L., and David T. Mitchell. *Cultural Locations of Disability*. Chicago: U of Chicago P, 2006.
Solove, D. J. "Melville's Billy Budd and Security in Times of Crisis." *Cardozo Law Review* 26, no. 6 (2005): 2443–70.
Spanos, William V. *The Errant Art of Moby-Dick: The Canon, the Cold War, and the Struggle for American Studies*. Durham, NC: Duke UP, 1995.
———. *Herman Melville and the American Calling: The Fiction after Moby Dick, 1851–1857*. Albany: SUNY P, 2008.
Spark, Clare. *Hunting Captain Ahab: Psychological Warfare and the Melville Revival*. Kent, OH: Kent State UP, 2001.
Spengemann, William C. "Melville the Poet." *American Literary History* 11, no. 4 (1999): 569–609.
Spiller, Robert, et al. *Literary History of the United States*. New York: MacMillan, 1948.
Stauffer, John. "Interracial Friendship and the Aesthetics of Freedom." *Frederick Douglass and Herman Melville: Essays in Relation*, edited by Robert S. Levine and Samuel Otter, 134–58. Chapel Hill: U of North Carolina P, 2008.
Stein, William Bysshe. *The Poetry of Melville's Late Years; Time, History, Myth, and Religion*. Albany: SUNY P, 1970.
Sten, Christopher. "City of Hope and Fear: Douglass and Melville in the Nation's Capital." *Leviathan: A Journal of Melville Studies* 10, no. 2 (2008): 23–36.

———. "Melville's Cosmopolitanism: A Map for Living in a (Post-) Colonialist World." In *Melville "Among the Nations,"* edited by Sanford E. Marovitz, and A. C. Christodoulou, 38–48. Kent, OH: Kent State UP, 2001.

———. *Savage Eye: Melville and the Visual Arts*. Kent, OH: Kent State UP, 1991.

———. "Vere's use of the "Forms": Means and Ends in *Billy Budd*." *American Literature* 47, no. 1 (1975): 37–51.

———. *The Weaver-God, He Weaves: Melville and the Poetics of the Novel*. Kent, OH: Kent State UP, 1996.

Stern, Milton R. *The Fine Hammered Steel of Herman Melville*. Urbana: U of Illinois P, 1957.

———. "Towards 'Bartleby the Scrivener.'" In *The Stoic Strain in American Literature*, edited by Duane J. Macmillan, 19–41. Toronto: U of Toronto P, 1979.

Stewart, George R. "The Two Moby-Dicks." *American Literature* 25, no. 4 (1954): 417–48.

Stewart, Randall. *American Literature and Christian Doctrine*. Baton Rouge: Louisiana State UP, 1958.

Stone, Geoffrey. *Melville*. Great Writers of the World series. New York: Sheed & Ward, 1949.

Stuckey, Sterling. *African Culture and Melville's Art: The Creative Process in "Benito Cereno" and "Moby-Dick."* Oxford: Oxford UP, 2009.

———. "Cheer and Gloom: Douglass and Melville on Slave Dance and Music." In *Frederick Douglass and Herman Melville: Essays in Relation*, edited by Robert S. Levine and Samuel Otter, 69–87. Chapel Hill: U of North Carolina P, 2008.

Suchoff, David. "Melville: Ironic Democracy." In *Critical Theory and the Novel: Mass Society and Cultural Criticism in Dickens, Melville, and Kafka*, 89–135. Madison: U of Wisconsin P, 1994.

Suggs, Robert C. "Melville's Flight to Taipi: Topographic, Archeological, and Historical Considerations." *ESQ: A Journal of the American Renaissance* 51, no. 1 (2005): 47.

Sundquist, Eric J. "*Benito Cereno* and New World Slavery." In *Reconstructing American Literary History*, edited by Sacvan Bercovitch, 93–122. Cambridge, MA: Harvard UP, 1986.

———. "Suspense and Tautology in *Benito Cereno*." *Glyph: Textual Studies* 8 (1981): 103–26.

———. *To Wake the Nations: Race in the Making of American Literature*. Cambridge, MA: Belknap Press of Harvard UP, 1993.

Sweet, Timothy. *Traces of War: Poetry, Photography, and the Crisis of the Union*. Baltimore: Johns Hopkins UP, 1990.

———. "'Will He Perish?': *Moby-Dick* and Nineteenth-Century Extinction Discourse." In *Above the American Renaissance: David S. Reynolds and the Spiritual Imagination in American Literary Studies*, ed. Harold K.

Bush and Brian Yothers, 87-103. Amherst, MA: University of Massachusetts Press, 2018.

Szendy, Peter. *Prophecies of Leviathan: Reading Past Melville*. Translated by Gil Anidjar. New York: Fordham UP, 2010.

Tally, Robert T. *Melville, Mapping and Globalization: Literary Cartography in the American Baroque Writer*. London; New York: Continuum, 2009.

Tamarkin, Elisa. "The Ethics of Impertinence: Douglass and Melville on England." In *Frederick Douglass and Herman Melville: Essays in Relation*, edited by Robert S. Levine and Samuel Otter, 181–206. Chapel Hill: U of North Carolina P, 2008.

———. "A Final Appearance with Elihu Vedder: Melville's Visions." *Leviathan: A Journal of Melville Studies* 18, no. 3 (2016): 68-111.

———. "A Final Appearance with Elihu Vedder: Melville's Visions." In *Melville's Philosophies*, ed. Branka Arsić and K. L. Evans, 261-300. New York: Bloomsbury, 2018.

Temple, Gale. "'Ineffable Socialities': Melville, Hawthorne, and Masculine Ambivalence in the Antebellum Marketplace." In *Hawthorne and Melville: Writing a Relationship*, edited by Leland S. Person, 113–31. Athens: U of Georgia P, 2008.

Thomas, Brook. *Cross-Examinations of Law and Literature: Cooper, Hawthorne, Stowe, and Melville*. Cambridge; New York: Cambridge UP, 1987.

Thompson, G. R., ed. "Melville in the Marquesas: Actuality of Place in *Typee* and Other Island Writings." Special issue, *ESQ: A Journal of the American Renaissance* 51, nos. 1–3 (2005).

Thompson, G. R., and Eric Carl Link. *Neutral Ground: New Traditionalism and the American Romance Controversy*. Baton Rouge: Louisiana State UP, 1999.

Thompson, Lawrance Roger. *Melville's Quarrel with God*. Princeton, NJ: Princeton UP, 1952.

Thomson, Shawn. *The Romantic Architecture of Herman Melville's Moby-Dick*. Madison NJ: Fairleigh Dickinson UP, 2001.

Thorp, Willard, ed. *Herman Melville: Representative Selections, with Introduction, Bibliography, and Notes*. New York: American Book Co., 1938.

Tolchin, Neal L. *Mourning, Gender, and Creativity in the Art of Herman Melville*. New Haven, CT: Yale UP, 1988.

Tompkins, Jane P. *Sensational Designs: The Cultural Work of American Fiction, 1790–1860*. New York: Oxford UP, 1985.

Trilling, Lionel. *The Liberal Imagination: Essays on Literature and Society*. New York: Viking Press, 1950.

Trodd, Zoe. "A Hid Event, Twice Lived: The Post-War Narrative Sub-Versions of Douglass and Melville." *Leviathan: A Journal of Melville Studies* 10, no. 2 (2008): 51–68.

Vendler, Helen. "Desert Storm." Review of *Clarel*, by Herman Melville, and *Journals*, by Herman Melville. *New Republic*, 7 December 1992, 39–42.

———. "Melville and the Lyric of History." *Southern Review* 35, no. 3 (1999): 579–94.

Vincent, Howard Paton. *The Tailoring of Melville's "White-Jacket."* Evanston, IL: Northwestern UP, 1970.

———. *The Trying-Out of "Moby-Dick."* Carbondale: Southern Illinois UP, 1965.

Wadlington, Warwick. *The Confidence Game in American Literature.* Princeton, NJ: Princeton UP, 1975.

Wald, Priscilla. "Hearing Narrative Voices in Melville's *Pierre.*" *Boundary 2* 17, no. 1 (1990): 100–132.

Walker, Franklin. *Irreverent Pilgrims: Melville, Browne, and Mark Twain in the Holy Land.* Seattle: U of Washington P, 1974.

Wallace, Robert K. "Ben-Ner's Moby Dick and Melville's Mechanism of Projection." *Leviathan: A Journal of Melville Studies* 9, no. 1 (2007): 43–59.

———. *Douglass and Melville: Anchored Together in Neighborly Style.* New Bedford, MA: Spinner Publications, 2005.

———. "Eckert's Great Whales as Homage and Prophecy." In *Ungraspable Phantom: Essays on Moby-Dick*, edited by John Bryant, Mary K. Bercaw Edwards, and Timothy Marr, 321–36. Kent, OH: Kent State UP, 2006.

———. "Fugitive Justice: Douglass, Shaw, Melville." *Frederick Douglass and Herman Melville: Essays in Relation*, edited by Robert S. Levine and Samuel Otter, 39–68. Chapel Hill: U of North Carolina P, 2008.

———. *Heggie and Scheer's Moby-Dick: A Grand Opera for the Twenty-First Century.* Denton, TX: University of North Texas Press, 2013.

———. *Melville & Turner: Spheres of Love and Fright.* Athens: U of Georgia P, 1992.

Wallace, Robert K., and Ivy G. Wilson, eds. "Frederick Douglass and Herman Melville." Special issue, *Leviathan: A Journal of Melville Studies* 10, no. 2 (2008): 3–83.

Warner, Michael. "What Like a Bullet can Undeceive?" *Public Culture* 15, no. 1 (2003): 41–54.

Warren, Robert Penn. "Melville the Poet." *Kenyon Review* 8, no. 2 (1946): 208–23.

———, ed. *Selected Poems of Herman Melville.* New York: Random House, 1967.

Warren, Rosanna. "Dark Knowledge: Melville's Poems of the Civil War." *Raritan: A Quarterly Review* 19, no. 1 (1999): 100–121.

Watson, E. L. Grant. "Melville's Testament of Acceptance." *New England Quarterly* 6, no. 2 (1933): 319–27.

Weaver, Raymond M. *Herman Melville: Mariner and Mystic.* 1920. Reprint, New York: Cooper Square, 1961.

Weinauer, Ellen. "Women, Ownership, and Gothic Manhood in *Pierre.*" In *Melville and Women*, edited by Elizabeth A. Schultz, and Haskell S. Springer, 141–60. Kent, OH: Kent State UP, 2006.

Weir, Charles, Jr. "Malice Reconciled: A Note on *Billy Budd.*" *University of Toronto Quarterly* 13 (1944): 276–85.

Weisberg, Richard H. "Accepting the Inside Narrator's Challenge: *Billy Budd* and the 'Legalistic' Reader." *Cardozo Studies in Law and Literature* 1, no. 1 (1989): 27–48.

———. *The Failure of the Word: The Protagonist as Lawyer in Modern Fiction.* New Haven, CT: Yale UP, 1984.

———. "How Judges Speak: Some Lessons on Adjudication in *Billy Budd, Sailor* with an Application to Justice Rehnquist." *N.Y.U. Law Review* 57 (1982): 1–69.

Wenke, John Paul. *Melville's Muse: Literary Creation and the Forms of Philosophical Fiction.* Kent, OH: Kent State UP, 1995.

Werge, Thomas. "*Moby-Dick* and the Calvinist Tradition." *Studies in the Novel* 1, no. 4 (1969): 484–506.

Westover, Jeff. "The Impressments of *Billy Budd.*" *Massachusetts Review: A Quarterly of Literature, the Arts and Public Affairs* 39, no. 3 (1998): 361–84.

Wiegman, Robyn. "Melville's Geography of Gender." *American Literary History* 1, no. 4 (1989): 735–53.

Williams, John B. *White Fire: The Influence of Emerson on Melville.* Long Beach: California State University, Long Beach, 1991.

Wilson, Edmund. *Patriotic Gore: Studies in the Literature of the American Civil War.* New York: Oxford UP, 1962.

Wilson, Ivy G. "'No Soul Above': Labor and the 'Law in Art' in Melville's 'The Bell-Tower.'" *Arizona Quarterly: A Journal of American Literature, Culture, and Theory* 63, no. 1 (2007): 27–47.

———. *Specters of Democracy: Blackness and the Aesthetics of Politics in the Antebellum U.S.* New York: Oxford UP, 2011.

Wineapple, Brenda. "Hawthorne and Melville: Or, the Ambiguities." In *Hawthorne and Melville: Writing a Relationship*, edited by Leland S. Person, 51–69. Athens: U of Georgia P, 2008.

Winters, Yvor. "Herman Melville and the Problems of Moral Navigation." In *In Defense of Reason*, 200–240. New York: The Swallow Press, 1947.

Withim, Phil. "Billy Budd: Testament of Resistance" *Modern Language Quarterly* 20 (1959): 115–27.

Wright, Nathalia. *Melville's Use of the Bible.* New York: Octagon Books, 1949.

Yothers, Brian, ed. *Billy Budd, Sailor: Critical Insights.* Ipswich, MA: Salem Press, 2017.

———. "Melville's Asia, Melville's Missionaries." In *Visionary of the Word: Melville and Religion*, ed. Jonathan A. Cook and Brian Yothers, 185-210. Evanston, IL: Northwestern University Press, 2017.

———. "One's Own Faith: Melville's Reading of *The New Testament and Psalms.*" *Leviathan: A Journal of Melville Studies* 10, no. 3 (2008): 39–59.

———. *The Romance of the Holy Land in American Travel Writing, 1790–1876.* Burlington, VT: Ashgate, 2007.

———. *Sacred Uncertainty: Religious Difference and the Shape of Melville's Career.* Evanston, IL: Northwestern University Press, 2015.

Young, Philip. *The Private Melville.* University Park: Pennsylvania State UP, 1993.

Zettsu, Tomoyuki. "Cannibal Connections: A Buddhist Reading of 'The Encantadas.'" *Leviathan: A Journal of Melville Studies* 8, no. 3 (2006): 43–50.

Ziff, Larzer. *Literary Democracy: The Declaration of Cultural Independence in America*. New York: Viking, 1981.

Zimmerman, Brett. *Herman Melville: Stargazer*. Montreal: McGill-Queen's UP, 1998.

Zoellner, Robert. *The Salt-Sea Mastodon: A Reading of "Moby-Dick."* Berkeley: U of California P, 1973.

Index

Aaron, Daniel, 143–44
Adler, George J, 84
Adler, Joyce, 144–45
aesthetics, 4, 23, 29–58, 92, 136, 161, 169, 173
Alter, Robert, 90
American Studies, 16, 23, 119, 125
Anderson, Charles R., 4, 9, 34, 59, 102, 154
Arac, Jonathan, 148n1, 160, 168
Arendt, Hannah, 173n1
Argersinger, Jana L., 111
Arsic, Branka, 91–92
Arvin, Newton, 16–17, 40, 93–94, 105, 134
Auden, W. H., 17, 67, 75, 89
Avallone, Charlene, 101, 117n3, 166

Baird, James, 14, 71–73
Baker, Anne, 165, 169
Balaam, Peter, 101, 118n8
Barnum, Jill, 14, 166
Barrett, Faith, 147
Baym, Nina, 6, 44, 51, 53, 97
Bell, Michael Davitt, 126
Bell, Millicent, 65
Bellis, Peter J., 113
Bercaw, Mary K. *See* Edwards, Mary K. Bercaw
Bercovitch, Sacvan, 77, 125–27, 135, 148n3
Bernard, Fred V., 164
Bernardini, Craig, 178
Berthoff, Warner, 29, 38–41, 59, 82, 89, 93n1
Berthold, Dennis, 48, 56, 171–72
Berthold, Michael, 157
Bewley, Marius, 122

Bezanson, Walter E., 14, 24, 34–35, 41–42, 53–54, 56, 78–79
bibliographical studies, 4
Bickley, Robert Bruce, 43–45
biography, 8–24, 28n4. 28n5, 61, 76, 93n3, 96, 104, 112, 117n5, 146, 177
Blackmur, R. P., 29, 31–32, 35–36, 38–40, 49, 54, 76, 90, 125
Blum, Hester, 132, 139, 170
Boone, Daniel, 143
Boone, Joseph Allen, 106, 117–18n7
Bowen, Merlin, 72–73
Braswell, William, 62–64, 66, 69
Bredahl, A. Carl, 57n4
Brodhead, Richard H., 124–25
Brodtkorb, Paul, 75–76, 78
Brodwin, Stanley, 94n10
Brooks, Van Wyck, 120–21
Browne, J. Ross, 15, 79
Browne, Ray B., 77
Browne, Sir Thomas, 30, 57n1, 84
Brumm, Ursula, 77–78
Bryant, John, 25, 28n9, 40, 47–48, 118n9, 165, 167, 176, 177, 178
Budick, Emily Miller, 157, 172
Buell, Lawrence, 53, 82, 89, 94n12, 131–32, 146, 159–60
Busch, Frederick, 117n1

Calder, Alex, 164
Cameron, Sharon, 112–13
Camus, Albert, 67–68, 75, 79, 86, 94n8
Castiglia, Christopher, 111–12, 161
Castronovo, Russ, 160–61
Chai, Leon, 46
Charvat, William, 14, 128

Chase, Richard Volney, 16, 38, 102–5, 108–9, 113, 122, 123, 129, 140
Cohen, Hennig, 42, 56
Colacurcio, Michael, 90–91
Colatrella, Carol, 138, 178
Cook, Jonathan A., 85
Cover, Robert M., 136
Cowan, Bainard, 81, 94n11
Cowen, Walker, 26, 87–88
Crain, Caleb, 110–11
Creech, James, 108–9
Crews, Frederick, 131

Davidson, Cathy N., 20
Davis, Clark, 113
Davis, Merrell R., 9, 14, 34, 51, 76
deconstruction, 126, 128
Delbanco, Andrew, 16, 23–34, 93n3, 177
Deleuze, Gilles, 91, 108
Derrida, Jacques, 49, 95
Dettlaff, Shirley M., 45, 48, 54
Dillingham, William B., 43, 76, 80
Dimock, Wai-Chee, 138, 157–60
Domnarski, William, 136
Douglas, Ann, 98, 109
Douglass, Frederick, 114, 149n8, 168–72, 175
Dryden, Edgar A., 40–41, 50, 52, 54–55, 58n8, 74, 124
Duban, James, 81–82, 87, 93n4
Duyckinck, Evert, 66, 79, 85, 133, 145

Eby, E. H., 117n6
Edwards, Mary K. Bercaw, 24, 28, 46, 177
Elliott, Emory, 41, 125
Ellis, Juniper, 164
Emerson, Ralph Waldo, 26, 30, 45, 64–65, 71, 82–83, 85, 94n13, 121, 123–24, 127–28
ethnic studies, 120, 148, 150–62
Evans, Kim Leilani, 94n9
Evelev, John, 139

Fabricant, Carole, 117n6
Feidelson, Charles, 14, 30, 35–36, 38, 51, 76, 129

feminist criticism, 102–7
Ferguson, Robert A, 136, 141
Fiedler, Leslie A, 103–6, 107, 117n6
Finkelstein, Dorothee Metlitsky, 89, 95n15, 153
Fisher, Marvin, 43, 134
Flory, Wendy Stallard, 101
Fogle, Richard Harter, 37, 41, 44
Foley, Brian, 57n1
Foster, Charles H, 133
Foster, Elizabeth S, 14, 70
Foucault, Michel, 113, 138
Franchot, Jenny, 83–84
Frankel, Matthew Cordova, 57
Franklin, H. Bruce, 50, 73–75, 79, 82, 88, 124, 130, 138, 142
Frederick, John T., 94n6
Fredericks, Nancy, 137–38
Freeman, F. Barron, 24, 61, 138
Freeman, John, 12
Friedman, Maurice S, 94n8
Fuller, Randall, 149n7

Garner, Stanton, 20, 145, 147
gender, 23, 89, 96–112, 149, 157, 170
Giles, Paul, 164–65
Gilman, William H, 9, 14–16, 19, 34, 38, 51, 76
Gilmore, Michael T., 128
Gleim, William S, 69
Goldman, Stan, 83, 87, 89
Greenberg, Amy S., 166
Grey, Robin, 87
Grossman, Jay, 148n1
Gunn, Giles B., 94n11

Haberstroh, Charles, 104, 107, 108, 113
Hardack, Richard, 94n13
Hardwick, Elizabeth, 22–23
Harvey, Bruce A., 162, 165
Hawthorne, Nathaniel, 16, 19, 23–25, 30, 33, 44, 46, 52, 60, 61, 63, 75, 79, 85–86, 97, 101, 104, 109, 111–12, 119, 121, 123, 124, 126–28, 131, 133, 135, 140, 157, 163
Hawthorne, Sophia Peabody, 101
Hayes, Kevin J., 57n3

Hayford, Harrison, 14, 18, 19, 24, 44, 47, 78
Heath, William, 118n9, 155
Heflin, Wilson L, 9, 14–16, 19
Heidmann, Mark, 93
Heimert, Alan, 133–34, 140
Herbert, T. Walter, 79–80, 90, 118n9, 154–55
Higgins, Brian, 7, 24, 27, 60, 93n2, 142
Hoffman, Daniel, 37–38, 41, 45, 47
Howard, Leon, 16–17
Hsu, Hsuan, 57n6
Hughes, Henry, 28n3, 110

Inge, M. Thomas, 177
Irwin, John T, 94n11
Ives, C. B., 136

Jackson, Virginia, 55
James, C. L. R., 151–53, 157, 159
Jehlen, Myra, 125, 128
Johnson, Barbara, 134–36

Kaiwi, Monica A. Ka'imipono, 166
Karcher, Carolyn L., 154–56
Kato, Yuji, 167
Kaul, A. N., 154
Kazin, Alfred, 86, 93n1, 174
Kelley, Wyn, 23–24, 27n2, 102, 139, 161, 166, 174, 177
Kenny, Vincent S, 79
Kleitz, Dorsey, 167
Knapp, Joseph G., 79
Koffler, Judith Schenck, 137
Konefsky, Alfred S., 140
Kramer, Michael P., 131
Kring, Walter Donald, 20, 84–85, 99, 117n2
Kulkarni, Hemant Balvantrao, 75

Laist, Randy, 178
Lawrence, D. H., 33, 120, 131, 148
Lazo, Rodrigo, 170
Lebowitz, Alan, 28n4
Ledbetter, Jack W, 136
Lee, A. Robert, 167
Leverenz, David, 107–8
Levin, Harry, 122

Levine, Robert S, 159, 169, 170
Lewis, R. W. B., 12, 61, 85, 123, 133
Leyda, Jay, 17–19, 37
Lowell, Robert, 159
Lyons, Paul, 166

Mailloux, Steven, 137, 169
Maloney, Ian S, 58n9
Mankino, Arimichi, 167
Marovitz, Sanford E, 14, 48, 161
Marr, Timothy, 89, 162, 177
Marrs, Cody, 147
Martin, Robert K, 104–9, 111–12, 117–18n7
Marx, Leo, 37, 91, 123, 144
Mason, Ronald, 68, 93n3
Matteson, John T, 140–41
Matthiessen, F. O., 30–36, 38, 57n2, 121–22, 130, 148n1
McCall, Dan, 46–47
McLoughlin, Michael, 94n13
McWilliams, John P, 127–28
Melvill, Allan, 21, 62, 101, 106
Melville, Elizabeth Shaw, 20–21, 28, 80, 85, 96–102, 175
Melville, Gansevoort, 18, 19, 21, 62, 102, 104, 106, 135, 145, 147, 158
Melville, Herman: and American nationalism, 5, 120, 150, 172; canonical status, 1, 7, 22, 37, 41, 43, 45, 56, 58n8, 78, 82, 86, 97–99, 117n3, 120–24, 129, 131, 137, 148, 158, 164; Civil War and, 6, 20, 55, 57, 87, 140–49, 155, 156, 168; family relationships, 3, 4, 9, 10, 11, 17–22, 28n5, 62, 99–100, 104, 113, 123, 132, 133, 135, 139, 140, 145; friendship with Hawthorne, 16, 19, 23–25, 60–61, 63, 75, 79, 85, 86, 97, 101, 104, 109, 111–12; religious views, 4, 12, 20, 22, 31–32, 36, 44, 48, 59–91, 134, 137, 138, 144, 147, 153, 162, 172–73; in the South Seas, 11, 15, 28, 105, 154, 163–66; sexuality, 96–112; views on race and slavery, 5–6, 114, 133–34, 147, 150–73; women and alleged misogyny, 4, 21, 96–97, 101

Melville, Herman, works by: "Bartleby the Scrivener," 1, 2, 5, 12, 22, 37, 43, 46, 50, 73, 91–92, 95, 108, 127, 128, 136, 138, 141, 148n4, 152, 177, 178; *Battle-Pieces*, 5, 10, 27, 32, 33, 42–43, 55, 57n6, 63, 87, 113, 127, 141–48, 169; *Benito Cereno*, 5, 12, 37, 68, 83, 94n13, 136, 149, 152, 156–57, 159, 161, 163–64, 171, 173n2; *Billy Budd*, 1, 5, 10–13, 17, 24, 27, 31, 42, 43, 54, 61–64, 66–74, 77, 80, 82, 83, 86, 88, 89, 92, 93n3, 94n6, 98, 102, 103, 105, 108–11, 115, 124, 134–46, 150, 158, 160, 169, 177, 178; *Clarel*, 5, 10, 12, 22, 27, 32, 34, 41–43, 48, 49, 52–55, 61, 63–64, 68, 70, 72–73, 78–79, 82–84, 86–90, 94n10, 95n14, 97–98, 112, 113, 127, 139, 144, 150, 153, 160–62, 164, 172, 173n4; *The Confidence-Man*, 10, 13, 38, 41, 47–48, 50, 55–56, 60, 63, 67, 68, 70, 73–74, 82, 84, 85, 94n13, 108, 113–14, 116, 124–27, 135–36, 145, 148, 155, 158, 160, 168; *The Encantadas*, 12, 38, 150, 154, 167, 170; *Israel Potter*, 38, 158, 160, 169; *John Marr and Other Sailors*, 32, 43, 57, 63, 144, 150; *Mardi*, 2, 5, 17, 34, 36, 53, 62, 63, 68, 71, 73, 74, 84, 88, 104, 133, 144, 152, 156, 158, 172; *Moby-Dick*, 1, 2–3, 5–6, 7–11, 13, 15–19, 22, 24–28, 29, 31–41, 43–50, 52–53, 55–58, 60–61, 63, 65, 67–71, 73–76, 78–82, 84–87, 89, 90, 92, 93n4, 95n16, 100, 103–18, 119–22, 124–35, 140–44, 148, 150–54, 157–68, 171, 174–78; *Omoo*, 5, 9, 12, 15, 17, 36, 38, 51, 63, 104, 105, 120, 160, 166; "The Paradise of Bachelors and The Tartarus of Maids," 92, 100, 110, 117n6, 138; "The Piazza," 10, 37, 45, 91, 101, 124, 152; *Piazza Tales*, 10, 37, 91, 101; *Redburn*, 5, 9, 12, 15, 17, 34, 44, 52, 91, 103– 5, 108, 109, 139, 150, 155, 158, 172; "Shiloh," 147; *Timoleon, Etc*, 32, 33, 43, 57, 63; *Typee*, 5, 8–10, 12, 15–16, 25, 27, 28n3, 28n5, 36, 38, 45, 47, 50, 51, 60, 63, 68, 69, 71, 92, 104–6, 108–11, 114, 120, 121, 135, 139, 144, 160, 162–67; *Weeds and Wildings*, 43, 57; *White-Jacket*, 5, 15, 30, 31, 34, 63, 64, 104, 114, 126, 136, 139, 144, 150, 155, 158, 160

Melville, Maria Gansevoort, 19, 104, 106

Melville Revival, 4, 7–8, 11, 14–15, 37, 54, 57, 98, 99, 102, 120, 121, 140, 165, 178

Metcalf, Eleanor Melville, 9, 11, 18–19, 28n2

Michaels, Walter Benn, 128

Middleton-Kaplan, Richard, 177

Milder, Robert, 88, 111, 140

Miller, Edwin Haviland, 18–20, 104, 113, 135

Miller, Perry, 132–33, 139

Mitchell, David, 115–16

Montas, Roosevelt, 169

Moore, Richard S, 45

Morrison, Toni, 1, 157

Mumford, Lewis, 12–13, 16, 19, 23, 61

Murray, Henry A, 68, 99, 117n4, 140, 175

Mushabac, Jane, 57n5

Nabers, Deak, 141

Naslund, Sena Jeter, 117n1, 178

New, Elisa, 86–87

New Americanists, 126–31, 140, 148, 153, 158, 168

New Criticism, 4, 35

New Historicism, 15, 127

Ngai, Sianne, 50, 148n4

Nichol, John W, 30

Obama, Barack, 1, 6n1, 148

Obenzinger, Hilton, 87, 89, 161, 162, 165

Olsen-Smith, Steven, 26, 176

Olson, Charles, 33–36, 57n2, 120, 140, 165
Oshima, Yukiko, 161, 168
Otter, Samuel, 28n3, 38, 40, 53–54, 58n10, 114–15, 158, 160, 166, 169–71, 177

Paglia, Camille, 117–18n7
Pardes, Ilana, 89–90
Parini, Jay, 117n1
Parker, Hershel, 7, 8, 16, 17, 19, 20, 21–27, 28n7, 42, 47, 60, 78, 84, 93n2, 97, 100, 102, 117n2, 142, 178
Parrington, Vernon Louis, 121
Pease, Donald E, 128–31, 153
Peeples, Scott, 168–69
Percival, Milton Oswin, 75
Peretz, Eyal, 95n18
Person, Leland, 110–11
philosophy, 1, 13, 15, 32, 64–65, 67, 75–76, 78, 88, 91, 121, 140, 145
Plato, 64–65, 71, 103
Pommer, Henry, 14, 87
Porte, Joel, 123–24
Posner, Richard A, 137
postcolonial studies, 154, 158–68
Post-Lauria, Sheila, 51, 100
Potter, William, 88–89

queer theory, 109, 116

race, 22, 113–14, 120, 149, 153–69
Rahv, Philip, 148n2
Reich, Charles A, 136
Religion, 1, 4, 13, 22, 59–94, 125, 140, 147, 172
Renker, Elizabeth, 20, 53–55, 58n7, 58n8, 99–100, 109
Reynolds, David S, 51
Reynolds, Larry J, 173n6
Robertson-Lorant, Laurie, 17, 19, 21, 97, 100, 101, 111
Robillard, Douglas, 48, 52, 55, 57, 57n6, 87
Rogin, Michael Paul, 19, 28n5, 135–36
Rosenberg, Warren, 97

Rosenberry, Edward H, 36, 38, 47, 48, 113
Rowe, John Carlos, 126, 135, 164
Ryan, James Emmett, 115–16
Rysten, Felix S. A., 94n8

Said, Edward W, 159
Saiki, Ikuno, 168
Samson, John, 158–60
Samuels, Ellen, 116
Sanborn, Geoffrey, 28n3, 58n10, 163–64
Sandberg, Robert, 176–77
Schiffman, Joseph, 62, 93n3
Schueller, Malini Johar, 89, 95n15, 160, 162, 165
Schultz, Elizabeth A, 52–53, 100, 177
Sealts, Merton M, 14, 19, 24, 25, 26, 52, 57n2, 64–65, 80, 82, 84
Sedgwick, Catharine Maria, 101, 118n8
Sedgwick, Eve Kosofsky, 109–10
Sedgwick, William Ellery, 32–33, 41, 53, 62–64, 68, 69
Seelye, John D, 42–43, 51
Sewall, Richard Benson, 122
sexuality, 21, 25, 54, 96–118, 140, 148n1, 149n6, 155, 162, 163, 167, 169
Shakespeare, William, 26, 29, 30–34, 40, 52, 57n2, 93, 119
Shattuck, Roger, 86
Sherrill, Rowland A, 80–81
Short, Bryan C, 48–49, 166, 170
Shulman, Robert, 117, 135
Shurr, William, 43, 54, 57
Slotkin, Richard, 142–43
Smith, Henry Nash, 134
Snyder, Sharon L, 115–16
Solove, D. J., 138–39
Spanos, William V, 130–31, 168
Spark, Clare, 11, 140
Spengemann, William C, 53, 58n7
Stauffer, John, 169
Stein, William Bysshe, 42, 57
Sten, Christopher, 48, 51, 136, 161, 166, 169
Stern, Milton R, 70–71

Stewart, George R, 44
Stewart, Randall, 93
Stone, Geoffrey, 64, 66, 69, 83
Stuckey, Sterling, 169–71
Suchoff, David, 138
Suggs, Robert C, 28n3, 165–66
Sundquist, Eric J, 156–57, 170, 172, 173n2
Sweet, Timothy, 148n5
Szendy, Peter, 92, 95, 148

Tally, Robert T, 168
Tamarkin, Elisa, 169
Temple, Gale, 111
textual criticism, 4, 7, 11–12, 24–28, 29, 34, 44, 47, 78, 86–88, 100–101, 109, 112, 153, 162, 167, 176
Thomas, Brook, 136
Thompson, G. R., 28n3, 131, 136, 165, 166
Thompson, Lawrance, 69–70, 76, 77, 79, 82–84, 86, 89, 90
Thomson, Shawn, 58n9
Thorp, Willard, 13, 62
Tolchin, Neal L, 106–7
Tompkins, Jane P, 98–99
transnational studies, 5–6, 150–73
Trilling, Lionel, 122
Trodd, Zoe, 168–69

Vendler, Helen, 49, 53, 146
Vincent, Howard P, 9, 51, 76
visual arts, 3–4, 29–58, 76, 100, 136, 171, 177

Wadlington, Warwick, 125
Wald, Priscilla, 50
Walker, Franklin, 79
Wallace, Robert K, 40, 48, 52, 56, 168–69, 177
Warner, Michael, 146–47
Warren, Robert Penn, 32, 42, 53, 56, 146
Warren, Rosanna, 146
Watson, E. L. Grant, 61
Weaver, Raymond M, 8–14, 16, 19, 23, 24, 27n2
Weinauer, Ellen, 101
Weir, Charles, Jr, 62
Weisberg, Richard H, 136–37
Wenke, John Paul, 84
Werge, Thomas, 79
Westover, Jeff, 138
Wiegman, Robyn, 117–18n7
Williams, John B, 82
Wilson, Edmund, 142–43
Wilson, Ivy G, 168, 173n5
Wineapple, Brenda, 111
Winters, Yvor, 121
Withim, Phil, 62
Wright, Nathalia, 14, 66

Yothers, Brian, 173
Young, Philip, 104

Zettsu, Tomoyuki, 167
Ziff, Larzer, 135
Zimmerman, Brett, 94n7
Zoellner, Robert, 78

www.ingramcontent.com/pod-product-compliance
Lightning Source LLC
Chambersburg PA
CBHW070802230426
43665CB00017B/2460